陕西推进"一带一路"建设蓝皮书

（2013—2023）

Blue Book of Shaanxi Province Promoting the Belt and Road Initiative (2013—2023)

陕西省推进"一带一路"建设工作领导小组办公室
新 华 社 中 国 经 济 信 息 社 ◎编著

新华出版社

图书在版编目（CIP）数据

陕西推进"一带一路"建设蓝皮书：2013-2023 / 陕西省推进"一带一路"建设工作领导小组办公室，新华社中国经济信息社编著. -- 北京：新华出版社，2023.12
ISBN 978-7-5166-7260-0

Ⅰ. ①陕…　Ⅱ. ①陕…②新…　Ⅲ. ①区域经济发展—研究报告—陕西—2013-2023　Ⅳ. ① F127.41

中国国家版本馆 CIP 数据核字（2023）第 250388 号

陕西推进"一带一路"建设蓝皮书：2013—2023

编　　著：	陕西省推进"一带一路"建设工作领导小组办公室
	新华社中国经济信息社
出 版 人：	匡乐成
责任编辑：	胡卓妮　唐波勇
选题策划：	唐波勇
封面设计：	华兴嘉誉
出版发行：	新华出版社
地　　址：	北京石景山区京原路 8 号
邮　　编：	100040
网　　址：	http://www.xinhuapub.com
经　　销：	新华书店、新华出版社天猫旗舰店、京东旗舰店及各大网店
购书热线：	010-63077122　中国新闻书店购书热线：010-63072012
照　　排：	华兴嘉誉
印　　刷：	北京明恒达印务有限公司
成品尺寸：	170mm × 240mm
印　　张：	27.25
字　　数：	280 千字
版　　次：	2023 年 12 月第一版
印　　次：	2023 年 12 月第一次印刷
书　　号：	ISBN 978-7-5166-7260-0
定　　价：	98.00 元

版权专有，侵权必究。如有质量问题，请与出版社联系调换：010-63077124

《陕西推进"一带一路"建设蓝皮书（2013—2023）》
编委会

主　　　任：徐玉长　曹文忠

副 主 任：李　月

主　　　编：陈　瑜　张亚强

副 主 编：冯　国　毛海峰

执 行 主 编：陆晓明　胡　柳　尹　亮

编委会成员：

　　　　　　安　航　翟淑睿　雷肖霄　董道勇　上　庆

　　　　　　曹家宁　马玉竹　荣忠霞　魏　薇　沈忠浩

　　　　　　李晓慧　邱　俊　汪慕涵　张　歌　罗婧婧

　　　　　　张　斌　刘　雨　杨　翼　刘　辉

学术支持：

西北大学经济管理学院

西北大学丝绸之路研究院

Editorial Board of the Blue Book of Shaanxi Province Promoting the Belt and Road Initiative (2013—2023)

Directors: Xu Yuchang, Cao Wenzhong

Deputy Director: Li Yue

Chief Editors: Chen Yu, Zhang Yaqiang

Associate Editors: Feng Guo, Mao Haifeng

Executive Editors: Lu Xiaoming, Hu Liu, Yin Liang

Members of the Editorial Board:
An Hang, Zhai Shurui, Lei Xiaoxiao, Dong Daoyong, Shang Qing, Cao Jianing, Ma Yuzhu, Rong Zhongxia, Wei Wei, Shen Zhonghao, Li Xiaohui, Qiu Jun, Wang Muhan, Zhang Ge, Luo Jingjing, Zhang Bin, Liu Yu, Yang Yi, Liu Hui

Academic Support:
School of Economics & Management, NWU
Institute of Silk Road Studies, NWU

奋进新时代开启新征程
书写陕西"一带一路"开放新篇章

2013年秋,习近平总书记提出共建"丝绸之路经济带"和"21世纪海上丝绸之路"。随着世界进入百年未有之大变局,人类文明发展面临越来越多的问题和挑战。中国高举构建人类命运共同体旗帜,因应全球发展及各国期待,继承和弘扬丝路精神这一人类文明的宝贵遗产,提出共建"一带一路"倡议。这一倡议,连接着历史、现实与未来,源自中国、面向世界、惠及全人类。

2100多年前,汉朝使者张骞从长安,也就是今日的陕西西安出发,出使西域,带动形成了著名的"丝绸之路"。这条连接东西、沟通有无、繁荣世界的历史之路,历经数千年的风雨洗礼,几经中断,如今又书新篇。作为古丝绸之路东方起点的陕西,如今再次成为21世纪共建"一带一路"的重要节点。

共建"一带一路"倡议,为"不沿边、不靠海"的陕西走向开放前沿创造了重大历史机遇。十年来,在习近平新时代中国特色社会主义思想的指引下,陕西深入贯彻落实习近平总书记关于共建"一带一路"重要论述和来陕考察重要讲话指示精神,积极打造内陆改革开放高地,全力建设"一带一路"交通商贸物流、国际产能合作、科技教育合作、国际文化旅游、丝绸之路金融五大中心,深度融入共建"一带一路"大格局，取得一系列具有陕西特色的显著成果。

《陕西推进"一带一路"建设蓝皮书（2013—2023）》由陕西省推进"一带一路"建设工作领导小组办公室和新华社中国经济信息社联合编著，是全面梳理十年来陕西省推进"一带一路"工作的系统性著作。通过陕西省政府主管部门和国家通讯社的专业机构紧密合作，系统梳理十年来陕西推进"一带一路"建设工作的成效，展望未来发展的方向和路径。这不仅对陕西地方推动"一带一路"工作能够有所促进，也是作为共建"一带一路"倡议的重要节点的陕西应尽的义务，同时能够更好服务国家共建"一带一路"倡议大局。功在当下，利在千秋，是一件值得庆贺的事情。

奋进新时代，开启新征程。今年5月，中国-中亚峰会在西安成功举办，为世界彰显了共建"一带一路"的伟大成绩与重要意义，为新时代新征程陕西融入共建"一带一路"大格局注入了新的动力。值此新书出版之际，让我们再次重温习近平总书记的重要讲话精神：陕西"要着力扩大对内对外开放，打造内陆改革开放高地。更加主动融入和服务构建新发展格局，更加深度融入共建'一带一路'大格局，在扩大对内对外开放中强动力、增活力，打开发展新天地"。

希望此书的出版能够让陕西全体从事"一带一路"事业的干部群众精神更加振奋，始终牢记习近平总书记的殷殷期盼，低调务实、埋头苦干，继续书写陕西"一带一路"开放新篇章。

是为序。

陕西省推进"一带一路"建设工作领导小组办公室

2023年11月

Embarking on a New Journey in the New Era and Writing a New Chapter in the Opening-Up of Shaanxi in the Belt and Road Initiative

In the autumn of 2013, Xi Jinping, General Secretary of the Communist Party of China (CPC) Central Committee, proposed the initiatives of jointly building the "Silk Road Economic Belt" and the "21st Century Maritime Silk Road". As the world enters a stage with great changes unseen in a century, the humankind is faced with an increasing number of issues and challenges to civilization development. Holding high the banner of building a community with a shared future for mankind, China meets the needs for global development and the expectations of all countries and regions, upholds and carries forward the spirit of the Silk Road - a precious heritage of human civilization, and puts forward the Belt and Road Initiative (BRI), which connects history, the reality and the future. It is truly an initiative from China and aims to benefit the whole mankind and make the world a better place.

Over 2,100 years ago, Zhang Qian, a Han Dynasty envoy, was commissioned with extraordinary powers and made his journey twice to the Western Regions from Chang'an (Xi'an City in Shaanxi today). Hence the world-renowned Silk Road came into existence. The overland route connecting the East and the West once brought prosperity to the world. During thousands of years of trials and vicissitudes, the route was interrupted several times. Now, it is turning a new leaf of life. As the starting point of the ancient Silk Road in the East, Shaanxi once again stands as a key node on the journey of the BRI cooperation in the 21st century.

The BRI has provided major historic opportunities for Shaanxi, an inland province neither on the border nor along the coast, to move toward the forefront of opening up. Over the past 10 years, under the guidance of Xi Jinping Thought on Socialism with Chinese Characteristics for a New Era, Shaanxi has earnestly implemented General Secretary Xi Jinping's important discussions on the BRI cooperation and the key speeches delivered during his inspection to Shaanxi, actively developed the inland province into a highland for the reform and opening up, in an all-out effort to build the centers for transportation, commerce and logistics, international industrial capacity cooperation, scientific and educational cooperation, international cultural tourism and Silk Road finance, and deeply integrate into the BRI cooperation, and made a lot of notable achievements with Shaanxi features.

The Blue Book of Shaanxi Province Promoting the Belt and Road Initiative (2013-2023), co-compiled by the Office of the Leading Group for Promoting the Belt and Road Initiative in Shaanxi and the China Economic Information Service of Xinhua News Agency, is systemic works that gives a comprehensive description of the progress Shaanxi has made in promoting the BRI over the past ten years. Through the close collaborations between the competent departments of the People's Government of Shaanxi Province and the professional institution of the national news agency, the Blue Book presents the achievements of Shaanxi in this regard and charts the direction and path for future development. This will not only help boost the efforts of Shaanxi in promoting the BRI, but also represent the bounded duty of Shaanxi as a key node in the BRI cooperation. Meanwhile, it will better serve the national endeavor in promoting the BRI. It is a cause for celebration, which will benefit both the current and future generations.

Shaanxi is embarking on a new journey in the new era. This May, the China-Central Asia Summit was held successfully in Xi'an, showcasing the great achievements that have been made in the BRI cooperation as well as the key significance of the BRI and injecting new impetus into Shaanxi's endeavor to promote the BRI in the new era. Upon the publication of the Blue Book, let's review the spirit of important speeches of General Secretary Xi Jinping: Shaanxi "should open up wider and develop the inland province into a highland for the reform and opening up, integrate and serve the new development pattern more proactively, and be more deeply integrated into the overall pattern of jointly building the BRI, so as to strengthen Shaanxi's momentum and vitality in expanding opening up and open a new development landscape."

It is hoped that the publication of the Blue Book will bring even more energy to all cadres and masses in Shaanxi, and encourage them to bear in mind the ardent expectations of General Secretary Xi Jinping, work earnestly and in a down-to-earth manner, to continue writing newer chapters of Shaanxi's BRI endeavor.

This is the preface.

Office of the Leading Group for Promoting the Belt and Road Initiative in Shaanxi

November 2023

目 录

奋进新时代开启新征程　书写陕西"一带一路"开放新篇章 ····· 1

全景篇

概要 ··· 003

一、陕西"一带一路"建设的愿景目标 ···························· 010

　　（一）明确目标定位，规划建设蓝图 ························· 010

　　（二）加强统筹协调，优化服务保障 ························· 014

二、陕西"一带一路"建设的实践成效 ···························· 018

　　（一）畅通道，实现硬联通 ···································· 019

　　（二）优服务，推动软联通 ···································· 022

　　（三）汇人文，促进心联通 ···································· 026

　　（四）强经贸，深化产能合作 ································· 029

主题篇

一、交通商贸物流中心枢纽功能彰显 ······························ 038

　　（一）加快形成亚欧陆海贸易大通道 ························· 038

（二）打造高效便捷物流集疏体系⋯⋯⋯⋯⋯⋯⋯⋯⋯⋯ 044

　　（三）助力对外贸易实现跨越发展⋯⋯⋯⋯⋯⋯⋯⋯⋯⋯ 047

二、国际产能合作中心建设稳步推进⋯⋯⋯⋯⋯⋯⋯⋯⋯⋯⋯⋯ 052

　　（一）雄厚基础拓展合作领域⋯⋯⋯⋯⋯⋯⋯⋯⋯⋯⋯⋯ 052

　　（二）"走出去"深度参与国际产业分工⋯⋯⋯⋯⋯⋯⋯⋯ 055

　　（三）"引进来"着力打造特色产业集群⋯⋯⋯⋯⋯⋯⋯⋯ 059

　　（四）纵深推进国际产能合作中心建设⋯⋯⋯⋯⋯⋯⋯⋯ 063

三、科技教育中心交流合作拓点扩面⋯⋯⋯⋯⋯⋯⋯⋯⋯⋯⋯⋯ 065

　　（一）搭建科技人文交流桥梁⋯⋯⋯⋯⋯⋯⋯⋯⋯⋯⋯⋯ 065

　　（二）深化教育国际交流合作⋯⋯⋯⋯⋯⋯⋯⋯⋯⋯⋯⋯ 070

　　（三）继续提升科教开放水平⋯⋯⋯⋯⋯⋯⋯⋯⋯⋯⋯⋯ 076

四、国际文化旅游中心活力与日俱增⋯⋯⋯⋯⋯⋯⋯⋯⋯⋯⋯⋯ 078

　　（一）发挥优势打造文旅中心⋯⋯⋯⋯⋯⋯⋯⋯⋯⋯⋯⋯ 078

　　（二）砥砺奋进谱写文旅新篇⋯⋯⋯⋯⋯⋯⋯⋯⋯⋯⋯⋯ 080

　　（三）多管齐下讲好陕西故事⋯⋯⋯⋯⋯⋯⋯⋯⋯⋯⋯⋯ 087

五、丝绸之路金融中心探索试点创新⋯⋯⋯⋯⋯⋯⋯⋯⋯⋯⋯⋯ 090

　　（一）以要素集聚打造区域金融中心⋯⋯⋯⋯⋯⋯⋯⋯⋯ 090

　　（二）以服务创新强化金融支撑功能⋯⋯⋯⋯⋯⋯⋯⋯⋯ 093

　　（三）以开放合作打破未来发展瓶颈⋯⋯⋯⋯⋯⋯⋯⋯⋯ 096

目录

专题篇

一、健康新领域共筑卫生健康共同体 ············ 104
   （一）陕西迎来医疗产业升级 ············ 104
   （二）中医药国际合作格局基本形成 ············ 107
   （三）跨境医疗卫生合作稳步推进 ············ 112
   （四）提质"走出去"还需协同发力 ············ 113

二、绿色新领域探索生态环境治理样本 ············ 116
   （一）逐步构建生态安全新屏障 ············ 116
   （二）不断拓展绿色领域国际合作 ············ 119
   （三）"一盘棋"布局绿色开放合作 ············ 122

三、数字新领域面向未来推动国际合作 ············ 125
   （一）筑牢数字经济发展的制度基础 ············ 125
   （二）数字经济助力共建"一带一路" ············ 127
   （三）跨境电商产业链和生态圈初步形成 ············ 130
   （四）"一带一路"高质量发展需要数字动能 ············ 131

展望篇

一、明确主攻方向补齐开放不足最大短板 ············ 138
   （一）纵横汇通的交通物流枢纽作用更突出 ············ 138

（二）面向中亚南亚西亚的重点方向更明确 ······· 139
　　（三）打造"内陆改革开放高地"更主动 ············ 140

二、发挥自身特色实现重点领域新的突破 ············ 141
　　（一）"一带一路"农业领域合作更务实 ············ 141
　　（二）健康绿色等新领域合作更深入 ··············· 142
　　（三）实现文明互鉴的"区域窗口"更清晰 ········ 142

三、深化创新驱动、释放高质量发展内生动力 ······ 144
　　（一）西安"双中心"辐射作用更明显 ··············· 144
　　（二）"秦创原"科技成果转化能效更强大 ········ 145
　　（三）数字化牵引作用更强劲 ························ 146

四、锚定目标推进高质量共建"一带一路" ············ 147
　　（一）高标准、可持续、惠民生的目标更可期 ··· 147
　　（二）能盈利促双赢的外向型经济更多元 ········ 148
　　（三）高层次高品质的论坛活动更丰富 ············ 149

结语 ··· 150

陕西推进"一带一路"建设大事记（2013—2023） ············ 152

Table of Contents

Embarking on a New Journey in the New Era and Writing a New Chapter in the Opening-Up of Shaanxi in the Belt and Road Initiative ··· 3

Panorama

Overview ·· 171

I. Shaanxi's Vision and Goals of Building the Belt and Road Initiative(BRI) ·· 183

   (i) Specifying Goals and Positioning and Drawing up the Blueprint ····· 183

   (ii) Strengthening Overall Planning and Coordination, and Optimizing Service Support ·· 188

II. Practical Achievements of BRI Building in Shaanxi ············· 195

   (i) Removing Barriers to Achieve Hard Connectivity ················· 196

   (ii) Improving Service to Promote Soft Connectivity ················· 202

   (iii) Promoting People-to-people Exchanges and Connectivity ······· 207

   (iv) Strengthening Economy and Trade to Deepen Production Capacity Cooperation ·· 213

Theme Chapter

I. The Function of the Center for Transportation, Trade and Logistics as a Hub Becomes Prominent ······ 225

 (i) Speeding up the Formation of Asia-Europe Land-sea Trade Corridor ······ 226

 (ii) Building an Efficient and Convenient Logistics Collection and Distribution System ······ 234

 (iii) Fostering Foreign Trade to Achieve Leapfrogging Development ··· 239

II. Steady Progress in Building an International Production Capacity Cooperation Center ······ 247

 (i) Solid Foundation for Expanding Cooperation ······ 248

 (ii) "Go Global" to Deeply Participate in the International Industrial Division of Labor ······ 252

 (iii) "Bring in" to Build Characteristic Industrial Clusters ······ 258

 (iv) Promoting the Construction of International Production Capacity Cooperation Center ······ 263

III. Expanding Exchanges and Cooperation of Science and Technology Education Center ······ 267

 (i) Building Bridges for Technology and People-to-people Cultural Exchanges ······ 268

 (ii) Deepening International Exchange and Cooperation in Education ······ 276

 (iii) Continuing to Enhance the Openness of Science and Education ···· 285

IV. The Vitality of Shaanxi as the International Cultural Tourism Center is Increasing Day by Day ········· 288

   (i) Building a Cultural and Tourism Center by Taking Advantage of the Strengths ········· 289

   (ii) Building on the New Chapter of Culture and Tourism ········· 292

   (iii) Telling the Story of Shaanxi with Multiple Approaches ········· 303

V. Silk Road Financial Center Pilot Explores Innovations ········· 307

   (i) Building a Regional Financial Center Through Factor Clustering ········· 308

   (ii) Strengthening Financial Support Functions Through Service Innovation ········· 311

   (iii) Breaking the Bottleneck of Future Development Through Openness and Cooperation ········· 317

Special Topics

I. Building a Health Community in New Areas ········· 324

   (i) Shaanxi Ushers in the Upgrading of the Medical Industry ········· 325

   (ii) The Pattern of International Cooperation in Chinese Medicine has Basically Taken Shape ········· 329

   (iii) Cross-border Medical and Health Cooperation Progresses Steadily ········· 336

   (iv) Improving the Quality of Go Global Requires Concerted Efforts ········· 338

II. Exploration of Ecological Environment Governance Samples in Green New Fields ········ 342

(i) Gradually Build a New Barrier for Ecological Security ············ 343

(ii) Continuously Expanding International Cooperation in the Green Field ········ 346

(iii) Coordinated Layout for Green and Open Cooperation ············ 351

III. Promoting International Cooperation in New Digital Fields for the Future ········ 354

(i) Building a Solid Institutional Foundation for the Development of the Digital Economy ········ 354

(ii) Digital Economy Helps Build the Belt and Road ················ 357

(iii) The Cross-Border E-Commerce Industry Chain and Ecosystem are Initially Formed ········ 362

(iv) High-quality Development of the BRI Requires Digital Momentum ········ 364

Prospect

I. Clarifying the Main Direction and Making up for the Biggest Shortcomings of Openness ········ 371

(i) The Role as Transportation and Logistics Hub is More Prominent ··· 372

(ii) The Key Directions towards Central Asia, South Asia and West Asia are Clearer ········ 372

(iii) Developing the Inland Province into a Highland for Reform and Opening up is more Proactive ········· 374

II. Giving Full Play to its Own Characteristics to Achieve New Breakthroughs in Key Areas ········· 375

(i) Cooperation in the Agricultural Field of the BRI is More Pragmatic ····· 375

(ii) Cooperation in Health, Green Development and Other New Fields is closer ········· 376

(iii) The "Regional Window" for Realizing Mutual Learning Among Civilizations is Clearer ········· 377

III. Deepen Innovation and Release Endogenous Power for High-Quality Development ········· 379

(i) The Radiation Effect of Xi'an as "Double Centers" is More Obvious ········· 379

(ii) "Qinchuangyuan" Scientific and Technological Achievements are Transformed More Efficiently ········· 380

(iii) Digitalization Provides a Stronger Guiding Effect ········· 381

IV. Anchor Goals to Promote High-Quality Development of the BRI ········· 383

(i) The Goal of High Standards, Sustainability and Benefiting People's Livelihood is More Promising ········· 383

(ii) Export-oriented Economy that can Make Profits and Promote Win-Win Results is More Diversified ········· 384

(iii) High-level and High-quality Forum Activities Increase ·········· 385

Conclusion ·· 387

Major Events in Shaanxi's Advance of the Belt and Road Initiative (2013—2023)·· 389

全景篇

概　要

2100多年前，汉使张骞两次从长安出发，持节出使西域，历时20余年，开通了一条连接中国、中亚、西亚的通道，史称"凿空之旅"。这条横贯东西的通道后来进一步西延至欧洲，成为沿线国家和地区经贸往来与人文交流的繁荣之路，得名"丝绸之路"，成就千年丝路传奇。

2013年9月7日，中国国家主席习近平出访中亚时在哈萨克斯坦纳扎尔巴耶夫大学发表演讲，首次提出共同建设"丝绸之路经济带"倡议，让古老的丝绸之路焕发新的生机活力，把中国同欧亚国家的互利合作推向新的历史高度。习近平主席深情回忆："我的家乡陕西，就位于古丝绸之路的起点。站在这里，回首历史，我仿佛听到了山间回荡的声声驼铃，看到了大漠飘飞的袅袅孤烟。"当年10月3日，习近平主席出访东南亚时在印度尼西亚国会发表演讲，提出共同建设"21世纪海上丝绸之路"倡议，使沿线各国经济联系更加紧密、相互合作更加深入、发展空间更加广阔，造福各国人民。

源自中国、属于世界，共建"一带一路"倡议得到国际社会广泛响应。据国务院新闻办公室发布的《共建"一带一路"：构建人类命运共同体的重大实践》白皮书数据，截至2023年6月底，中国已与五大洲的150多个国家、30多个国际组织签署了200多份共建"一带一路"合作文件。"一带一路"已成为加强共建国家经贸往来、产业合作、人文交流的重要纽带，促进共建国家政策沟通、设施联通、贸易畅通、资金融通、民心相通的重要机制，推动共同发展、完善全球治理、构建人类命运共同体的重要实践。

陕西作为古丝绸之路的起点，如今再次成为21世纪共建"一带一路"的重要节点。在习近平主席提出共建"丝绸之路经济带"倡议的当月，西安市与12个城市共同签署《共建丝绸之路经济带西安宣言》。2014年10月，陕西成立省长任组长的"推进丝绸之路经济带新起点建设工作领导小组"。十年来，陕西深入贯彻落实习近平总书记关于共建"一带一路"重要论述和来陕考察重要讲话指示精神，积极打造内陆改革开放高地，全力建设"一带一路"交通商贸物流、国际产能合作、科技教育合作、国际文化旅游、丝绸之路金融五大中心，畅通道、聚物流、促经贸、引产业、汇人文，深度融入共建"一带一路"大格局，取得一系列具有陕西特色的显著成果。

交通商贸物流中心建设率先取得突破。中欧班列长安号加速建设，运行质效持续提升。截至2023年9月，中欧班列长安号累计开行已超过2万列。目前长安号国际运输干线开行17条，已覆盖亚欧大陆45个国家和地区，国内开通"+西欧"集结线路21条，辐射全国主要货源地，成为国内运输时效最快、线路辐射最广、服务功能最全、综合成本最低、智能化程度最高的"五最班列",构筑起一条效率高、成本低、服务优的国际贸易"黄金通道";"空中丝绸之路"越织越密,西安咸阳国际机场累计开通客货运航线386条,其中国际客运航线83条,全货运航线45条,开通4条第五航权航线,加速构建"丝路贯通、欧美直达、五洲相连"航线网络格局。实现中亚"五国六城"通航全覆盖,西咸新区空港新城成为西北地区最大的航企聚集区、功能最全的空港型国家物流枢纽。

国际产能合作中心建设成效显著。高质量"引进来"推动陕西产业结构优化升级,电子信息、新能源汽车等新兴产业集群异军突起,高水平"走出去"助力共建国家地区提升发展水平,农业、能源、矿产等多领域合作实现双赢。2013—2022年,陕西对共建国家投资12.4亿美元,占同期全省对外投资总额的23.8%;在共建国家完成工程承包营业额135.7亿美元,占同期全省对外承包工程的52.6%。同时,充分发挥自由贸易区的先行先试功能,不断优化营商环境,依托中俄、中欧等国际产业合作园区,吸引三星、比亚迪、康佳等龙头企业在陕布局产能基地,着力打造有国际竞争力的特色产业集群。

科技教育中心建设持续推进。国际交流合作增量、拓点、扩面,150余所海内外高校加盟"丝绸之路大学联盟",超10万名外国留学生来陕留学。陕西已建立19个国家级、64个省级国际科技交流合作基地,成立陕西国际科技合作基地联盟,与40多个国家和地区的400多家机构建立了多层次合作关系。上合组织农业技术交流培训示范基地在陕西杨凌正式揭牌，与60多个国家开展现代农业合作，成功举办30余场上合组织现代农业发展圆桌会等交流活动，上合组织国家2.8万余名学员参加技术培训。

国际文化旅游中心建设亮点突出。"国风·秦韵"陕西文化周、非遗精品展等一批文化交流项目在海外引起强烈反响，文旅发展活力和国际影响力显著提升。十年来，陕西新增国际友城48对，已与41个国家建立了108对国际友城关系，其中共建"一带一路"国家友城54对。成功举办8届丝绸之路国际艺术节、3届世界文化旅游大会、7届西安丝绸之路国际旅游博览会。

丝绸之路金融中心建设不断创新。深化金融领域改革开放，持续提升金融外汇服务效能，不断积累符合共建"一带一路"倡议需求的金融产品和创新服务，以高水平开放推动共建"一带一路"高质量发展。陕西金融业增加值从2013年的791.1亿元增加到2022年的2109.7亿元，10年增长了2.7倍，年均增长率11.5%。陕西累计实现人民币跨境收付金额4536.99亿元，辐射148个国家和地区，其中覆盖96个共建"一带一路"国家，累计实现人民币跨境收付金额1813.17亿元，超全国平均水平约20个百分点。

打造"五大中心"，是陕西推动"一带一路"建设走深走实的具体抓手。十年来，陕西发挥统筹协调作用，先后制订了推进"一带一路"建设实施方案、专项规划等纲领性文件，连续9年配套出台年度工作要点，持续深化拓展"一带一路"五大中心建设内涵，陆续形成一系列富有特色的实践与经验：中欧班列（西安）成为全国中欧班列的排头兵,上合组织农业基地成为展示现代农业示范样板,丝绸之路大学联盟成为国际教育合作新典范,与中亚联合考古成为丝路"金名片",秦医秦药"走出去"深入沿线百姓人心,隆基绿能等陕企成为绿色丝路先行者,这些实践有力支撑了全省"一带一路"五大中心建设,推动陕西全面开放的新优势加速形成,在共建"一带一路"大格局中的作用日益突出。

十年来,陕西始终服从服务于中央部署,切实完成好党中央、国务院安排部署的各项任务。

在服务国家总体外交中勇担当。陕西配合中央部委圆满完成三十多位国家元首和政府首脑接待任务,与哈萨克斯坦、吉尔吉斯斯坦、乌兹别克斯坦等国元首家乡建立友好省州关系,在"元首家乡"外交带动下,"一带一路"重要节点作用更加凸显。中国—中亚峰会、"中国+中亚五国"外长第二次、第四次会晤等主场外交活动,以及亚洲文化遗产保护联盟大会、"一带一路"媒体合作论坛等重大外事活动在陕西成功举办,服务国家外交大局能力显著提升。

在承接重大战略任务后有作为。陕西以获批建设中欧班列集结中心示范工程为契机,高水平建设中欧班列西安集结中心,设立西安国际港站,上线运营长安号数字金融综合服务平台,与西部陆海新通道实现战略交汇,效率高、成本低、服务优的亚欧陆海贸易大通道加快形成。贯彻落实"加强同地区国家现代农业领域合作"重要指示,发挥杨凌发展现代农业的"国家队"作用,高水平推进上合组织农业基地实质性运营,与60多个国家开展现代农业合作,打造国际农业技术合作"示范田"。

在搭建国际交流平台时显特色。充分发挥自贸试验区改革开放综合试验平台作用,稳步扩大制度型开放,在经贸、人文等方面与共建"一带一路"国家开展一系列创新实践,36项典型经验在全国复制推广。依托最高法第二国际商事法庭、第六巡回法庭,司法部"三中心一基地"等重要平台,加快建设"一带一路"国际商事法律服务示范区,为对外经贸合作提供高质量的法律服务保障。持续提升完善丝博会、欧亚经济论坛等服务功能,为共建"一带一路"国家深化合作搭建国际交流平台。

共建"一带一路"为西部内陆地区走向开放前沿创造了重大历史机遇。陕西抢抓机遇,在"一带一路"建设中,开放开发形成新格局,社会经济发展迈上新台阶。对外贸易突飞猛进,全省进出口总额连续跨越2000亿元、3000亿元和4000亿元大关,年均增长14.7%;与共建"一带一路"国家进出口额翻两番,年均增长18.4%,在2022年首次突破1000亿元,同比增长41%;招商引资成效斐然,2014年以来战略新兴产业、高新技术产业固定资产投资翻一番,"十三五"以来年均实际利用外资比"十二五"期间翻一番;产业结构明显优化,近五年高新技术制造业增加值年均增长13.1%,比规模以上工业增加值平均增速高7个百分点;企业效益显著增强,2022年工业营收和工业利润比2013年双双翻番;经济发展水平全面提升,2022年人均GDP比2013年将近翻番。

长安复携手,再顾重千金。2023年5月,中国－中亚峰会成功举办，中国和中亚领导人聚首西安，同心筑梦，共谋发展。中亚是共建"一带一路"的首倡地，也是共建"一带一路"的示范区。在共建"一带一路"倡议提出十周年前夕，中国-中亚峰会进一步凝聚共识，峰会发表的"西安宣言"再次表达了各国共建"一带一路"的决心和信心，为共建"一带一路"注入了新的动力，也必将为陕西带来更多发展机遇。

凡为过往，皆成序章。十年来，陕西始终牢记习近平总书记对陕西开放发展作出的重要指示，坚持高位部署、统筹推进、发挥优势、彰显特色，打造国内大循环的重要支点和国内国际双循环的战略链接，助力陆海内外联动、东西双向互济的开放格局加快形成。未来，陕西将按照习近平总书记有关奋力谱写中国式现代化建设的陕西篇章的指示要求，更加深度融入共建"一带一路"大格局，充分发挥自贸试验区先行先试作用，继续扩大规则、规制、管理、标准等制度型开放，打造高能级开放平台；更加注重科技创新驱动，加力打造"秦创原"科技创新平台，聚合创新要素，扶持科技成果孵化、转化，让创新成为陕西发展的强大引擎；更加深入推进高标准、可持续、惠民生的高质量"一带一路"建设，更加注重数字、绿色、健康丝绸之路建设；更加深度融入共建"一带一路"大格局，高标准打造内陆改革开放高地，在扩大对内对外开放中强动力、增活力，打开发展新天地。

陕西"一带一路"建设的愿景目标

深度融入"一带一路"大格局,是习近平总书记对陕西的要求;实施共建"一带一路"倡议的重要节点,是习近平总书记对陕西的定位。发挥重要通道节点作用、探索建设西安"一带一路"综合试验区、打造内陆改革开放高地和开发开放枢纽,是国家赋予陕西的重大任务。

(一)明确目标定位,规划建设蓝图

十年来,习近平总书记多次对陕西"一带一路"建设作出明确指示,多份国家政策文件对陕西参与"一带一路"建设的目标任务提出具体要求,为陕西谋划"一带一路"建设提供了重要指南。

1. 深刻把握指示精神

2015年2月,习近平总书记在陕西考察时指出:陕西是"向西开放的前沿位置""陕西要找准定位,主动融入'一带一路'大格局"。

2020年4月，习近平总书记在陕西考察时指出，对陕西而言，开放不足是制约发展的突出短板。要深度融入共建"一带一路"大格局，发挥好自由贸易试验区先行示范作用，办好丝博会、欧亚经济论坛、杨凌农高会，建设中欧班列（西安）集结中心，加快形成面向中亚南亚西亚国家的通道、商贸物流枢纽、重要产业和人文交流基地，构筑内陆地区效率高、成本低、服务优的国际贸易通道。

2023年5月，习近平总书记在听取陕西省委和省政府工作汇报时强调，要着力扩大对内对外开放，打造内陆改革开放高地。更加主动融入和服务构建新发展格局，更加深度融入共建"一带一路"大格局，在扩大对内对外开放中强动力、增活力，打开发展新天地。稳步扩大规则、规制、管理、标准等制度型开放，推进自贸试验区高质量发展，积极打造高能级开放平台。积极参与西部陆海新通道建设，充分发挥中欧班列西安集结中心作用，加快形成面向中亚南亚西亚国家的重要对外开放通道，在联通国内国际双循环中发挥更大作用。着力营造市场化、法治化、国际化一流营商环境，提高招商引资的质量和水平。

2. 全面融入开放格局

2015年3月，国家发展改革委、外交部、商务部联合发布《推动共建丝绸之路经济带和21世纪海上丝绸之路的愿景与行动》提出，推进"一带一路"建设，中国将充分发挥国内各地区比较优势，实行更加积极主动的开放战略，加强东中西互动合作，全面提升开放型经济水平。其中明确要求，"打造西安内陆型改革开放新高地……形成面向中亚、南亚、西亚国家的通道、商贸物流枢纽、重要产业和人文交流基地"。

2020年5月，中共中央、国务院印发《关于新时代推进西部大开发形成新格局的指导意见》提出："支持陕西发挥综合优势，打造内陆开放高地和开发开放枢纽"，"在西安等重点城市探索建设'一带一路'综合试验区"，"支持陕西充分发掘历史文化优势，发挥丝绸之路经济带重要通道、节点作用"，"鼓励西安等加快建设国际门户枢纽城市"。

2020年10月，中共中央、国务院印发《黄河流域生态保护和高质量发展规划纲要》提出，"支持西安、郑州、济南等沿黄大城市建立对接国际规则标准、加快投资贸易便利化、吸引集聚全球优质要素的体制机制，强化国际交往功能，建设黄河流域对外开放门户"，"培育西安、郑州等中欧班列枢纽城市，发展依托班列的外向型经济"，"在沿黄省区新设若干农业对外开放合作试验区，深化与共建'一带一路'国家农牧业合作，支持有实力的企业建设海外生产加工基地"。

3. 精心规划建设蓝图

遵循习近平总书记指示，对标国家总体部署，陕西2016年出台《陕西省推进建设丝绸之路经济带和21世纪海上丝绸之路实施方案（2015—2020）》，首次提出打造"五大中心"，即"一带一路"上的交通商贸物流、国际产能合作、科技教育、国际旅游、区域金融中心。2021年印发《陕西省"十四五"深度融入共建"一带一路"大格局、建设内陆开放高地规划》，进一步提出构建"一核两翼四通道五中心多平台"联动开放格局。这两份陕西"一带一路"建设的顶层设计文件，明确了全省"一带一路"建设的任务书、时间表和路线图。

按此规划和方案，陕西"一带一路"建设的近期目标是，用3—5年的时间，夯实基础，彰显优势。到2020年，与共建"一带一路"国家的合作交流机制进一步健全，合作平台进一步完善，经济外向度明显提升，五大中心建设初见成效，基本形成宽领域、多层次、高水平的全面开放新格局。中期目标是，到2025年，建成连通内外、便捷高效的海陆空国际综合大通道；建成具有陕西特色的现代产业体系；建成具有陕西特点和优势的创新发展体系；建成丝绸之路风情体验旅游核心区；建成丝绸之路经济带上的金融聚集区。远期目标是，到21世纪中叶，全面形成陕西与共建国家的合作交流网络，经贸往来更加活跃、人文交流更加密切、能源合作更加广泛，全面提升综合经济竞争力和文化软实力，全面实现"一带一路"五大中心的战略目标，全面建成内陆改革开放新高地。

（二）加强统筹协调，优化服务保障

在找准定位、明确目标的基础上，陕西分解重点任务，建立工作机制，加强政策引导，强化统筹协调，完善服务保障，久久为功，扎实推进"一带一路"建设。

1.细化目标分解重点任务

落实规划蓝图，需要分解重点任务，形成抓手。陕西已经明确，"十四五"期间，全省"一带一路"建设的重点任务是，形成"一核两翼四通道五中心多平台"的全方位联动开放布局，打造五大中心，建设数字、绿色、健康丝绸之路，实施九大工程。

"一核两翼四通道五中心多平台"是从空间上进行的战略布局。"一核"包括西安主城区、咸阳主城区、西咸新区；"两翼"指陕北能源化工之翼、陕南生态之翼；"四通道"是新亚欧大陆桥"亚欧干线"通道、蒙俄—东盟"南北干线"通道、亚欧干线中巴"南亚支线"通道、亚欧干线地中海"西亚支线"通道；"五中心"即交通商贸物流、国际产能合作、科技教育合作、国际文化旅游、丝绸之路金融中心；"多平台"指自贸试验区、经济开发区、保税区、上合农业技术交流培训示范基地等开放平台。

五大中心建设的具体任务是，将陕西打造成为国际性商贸物流枢纽和国际陆海贸易大通道的运营组织中心；建成具有国际竞争力的产业基地，形成强大的开放型产业集群，构建内外需并重的现代产业体系；建成具有陕西特点和优势的创新发展体系，成为全国创新创业的核心区域；建成中华文明—丝绸之路旅游核心区，成为彰显华夏文明的历史文化首选地；建成丝绸之路经济带上的金融聚集区，成为具有重要影响、鲜明特色、辐射西部和欧亚国家的区域性金融中心。

在培育拓展开放合作新优势、新方向、新领域方面，加强数字丝绸之路建设，建设大数字技术应用及基础设施，推动科技创新，搭建国际数字合作平台；加强健康丝绸之路建设，推进中医药国际化发展，拓展卫生健康合作领域，参与全球公共卫生治理；加强绿色丝绸之路建设，深化生态环境保护国际合作，提高生态环境保护能力，参与生态环境保护全球治理。

实施九大工程是指，建设一批面向国际的开放合作基地、中心、平台：探索建设西安"一带一路"综合试验区；构筑完善亚欧陆海贸易大通道；高质量建设中欧班列西安集结中心；创新建设陕西自由贸易试验区；高标准建设上海合作组织农业技术交流培训示范基地；加快建设西安临空经济示范区；打造"一带一路"大宗商品交易中心；着力建设西安丝路科创中心；推动建设"一带一路"文化贸易展示中心。

2. 统筹协调加强政策引导

高效的工作机制是推进重点任务、实现规划蓝图的重要基础。

2014年10月，响应共建"丝绸之路经济带"倡议，陕西成立"推进丝绸之路经济带新起点建设工作领导小组"（现更名为"推进'一带一路'建设工作领导小组"），省长任组长，相关职能部门和重点城市负责人参加。省领导小组办公室多次召开全体会议，统筹协调全省"一带一路"建设工作，在各个时间节点上为全省推进"一带一路"建设工作提供关键指引。

省领导小组成立不久就印发了陕西《丝绸之路经济带新起点建设重点工作实施方案》，提出40条工作措施。十年间，省领导小组指导省相关部门出台多项具体工作层面的政策措施，如《关于推动交通物流融合发展的实施方案》《关于统筹推进新冠肺炎疫情防控和"一带一路"建设高质量发展的若干措施》《支持中欧班列长安号高质量发展的若干措施》《西安丝绸之路金融中心发展行动计划（2020—2022年）》等。

2015年以来，省领导小组办公室连续9年印发年度行动计划，明确当年工作要点并安排责任部门分工；省级相关部门、单位和各市（区）根据分工推进工作，及时向省领导小组办公室报送重点任务和重大项目进展情况；省领导小组办公室每半年向省政府报告一次工作进展情况，年底全面盘点和梳理工作推进和完成情况，并积极谋划下一年度工作。

十年间，省领导小组办公室先后建立年度重点工作台账、成员单位联络员、信息报送等制度和"一带一路"防风险工作机制，定期向国家"一带一路"建设领导小组办公室报送任务进展情况。国家"一带一路"建设工作领导小组办公室多次到陕西调研督导"一带一路"建设工作。

3.优化服务保障项目落实

统筹协调是落实重点任务的重要保障。为加强协同，凝聚合力，省领导小组办公室组织成员单位共同议定"一带一路"建设年度工作要点，按月调度重点任务推进情况，建立重大项目协调推进机制，利用新增地方政府债券等政策机遇，推动"一带一路"重要通道、重大平台项目建设。

在专业服务领域，不断健全服务支持体系：建设"一带一路"重大项目库，完善涉外经贸信息数据库，优化企业"走出去"综合服务平台，扩充驻外商贸服务机构，开展多层次人才培训，支持社会专业服务机构，多维度提升服务支持"一带一路"建设的能力和水平。

在风险防控方面，从省级层面完善重点领域风险跟踪、监测、预警体系，加强重大项目风险管理，培训提升企业应急处突能力，规范企业境外投资行为，加强对境外投资项目的指导和监督。

在宣介传播方面，在全国率先建立省级网络宣传平台——陕西一带一路网，精心推出各类重大宣介活动，统筹组织相关论坛、展会，畅通政府、企业、智库及民众之间信息沟通，讲好"一带一路"故事，推动建设经验分享，为各方共建"一带一路"创造合作机会。

POINT 二

陕西"一带一路"建设的实践成效

习近平总书记在第三次"一带一路"建设座谈会上指出,共建"一带一路",要把基础设施"硬联通"作为重要方向,把规则标准"软联通"作为重要支撑,把共建国家人民"心联通"作为重要基础,推动共建"一带一路"高质量发展,取得实打实、沉甸甸的成就。

十年来,陕西落实总书记指示精神,抢抓共建"一带一路"倡议助推西部地区走向开放前沿的历史机遇,践行"硬联通""软联通""心联通",全力推进"一带一路"交通商贸物流中心、国际产能合作中心、科技教育合作中心、国际文化旅游中心、丝绸之路金融中心五大中心建设,打造国内大循环的重要支点、国内国际双循环的战略链接,构建陆海内外联动、东西双向互济的开放格局,深度融入共建"一带一路"大格局,推动陕西社会经济发展迈上新台阶。

（一）畅通道，实现硬联通

交通先行，一通百通。陕西位于中国地理几何中心，承启东西，连接南北。立足区位优势，陕西"一带一路"建设以中欧班列（西安）为先手棋，打造国际陆港、空港等核心枢纽，建成陆海空多式联运的亚欧陆海贸易大通道。西安国际交通枢纽的承载能力和辐射能级显著提升。

1. 高质量发展中欧班列长安号

十年来，陕西高质量发展中欧班列，推动中欧班列长安号开行由"点对点"向"枢纽对枢纽"转变。截至2023年9月，中欧班列长安号累计开行已超过2万列。目前长安号国际运输干线开行17条，基本覆盖亚欧大陆全境，国内开通"+西欧"集结线路21条，辐射全国主要货源地。东向对接全球航运体系，常态化开通西安至青岛、宁波的国际海铁联运五定班列，满足东亚海运货物过境运输需求。南向开通中老、中越国际货运班列和西安至尼泊尔、巴基斯坦公铁联运线路。南北、东西国际物流通道实现在西安聚集融合，有效支撑了全国货源和进口物资的分拨集散需求。

为提升中欧班列长安号的聚集、辐射效应，陕西不断做大做强中欧班列西安集结中心。2020年，全国中欧班列西安集结中心示范工程获国家发展改革委批准；2022年，中欧班列长安号集拼中心获海关批准正式投用。2022年，中欧班列长安号运输的省外货物占比约70%，进口货物中约65%以上从西安国际港站发往全国各地。西安陆港设计集装箱年吞吐量达310万标箱，运力3850万吨，可支撑班列开行上万列。

在发展中欧班列的过程中，陕西坚持政府主导、市场化运行，出台多项政策，持续优化中欧班列长安号的运营组织。2016年10月，组建西安国际陆港多式联运有限公司，统一调度长安号运行。2018年7月，成立西安自贸港建设运营有限公司，进一步加强班列和集结中心的衔接。同时，陕西着力提升西安港枢纽集散功能，陆续引进中远海、中林、山东港、五矿、陕林、陕投等国内外物流及相关服务行业龙头企业，形成集集装箱运输、冷链物流、期货交割、大宗商品、整车运输等功能于一体的集结中心港口功能区；还着力完善集结中心综合服务功能，搭建中欧班列长安号数字金融综合服务平台，开发订舱、租箱、发运、报关、物流运输、集装箱动态、数字金融、跨境结算等数字化应用场景和功能，实现预约订舱与融资服务"一网通办"。中欧班列长安号及西安集结中心成为陕西"一带一路"建设的标杆项目。

2.加速建设国际航空枢纽

航空物流通道作为"一带一路"的重要载体，对服务构建新发展格局具有重要支撑作用。十年来，陕西加快建设西安临空经济示范区，航线网络持续拓展，"空中丝绸之路"不断织密，国际航空枢纽建设成效显著。

2015年,西安航空枢纽建设正式起航,当年西安咸阳机场年旅客吞吐量3297余万人次,货邮吞吐量20.8万吨,分别排名全国第8位和第21位。中国民用航空局发布的统计报告显示,2020年,西咸国际机场克服新冠疫情困难,实现货邮吞吐量37.6万吨,首次与旅客吞吐量一起跻身全国前十,"客多货少"局面初步扭转。

2021年11月,西安空港成为西北地区唯一获批的空港型国家物流枢纽。西咸新区空港新城管理委员会的数据显示,西安空港已累计开通客货运航线386条,其中国际客运航线83条;全货运航线45条。其中,2019年5月,陕西开通首尔—西安—河内第五航权(即第三国运输权)货运航线,西安成为全国第二个获得并使用第五航权全货运航线的城市。截至2023年9月,陕西已开通3条第五航权货运航线和1条第五航权客运航线。

此外,西安咸阳国际机场三期扩建工程启动,分别于2019年1月和2020年1月获国家发改委立项批复和可研批复,2021年7月进入建设实施阶段,计划2025年全面建成投运。届时,西安咸阳国际机场将成为能保障年旅客8300万人次、货邮100万吨的超大型国际航空枢纽。

3. 创新探索多式联运模式

十年来,陕西连接全国的高铁、高速公路及航空交通网络日趋完善。其中,省内高铁营业里程达1019公里,形成西安直达北京、郑州、成都、兰州、银川等城市的"米"字形高速铁路网;高速公路通车里程达 6696 公里,形成连霍、京昆、包茂、福银、沪陕等高速公路快速辐射网;对接中欧班列、陆海联运班列、西部陆海新通道以及空港国内外航线,海陆空立体丝绸之路和国际物流枢纽日臻成型。

"多式联运"是发展综合交通运输体系和建设效率高、成本低、服务优的国际贸易通道的重要支撑,发货人只需同一个承运人订立一份合同,一次付费,通过一张单证即可完成全程运输。在夯实交通基础设施的同时,陕西积极探索铁路、公路、水运、航空等多种运输方式高效联动,主动承担空铁、海铁、公铁多式联运试点示范。

目前,西安港"一带一路"内陆中转枢纽和中铁联集"陆海联动、多点协同"集装箱智能骨干网已成为国家示范工程,西安空港也入选全国首批 29 家"全国示范物流园区",省内陆港、空港联动发展的集装箱疏运体系初步形成,西安、宝鸡、延安入选全国物流枢纽承载城市,全省 A 级物流企业总数突破 230 家。

(二)优服务,推动软联通

充分发挥"硬联通"效益,需要破除"软联通"壁垒,陕西在推动"软联通"上积极作为,先行先试,在中欧班列陆上贸易规制、空中运输航权等领域开展规则探索,扩大规则、规制、管理、标准等制度型开放,加快与区域全面经济伙伴关系协定(RCEP)、中欧投资协定等国际高标准经贸规则衔接。中国（陕西）自贸试验区自2016年8月获批设立以来，累计形成创新案例620项。

1. 便利通关　助力跨境货运提效

在促进"软联通"方面，陕西率先发力通关便利化改革，贸易通关便捷化水平不断提升。"单一窗口"主要业务功能应用率已达100%，"铁路运输方式舱单归并新模式""大型机场运行协调新机制"等31项改革试点经验在全国复制推广。

为提升中欧班列进口通关效率，西安陆港与海关首创铁路运输进口货物"舱单归并、合并申报"，将原来"一柜一单"进口申报模式改为"舱单归并"，同一公司、同一合同、同一品名、同一规格、同一批次的大宗进口货物归并成一个舱单，企业报关时仅需填写一份报关单，可节省90%以上的通关费用和时间。经海关总署批准，西安港务区启动"铁路进出境快速通关业务"，海关对铁路舱单电子数据进行审核、放行、核销，进出境货物可在西安车站海关办结所有通关手续，从阿拉山口、霍尔果斯等边境口岸直接通行，无须另行申报办理转关手续，通关时间压缩一半，班列转关滞留时间大幅缩短。此外，西安落地全国首个"陆路启运港退税"试点，企业自铁路场站出口集装箱货物，在启运报关出口后即可申请退税，与一般货物离境后退税对比，退税时间从平均30天压缩至最快两天，大幅缩短了企业资金被挤占的时间。

西安空港创新国际货物24小时机坪"直提直装"改革，改变以往国际货物抵达机场后须先运至机场货运仓库、经查验后提货的流程，企业在飞机入境前即办理货物报关手续，海关提前审验抵港前已完税或具备税款担保资格企业非开箱查验类货物，发放运抵放行许可，允许在机坪直提直装，实现国际货物24小时"随到随提、随到随装"，比之前在仓库提货可提前2-3天，满足企业对物流时效和特殊商品安全运输"零延时"的迫切要求。

西安空港还先后取得全省首例国际保税维修、大型设备保税融资租赁首单、跨境电商保税备货业务首单、增值税一般纳税人资格试点首单等一批突破性成果。目前，西咸空港综合保税区进口通关平均时间25小时，出口通关平均2.7小时，高于全国平均通关时效。

2. 完善法治　保障畅通经济合作

近年来，陕西积极推进"一带一路"国际商事法律服务示范区建设，构建全功能、全生态链的国际商事法律服务保障，让法治为共建"一带一路"保驾护航。

"一带一路"国际商事法律服务示范区位于西安国际港务区，以国际商事诉讼、调解、仲裁、法律服务、司法人才合作及国际法查明研究为核心功能，是全国唯一面向"一带一路"的法律服务示范区。自2018年12月获准建设以来，示范区已引入一大批专业化、国际化法律平台和服务机构入驻，包括中国—上海合作组织法律服务委员会西安中心、"一带一路"律师联盟西安中心、西安"一带一路"国际商事争端解决中心、国家生物安全证据基地、最高人民法院第二国际商事法庭、最高人民法院第六巡回法庭、西安知识产权法庭、陕西自贸试验区仲裁院以及知名律师事务所等，为示范区核心功能提供重要支撑。

示范区高度重视知识产权保护，组建"一带一路"产业知识产权联盟，探索建设"一带一路"知识产权保护示范区。17家入驻法律服务机构成立陕西省"一带一路"知识产权法律服务协作体。此外，示范区发挥在中国（陕西）自贸试验区实施律师制度政策创新的引领作用，探索创新国际商事争端诉讼、仲裁、调解"一站式"解决新模式，还制订了《支持中国律师"走出去"服务我国全方位对外开放大局的实施方案》。

3. 标准对接　破解市场交易壁垒

标准碎片化是共建"一带一路"国际合作的一大制约。陕西发挥省内科研机构在相关领域的技术优势，积极开展标准研究，双向推动中国标准与国际接轨和中国标准"走出去"，为中外标准对接互认贡献"陕西力量"。

2017年9月，陕西获准设立"一带一路"国家计量测试研究中心（陕西），依托西北国家计量测试中心、陕西省计量科学研究院的技术能力，构建国际计量交流合作平台，发挥计量的基础保障、技术支撑和质量引领作用，提升计量服务对共建"一带一路"的贡献。2021年5月，该中心正式揭牌，成为全国唯一一家服务共建"一带一路"倡议的国家级计量技术研究机构。

"一带一路"国家计量测试研究中心（陕西）筹建以来，已整理共建"一带一路"国家和地区计量法律法规和管理制度200余部；收集编印共建"一带一路"国家和地区背景资料3册；应"走出去"企业计量需求，完成斐济公路项目、马里水电站项目等设备检定，帮助企业降低项目成本；与西北政法大学国际法学院共同开展共建"一带一路"国家和地区计量法律法规研究，研究重点国家的计量法律法规体系，推动我国计量体系国际化。

（三）汇人文，促进心联通

国之交在于民相亲。十年来，陕西发挥文化历史深厚、科教资源丰富的优势，持续推动人文交流和科教合作，助力共建"一带一路"国家和地区人民"心联通"。陕西积极组织丝路考古，推动文明交流互鉴；有力推动了国际教育合作，已使陕西成为中亚国家学生出国留学热门目的地；大力发展跨境旅游，促进中外人民友好往来；积极搭建科创平台，创立示范基地，推广科技成果惠及民生；有力支持了民间筹建人文交流联盟，增进相互了解和传统友谊。十年来，陕西新增国际友城48对，已与41个国家建立了108对国际友城关系，其中共建"一带一路"国家友城54对。

1. 丝路文旅推动文明互鉴

凤鸣岐山，冠盖长安，周礼秦制，汉风唐韵。依托独特的文旅资源，陕西着力打造弘扬华夏文明、传承丝路精神的国际文化旅游中心。

为挖掘丝路文明，西北大学成立"丝绸之路考古中心"，获批建设"中国-中亚人类与环境'一带一路'联合实验室"，已与30多个国家的知名高校和文博机构建立交流合作关系。西北大学考古队在全国率先走出国门，开展境外考古发掘研究，已完成乌兹别克斯坦拉巴特遗址、塔吉克斯坦贝希肯特谷联合考古发掘和调查，正兵分五路开展乌兹别克斯坦大遗址文物发掘整理和保护调研、土库曼斯坦考古项目考察、"一带一路"国际联合实验室建设等工作，还将恢复或启动在哈萨克斯坦、尼泊尔、缅甸、伊朗等地的考古和文化遗产保护项目。

十年来，陕西省成功举办8届丝绸之路国际艺术节、3届世界文化旅游大会、7届西安丝绸之路国际旅游博览会。"国风·秦韵"陕西文化周先后走进意大利、白俄罗斯等20多个国家和地区的友好城市；"从长安到罗马"系列展演等文化交流项目在海内外广受好评；"丝绸之路：长安—天山廊道的路网"成为首例跨国合作、成功申遗的世界文化遗产项目。

为方便人员往来，陕西与联合国世界旅游组织、亚太旅游协会等国际机构合作，联合北京、上海建立了国内首个入境旅游省际合作机制。西安与厦门达成旅游战略合作，推动"海丝陆丝"联动。世界城市和地方政府联盟首个地方行动港——青年教育与对话港落地西安。西安领事馆区加速建设，泰国、韩国、柬埔寨、马来西亚4个国家设立总领事馆,法国、英国、德国等32个国家设立签证中心。

2. 教研合作促进相知相亲

共建"一带一路"的未来属于青年。陕西依托丰富的科教资源,面向未来和国际积极推动高等院校、职业教育学校开展中外合作办学,已连续举办6届丝绸之路教育合作交流会。目前,全省中外合作办学项目和机构达到50个,位居西部第一,全国第八。陕西成立国别和区域研究中心18所,获批教育部援外项目8个。十年来吸引超过10万名外国留学生来陕学习,为共建"一带一路"培养了大批"同路人"。

为加强校际交流,西安交通大学首倡"丝绸之路学术带",发起成立"丝绸之路大学联盟"。成立八年来,联盟持续推动共建"一带一路"国家和地区大学在人才培养、科研项目、文化沟通、政策研究、医疗服务等方面合作,联盟成员不断扩大,目前已有37个国家和地区的150余所高校入盟。陕西师范大学牵头成立了"丝绸之路教师教育联盟""丝绸之路人文社会科学联盟""丝绸之路图书档案出版联盟",已有7个国家的27所高校和研究机构加入联盟。

在共建"一带一路"研究方面,西安交通大学率先成立"丝绸之路经济带研究协同创新中心",西北大学牵头成立陕西高校"一带一路"智库机构联盟,西安财经学院发起成立"西部财经高校丝绸之路智库联盟"。相关智库取得一批法律、政治、社会和文化研究成果，为共建"一带一路"贡献智慧力量。

3. 科技交流赋能务实合作

创新是推动发展的重要力量。十年来，陕西深度参与"一带一路"科技创新行动计划，强化与共建"一带一路"国家在科技创新、成果转化、产业对接、人才交流等方面的合作。全省已建立19个国家级、64个省级国际科技交流合作基地，成立陕西国际科技合作基地联盟，与40多个国家和地区的400多家机构建立了多层次合作关系。2015年以来，全省各类创新主体与国外签订技术合同561项，合同总金额80多亿元。

2020年10月，上合组织农业技术交流培训示范基地在杨凌正式揭牌。基地聚焦"交流、培训、示范"核心功能，开展上合组织成员国间农业科研交流合作、现代农业科技人才培训、农业科技成果推广应用、国际农业产业园区建设，实现各方互利共赢。基地与60多个国家开展现代农业合作，在哈萨克斯坦、乌兹别克斯坦等国建成8个现代农业示范园区、1个农业科技产业园，成功举办30余场上合组织现代农业发展圆桌会等交流活动，上合组织国家2.8万余名学员参加技术培训。

（四）强经贸，深化产能合作

在"硬联通"和"软联通"的基础上，陕西加快融入全球产业链、供应链，对外贸易突飞猛进，自2013年以来全省进出口总额将近翻两番。招商引资和对外投资双向奔赴，高质量"引进来"推动形成先进制造业和现代服务业产业集群，自身产业结构持续升级优化；高水平"走出去"不断深化国际产能合作，助力共建"一带一路"国家和地区提升产业发展水平。

1. 对外贸易强劲增长

陕西积极培育国家外贸转型升级基地、省级特色出口基地等各类外贸集聚区，加快创建国家级进口贸易促进创新示范区。目前，全省国家级外贸转型升级基地达11家，省级外贸综合服务平台企业7家，带动小微企业开展外贸业务，对外贸易实现跨越式增长。

2022年，陕西进出口总额4835亿元，是2013年的3.88倍，期间年均增长18.5%，远超全国同期6.3%的年均增速；其中，出口3011亿元，年均增长21.5%；进口1824亿元，年均增长14.6%。陕西与共建"一带一路"国家和地区贸易增长尤为迅猛，"十三五"以来年均增长28.1%，超过全省进出口同期平均增速11.2个百分点；其中2022年对共建"一带一路"国家和地区进出口额突破1000亿元，比上年增长41%，占全省进出口总额比例从2015年的13.5%提升到23.3%。

随着跨境电子商务爆发式增长，陕西抢抓"网上新丝路"机遇，重点推进西安跨境电子商务综合试验区建设，推动外贸新业态、新模式蓬勃发展。截至2022年底，西安市拥有跨境电商及相关企业 1800 余家，全年跨境电商交易额达 144.27 亿元，同比增长 46.4%。

西安跨境电子商务综合试验区利用试点政策优势，打通"关、税、汇、检、商、物、融"交互通道和数据壁垒，实施跨境电商 1210 保税备货模式、9610 集货模式、9710B2B 直接出口模式、9810 出口海外仓模式等监管模式全覆盖。中欧班列长安号先后开行至杜伊斯堡、汉堡、莫斯科等的多条跨境电商专列，对跨境电商包裹实施即到、即查、即放行，24 小时内完成清关查验。2022 年，中欧班列长安号共开行跨境电商班列 198 列，同比增长超 60%。

2. 产业结构持续升级

"硬联通""软联通"推动陕西营商环境不断优化，招商引资吸引力不断增强。截至目前，世界 500 强企业累计在陕设立 144 家企业，三星、美光等外资巨头持续加大投资，扩大产能，2021 年全省实际利用外资首次突破 100 亿美元（含外商投资企业利润再投资），2013 年以来年均增长 18.3%。华为、中兴、比亚迪、吉利、创维、康佳等一批国内龙头企业入陕投资建厂，近五年高新技术制造业增加值年均增长 13.1%，是规模以上工业增加值平均增速的两倍多。高质量"引进来"有力推动了陕西产业结构升级优化，显著提升了陕西参与共建"一带一路"的能级。

陕西半导体协会公布的数据显示，在三星、美光、英飞凌等龙头企业带动下，陕西半导体产业销售额从 2011 年的 100 亿元增长到2022年的1228亿元，增幅超10倍，全国排名从第8位上升至第4位，仅次于江苏、上海和广东。国内外一大批硅片制造、显示器制造等大型加工贸易企业入陕，壮大了陕西新兴电子产业集群。

陕西新能源汽车发展迅速，形成省内又一个千亿级产业。2022年，西安新能源汽车产量在全国率先突破100万辆，超过上海成为全国新能源汽车产量第一城，其中比亚迪贡献产量99.5万辆。比亚迪还在商洛设立了电池生产基地，与宝鸡签订了战略合作协议，投资建设新能源汽车零部件基地。据不完全统计，截至2023年7月，比亚迪在陕累计投资超过550亿元，涵盖新能源乘用车及零部件、动力电池、智能终端及半导体研发中心等项目。西安已成为比亚迪继深圳总部外，发展质量最高、布局产业最全的北方基地。此外，西安"比亚迪专线"已开工，将铁路货运专线引入比亚迪四期厂区西侧的货场，将于2025年投入运营，届时可更方便工业区整车、零配件及高新区相关企业产成品通过中欧班列出口至中亚国家。

吉利汽车也积极扩大在陕产能，总投资78亿元的30万辆新能源整车项目落户西安，建成吉利全球首个全架构、全车系超级智能黑灯工厂，2022年首批车辆下线，2023年4月首次通过中欧班列长安号吉利汽车出口专列出口整车。

3.产能合作不断深化

借助共建"一带一路"，陕西对外投资稳步扩大，与共建"一带一路"国家和地区的务实合作持续深化。"十三五"期间，陕西年均对外直接投资 7.96 亿美元，比"十二五"年均提高 65.7%；年均新签对外承包工程合同金额 36.77 亿美元，比"十二五"年均翻番。

陕西一批龙头企业加快布局海外市场。陕西鼓风机（集团）系统解决方案和服务已遍及全球 100 多个国家和地区，隆基绿能科技已全球布局 32 个生产基地和 150 多个分支机构，陕西汽车集团重卡远销 110 多个国家和地区，陕西建设集团负责海外业务的全资子公司华山国际在 32 个国家（地区）设立了属地经营机构。

法士特集团是第一批国家级制造业单项冠军示范企业，其重型汽车变速器产销量连续 17 年稳居世界第一。法士特独资建设的首家海外工厂"法士特汽车传动（泰国）有限公司"于 2014 年 10 月全面投产，是目前东盟唯一一家重型变速器生产企业，以泰国为中心，以越南、印度为节点，建立覆盖东盟主要商用车市场的销售服务网络，同时辐射全球市场，成功加入戴姆勒、卡特彼勒、伊顿等世界著名汽车及零部件企业的全球供应链体系。2023 年，法士特将新一代新能源动力总成引入泰国市场，已获得 500 台新能源动力总成的订单。

光伏巨头隆基绿能于 2016 年在马来西亚投资 3.11 亿美元建设首个海外生产基地"隆基（古晋）有限公司"，2020 年以 17.8 亿元收购越南光伏项目，目前已在马来西亚建成拥有拉晶、切片、电池和组件四个工厂的全产业链基地，完成对越南电池和组件工厂的升级改造，正计划在印度设立电池和组件生产基地，有力支持了项目所在国扩大绿色能源产品出口，发展光伏发电。最近三年，海外收入已占隆基绿能营收总额的40%。

作为国家级农业产业化重点龙头企业，西安爱菊粮油工业集团依托西安国际港务区口岸功能和中欧班列长安号开放通道，与哈萨克斯坦开展产能合作，建设"哈萨克斯坦北哈州、新疆阿拉山口、西安国际港务区"三位一体农产品加工物流园，与北哈州签订150万亩"订单农业"协议，收购当地油料、小麦等，建成油料压榨、面粉加工年产能各30万吨，带动当地就业1000多人。2022年，爱菊集团从哈萨克斯坦累计进口农产品近30万吨，为哈萨克斯坦创汇1亿多美元。

乘着共建"一带一路"东风，近年来，承接海外工程项目的华山国际工程有限公司合同签约额以年均20%以上速度增长，其中2022年新签合同额120.85亿元，同比增长20.7%。华山国际近年荣获8项境外工程鲁班奖、4项境外工程国家优质工程奖，一批精品工程成为造福当地百姓的"民心工程"。例如，2018年建成的奥什医院是吉尔吉斯斯坦南部规模最大、现代化水平最高的医院，投用后改善了当地医疗基础设施落后的局面，缓解当地民众看病难；乌兹别克斯坦布斯坦渠道修复项目于2023年3月顺利通水，改善当地10多万公顷农田水资源短缺问题，灌溉效率提高60%，每年可节约水资源近3亿立方米。

主题篇

2016年印发的《陕西省推进建设丝绸之路经济带和21世纪海上丝绸之路实施方案（2015—2020）》，首次提出打造"一带一路"交通商贸物流、国际产能合作、科技教育、国际文化旅游、丝绸之路金融五大中心的主要目标，将打造"一带一路"五大中心作为贯彻落实国家"五通"要求的陕西实践。

十年来，陕西立足交通区位、产业、科教、历史文化等优势，围绕五大中心建设，出台政策、落实措施、投入资金、真抓实干，深度融入"一带一路"大格局，努力构建陆海内外联动、东西双向互济的开放格局。

如今，交通商贸物流中心建设率先取得重要突破，陕西作为"一带一路"商贸物流枢纽的作用凸显；持续稳步推进国际产能合作中心建设，"走出去""引进来"取得务实成效；着力构建"一带一路"科技教育中心，扎实推动科教人文的国际合作增量、拓点、扩面；发挥独特资源，国际文化旅游中心建设亮点突出，陕西文旅的发展活力与国际影响力与日俱增；丝绸之路金融中心建设着力于创新产品服务，积极开展试点，推动金融发挥对"一带一路"建设的支撑功能。

交通商贸物流中心枢纽功能彰显

十年来，陕西立足区位优势，出台政策措施，保证资金投入，以高水平通道建设为"先手棋"，效率高、成本低、服务优的亚欧陆海贸易大通道加快形成，面向国际的交通物流网络日渐成型，交通商务物流中心的枢纽功能日渐彰显。中欧班列长安号多项指标领跑全国，开行量累计突破20000列，常态化开行的17条国际线路通达45个国家和地区；"空中丝绸之路"织线成网，在全国率先实现中亚"五国六城"通航全覆盖；外贸盘子不断做大，不断完善海外仓、境外进出口商品仓储加工配送中心等布局，2013年至2022年，陕西与共建"一带一路"国家和地区进出口额年均增长18.4%。

（一）加快形成亚欧陆海贸易大通道

1. 中欧班列长安号领跑全国

共建"一带一路"倡议提出的当年，首趟中欧班列长安号于

2013年11月28日从西安开出。历经十年三个阶段的发展，中欧班列长安号年开行量由百余列增长到如今的4000余列，班列开行量、重箱率、货运量等多项指标稳居全国第一，常态化开行的17条国际线路通达45个国家和地区，开行21条"+西欧"线路，开行量占全国总量超20%。如今的中欧班列长安号已成为运输时效最快、智能化程度最高、线路辐射最广、服务功能最全、综合成本最低的"五最"班列。与此同时，中欧班列西安集结中心建设提速，构筑起一条效率高、成本低、服务优的国际贸易"黄金通道"。

起步探索期（2013—2017年）。中欧班列长安号开行之初，由中国铁路西安局集团公司负责组织运营，主要开行中亚方向班列；2016年，组建成立了长安号运营平台公司——西安国际陆港多式联运有限公司，开拓了西安至中亚五国、波兰、德国、匈牙利、俄罗斯5条干线通道，实现了首趟欧洲方向班列开行。这一阶段累计开行486列。

突破发展期（2018—2019年）。创新提出了政府主导、多平台运作、市场化运行的中欧班列开行思路，组建成立了西安自贸港建设运营有限公司，搭建了宏观可控的多平台运营模式。常态化运行西安至中亚五国、伊朗（阿富汗）、德国、波兰、捷克、芬兰、匈牙利、比利时、白俄罗斯、土耳其及俄罗斯等13条干线通道，向东稳定开行西安至青岛、宁波国际海铁联运班列，长安号辐射范围不断扩大。这一阶段，班列年度开行量迈上2000列台阶，累计开行3368列，跻身全国中欧班列开行城市的前列。

高质量发展期（2020年至今）。全面改造提升西安国际港务区的港口设施，不断创新中欧班列长安号的服务模式，提升运营水平，积极拓展境内外合作，推动港产港贸港城融合发展，加快建设中欧班列西安集结中心。新开通了跨黑海、里海线路，南向开通中老、中越班列，长安号国际运输干线达到17条，基本覆盖欧亚大陆全境，"+西欧"集结线路增加至21条；东向开通了西安至青岛的国际海铁联运五定班列，有效满足了日韩过境运输需求，实现南北、东西国际物流通道在西安聚集融合。2023年1—9月，中欧班列长安号开行3991列，同比增长29.54%，运送货物总重355.2万吨，同比增长35.2%。其中，中欧方向开行3541列，中亚方向开行450列。总体来看，中欧班列长安号的开行量、货运量、重箱率等核心指标稳居全国第一。

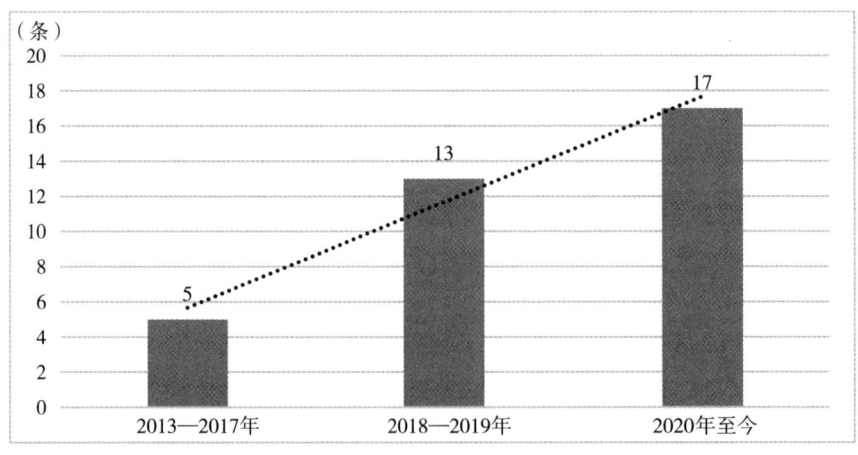

图1 2013—2023年中欧班列长安号开行线路数量

数据来源：陕西一带一路网。

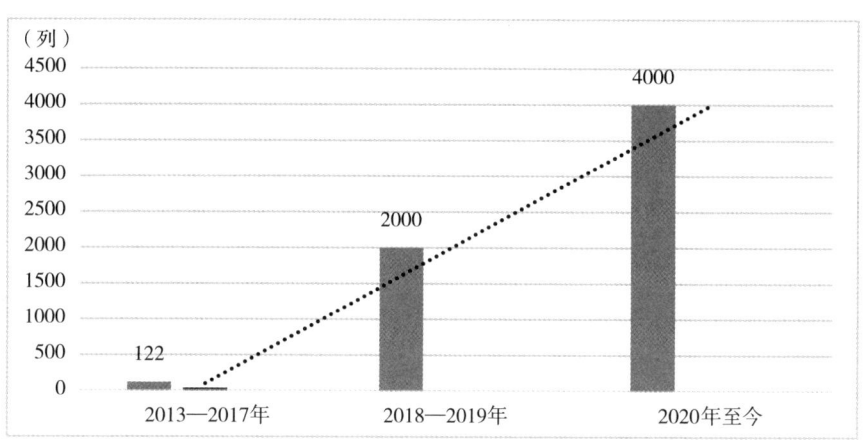

图2 2013—2023年中欧班列长安号年度平均开行列数

数据来源：陕西一带一路网。

作为便利快捷、安全稳定、绿色经济的新型国际运输组织方式，中欧班列长安号是陕西参与全球开放合作、融入"一带一路"大格局的主要实践，促进了陕西与共建"一带一路"国家之间的交流合作。新冠疫情期间，中欧班列长安号保持安全稳定运行并实现逆势增长，体现了陕西在稳定国际产业链供应链、助力国际抗疫合作中的担当，中欧班列长安号的战略作用也日益显现。

2."空中丝绸之路"织线成网

十年来，陕西主要依托西安咸阳国际机场和西咸新区空港新城，将"空中丝绸之路"织线成网，开通西安至乌兹别克斯坦首都塔什干、吉尔吉斯斯坦首都比什凯克、哈萨克斯坦首都阿斯塔纳、土库曼斯坦首都阿什哈巴德、塔吉克斯坦首都杜尚别的国际航线，在全国率先实现中亚"五国六城"通航全覆盖。

如今,西安咸阳国际机场累计开通386条客货运航线,其中国际客运航线83条,全货运航线45条,开通4条第五航权航线,加速构建"丝路贯通、欧美直达、五洲相连"航线网络格局。从西安出发,2小时航程可覆盖我国75%的领土和85%的经济资源,5小时航程可覆盖全亚洲城市,12小时航程可覆盖全欧洲城市,对陕西打造内陆开放高地形成有力支撑。

航空物流通道作为"一带一路"的重要载体,对服务"双循环"、发展新格局具有重要支撑作用。作为西北地区唯一的空港型国家物流枢纽,陕西省西咸新区空港新城通过建设空中货运走廊、打造国际贸易集散中心、创新通关监管模式等方式,加速构建辐射广、效率高、成本低、服务优的国际航空枢纽和贸易物流通道。

如今,西咸新区空港新城已成为西北地区最大的航企聚集区、功能最全的空港型国家物流枢纽,聚集普洛斯、丰树、日立和"三

图3 2014—2021年西安全货运航线数量

通一达"等近200家现代物流企业，建成投运物流园区13个，落户东航、海航等14家航空公司区域总部和芬兰航空、大韩航空等15家外航办事处。

图4　2015—2022年西安货邮吞吐量

数据来源：综合陕西省商务厅及互联网数据。

3.陆海空网联动协同渐成体系

陕西积极开展空铁、公铁、海铁多式联运试点示范，推进西安港"一带一路"内陆中转枢纽和中铁联集"陆海联动、多点协同"集装箱智能骨干网两个国家示范工程建设，全省空港、陆港联动发展的集疏运体系正加快形成。

开通首条TIR（国际公路运输系统）国际跨境公路货运线路。2023年6月，4辆标有TIR标示牌的卡车从陕西西咸空港综合保税区卡口出发，向目的地哈萨克斯坦驶去，标志着陕西省（西安—哈萨克斯坦）首条 TIR 国际跨境公路货运线路的开通。此举进一步完善了陕西到中亚乃至全球开放通道，填补了西安的陆空多式联运短板，有力促进了陕西与共建"一带一路"国家尤其是中亚国家的经贸合作。

路网布局进一步优化。着力推进以西安为中心的"米"字形陆路交通网建设，形成"安全便捷、衔接顺畅、绿色智能"的陆路交通体系。持续完善高速公路网络，2015 年以来先后建成延安至延川、太白至凤县、平利至镇平等高速公路，目前全省高速公路通车总里程达到 6696 公里，形成连霍、京昆、包茂、福银、沪陕等高速快速辐射网。持续完善高铁路网格局，郑西、宝兰、西成、西银等高铁先后开通运营，西延、西康、西十、延榆鄂高铁建设前期工作取得积极进展，高铁营业里程达到 1019 公里，实现了西安至北京、郑州、成都、兰州、银川等城市快速直达。

（二）打造高效便捷物流集疏体系

1. 集结中心提升枢纽集散功能

根据 2022 年 5 月印发的《中欧班列西安集结中心建设方案》，陕西落实国家"1+N+X"政策体系，围绕基础设施保障、信息化智能化建设、港产港贸港城融合发展三大领域，梳理谋划了 45 个重点项目，总投资 2241.57 亿元。如今，这些项目正在产生实效，集结中心的建设提速，提升了西安作为国际化物流枢纽的集散功能。

贸易通道体系建成达效，实现由"线"到"面"的转变。向西、向北创新开行跨两海线路，长安号干线通道增加至现在的17条，基本覆盖欧亚大陆全境；向东常态化开行西安至青岛、宁波国际海铁联运五定班列，有效满足了日韩过境运输需求，无缝对接全球航运体系；向南开通了中老、中越国际货运班列以及西安至尼泊尔、巴基斯坦公铁联运线路，实现南北、东西国际物流通道在西安聚集融合；通过"干支结合"的方式构建了"+西欧"集结体系，集结线路达到21条，资源要素的吸引力持续增强。

集结中心的综合服务功能持续完善。西安国际港站建成集装箱堆场69万平方米、铁路线路59条，日装卸作业能力3700标箱。以集结中心承载项目为牵引，不断完善港口功能，加快完善公铁快线、海关查验设施等，中欧班列长安号的集拼中心获批投用，西安国际港站拥有48条到发线，设计集装箱年吞吐量达310万标箱。

以集结中心建设为抓手，中欧班列服务陕西的聚集效应加速释放。近年来，西安国际港务区陆续引进了中林、山东港、五矿、陕林、陕投等行业龙头企业，建设了集集装箱运输、冷链物流、期货交割、大宗商品、整车运输等功能于一体的中欧班列西安集结中心港口功能区。截至目前，已引进世界500强企业31家、中国500强企业8家、中国民营500强企业5家。与此同时，快递、冷链、商贸、电商等重点物流领域聚集，京东"三大总部"、阿里巴巴丝路总部等一批企业总部或物流中转中心落户，陕西的A级物流企业突破230家。

2. 通关便利助力货运便捷直达

跨境电商综试区建设稳步推进，开行跨境电商专列。2022年1月1日，搭载着满载电子配件、跨境电商产品的50个集装箱，中欧班列长安号（西安—圣彼得堡—曼海姆）跨境电商专列驶出西安国际港，奔向德国曼海姆。跨境电商专列的开行，提高了国际货运物流效率，丰富了中欧班列西安集结中心的功能。截至目前，陕西已先后开行杜伊斯堡、汉堡、莫斯科等多条跨境电商专列和中欧班列长安号国际运邮专线，实现跨境货物直达欧洲20余个城市。2022年共开行跨境电商班列198列，同比增长60.9%，保持全国首位。

启动"铁路进出境快速通关业务"，落地全国首个陆路启运港退税试点。2022年4月，西安国际港务区成为全国首个陆路启运港退税试点的内陆港，中欧班列长安号成为首个享受启运港退税政策的铁路班列。跨境货物所有通关手续在西安车站海关即办即结，通关时间压缩1/2，退税时限从平均30天压缩至最快2天，有效降低了跨境贸易企业的综合物流成本。

信息化赋能高效通关。在西安国际港务区建设中欧班列长安号跨境电商集拼中心，信息化、可视化、智能化通关服务系统，实现信息化管理和高效通关。跨境电商散货通过"先报关，后装箱"的新模式，节约货物通关时间2至3天。实施跨境电商1210保税备货模式、9610集货模式、9710B2B直接出口模式、9810出口海外仓模式全覆盖，开通跨境电商"绿色通道"，对跨境电商包裹运输实施"优先装车、优先制票、优先挂运",实行货物即到、即查、即放行,实现24小时内完成清关查验。

3.服务平台帮助企业降本增效

依托铁路西安西站办事大厅,陕西将铁路运单审批与市场监管、税务、行政审批等服务内容进行"一厅集成式"办理,构建政策咨询、登记注册、纳税、货物发运、仓储等全链条综合服务体系。同时建设中欧班列长安号数字金融综合服务平台,开发订舱、租箱、发运、报关、物流运输、集装箱动态、数字金融、跨境结算等数字化应用场景和功能,实现预约订舱与融资服务"一网通办"。在德国、哈萨克斯坦、白俄罗斯等地布局建设8个跨境电商海外仓,衔接当地卡班网络、分拨中心等,为跨境商家提供"端到端、门到门"全链路物流服务,企业综合成本下降约10%。通过购买自备箱、减免跨境电商清单申报货物场站作业费、查验费等措施,实现跨境电商申报货物每柜查验费用平均降低1800元,大幅降低了企业运营成本。

(三)助力对外贸易实现跨越式发展

1.高端平台引领对外经贸合作

丝博会助力打造内陆对外开放新高地。从2016年起,中国东西部合作与投资贸易洽谈会正式更名为丝绸之路国际博览会暨中国东西部合作与投资贸易洽谈会。截至目前，已连续举办六届丝博会，先后有俄罗斯、英国、塞尔维亚等多个国家担任主宾国。丝博会展览面积、参展企业、展品数量连创新高，专业化、国际化、品牌化、信息化水平大幅提升，已经成为推动共建"一带一路"、推进西部大开发、促进东中西部地区联动发展的重要平台。前五届丝博会累计签订外资项目合同金额342亿美元，高新技术成果交易合同金额202亿元。第六届丝博会共有来自韩国、泰国、新加坡等70多个国家和地区的境外嘉宾与客商以及国内20多个省份的客商通过线上和线下结合的方式参会，并创新设置了区域全面经济伙伴关系协定（RCEP）专题展区，举办2022中国（陕西）——RCEP区域经贸合作圆桌会，进一步拓宽RCEP各成员国间的合作空间。

中国杨凌农业高新科技成果博览会引领高质量"一带一路"农业合作。杨凌农高会是国家5A级农业综合展会和国际展览业协会（UFI）认证展会，荣获中国驰名商标，品牌价值达871.19亿元。从1994年创办至今，杨凌农高会连续举办29届，是国内规模最大的农业综合性展会，集中展示国内外农业高新技术成果和先进适用技术。共建"一带一路"倡议提出以来，杨凌农高会的规模逐年扩大，国际化、市场化、专业化水平不断提升，已成为"国际知名、国内一流、市场认可、农民喜爱"的农科盛会。第29届中国杨凌农业高新科技成果博览会以线上线下相结合的方式在陕西成功举办，累计参观人数294.8万人次，征集签约项目338个，总金额突破988亿元，其中现场签约49个项目，签约金额295.08亿元。

欧亚经济论坛推动"一带一路"经贸频密互动。欧亚经济论坛是以上海合作组织国家为主体，面向广大欧亚地区的国家级大型机制性涉外论坛，每两年举办一届。西安是欧亚经济论坛的永久会址，自2005年以来已举办9届，成为促进相关国家地区经济文化发展的重要国际交流合作平台。通过论坛这一平台，与会各国先后签署了《西安共识》《西安倡议》《推进贸易安全与便利西安倡议》《共建丝绸之路经济带西安宣言》等一系列区域交流合作的纲领性文件，表达了与会各国共建"一带一路"的共同愿望和坚定信心，拓展了亚欧各国之间的合作空间。历届论坛先后签署或发布《上合组织发展报告》《中国企业欧亚国家投资报告》《丝绸之路黄金旅游走廊》等成果30余项，促成合作项目90余个。

2. 贸产融合增强物流商贸后劲

中欧班列的溢出效应日趋显著，服务企业超过1.65万家，推动港产、港贸、港城加速融合，西安国际港务区已落户康佳、汇芯等制造企业40余家，大宗贸易企业达886家。

加快港产融合。西安国际港务区依托国家加工贸易产业园和西安综合保税区，加快建设"一带一路"临港产业园，积极承接东南沿海产业转移。截至目前，临港产业园建设已全部完成，入园企业11家，京虹科技、硕达视创、思达智、威码逊、德世美、华展科技等9家企业已投产运营；康佳智能家电总部项目2022年10月投产运营，康佳丝路科技城、汇芯未来信息技术应用创新产业基地项目已开工建设。以西安国家医学中心建设为契机，主动谋划医工科技新兴产业，签约落地西部超导医工科技项目、联东U谷·医工科技/智能制造创新港项目等10亿元以上重大项目，布局国内首家超导重离子加速器研发和产业化基地。加速聚集科技创新氛围，引进汇芯国家级5G中高频器件创新中心西安分中心、康佳陕西研究院等11家优质研发企业；引进香港恒星联、深圳华晟物联等企业研发中心落户，打造中小企业科技研发区域中心。

加快港贸融合。加快建设金属、粮食、木材、冷链、整车等大宗商品交易中心，2022年大宗贸易营收规模1230亿元，同比增长17%；以国货崛起为契机，建设"丝路电商中心"，引进菜鸟国际、极兔国际、叮当快药3家估值过百亿的独角兽企业；夯实中欧班列长安号跨境电商全国集结中心，开行跨境电商高质量班列198列，同比增长61%，在全国率先开展跨境电商散货铁路集拼业务，引进菜鸟全球非空转运中心和世界500强CEVA全国铁路智慧集拼中心项目，促进园区进出口额稳步增长。抢抓外贸新赛道，大力发展跨境电商直播产业，围绕中央商务区打造"一带一路"电商创新中心，引进杭州配播、武汉声量、陕西微聚等14家龙头直播电商企业，打造集国内直播、跨境直播、短视频制作、主播培训为一体的直播电商生态圈。

加快港城融合。在建设招商局、华润、中电建、中粮等十大总部基础上，再引进中石化、国家电网、农行数字化等总部项目，打造中欧班列西安集结中心中央商务区。以第二国际商事法庭为核心的"一带一路"国际商事法律服务示范区高效运营,积极引进陕西云德、合恒等律师事务所,2022年度园区入驻律师事务所总体营收已突破1.3亿元;加快建设西安国际仲裁中心,西安仲裁委员会已顺利搬迁入区;在陕西法网成功开设了"一带一路"国际商事法律服务示范区专栏,"中欧班列线上综合服务平台"法律服务模块已上线调试。依托奥体中心、丝路国际体育文化交流培训基地,加快"国家综合体育训练基地"授予相关事宜,构建面向"一带一路"的文化、体育、教育、科技、法律的国家级人文交流平台,打造面向"一带一路"的城市会客厅。

初步形成临空经济全产业链。陕西西咸新区空港新城充分释放"临空、自贸、保税、跨境、口岸、航权"六大功能平台叠加优势,构建面向"一带一路"、辐射全球的货运航线网络。"阡陌纵横"的空中通道带来临空经济的爆发式增长。围绕"航空枢纽保障业、临空先进制造业、临空高端服务业"三大主导产业,聚集航空制造、电子信息、生物医药等产业项目,临空经济全产业链初步形成,正在成为"高精尖"产业发展的热土。截至2022年底,空港新城累计新增市场主体30626家,其中国家高新技术企业25家、其他科技型企业104家,申报科技型中小企业134家。西咸空港综合保税区自2020年1月经国务院正式批复成立以来,进出口额成倍增长至2022年的82.2亿元,年均增速83.4%;保税区业务趋向多元,临空经济产值突破120亿元。

国际产能合作中心建设稳步推进

十年来,作为能源大省和重要装备制造业基地,陕西充分发挥节点作用,积极融入全球产业链供应链,打造国际产能合作中心。一方面,高水平"走出去",深度参与国际产业分工,多家龙头企业加快海外布局,一批标志性工程统筹推进。2013—2022年,陕西对共建国家投资12.4亿美元,占同期全省对外投资总额的23.8%;在共建国家完成工程承包营业额135.7亿美元,占同期全省对外承包工程的52.6%。另一方面,高质量"引进来",充分发挥自由贸易区的先行先试功能,不断优化营商环境,依托中俄、中欧等国际产业合作园区,吸引三星、比亚迪、康佳等龙头企业在陕布局产能基地,着力打造有国际竞争力的特色产业集群。

(一)雄厚基础拓展合作领域

共建"一带一路"倡议提出以来,陕西得益于雄厚的能源及制造业产业基础优势,持续推动传统产业及高端装备制造业迈上新台阶，形成了一批竞争力强的企业集团，延长石油、陕煤、陕鼓、法士特、隆基绿能、爱菊等一批企业积极出海谋求新的发展空间。

1. 能源及高端装备制造业基础雄厚

优势产业是推进国际产能合作的基础，也是开展制度创新的前提。

在能源产业方面，陕西省原油、天然气产量稳居全国第一，原煤产量居全国第三，是全国重要能源基地。延长石油、陕煤集团入围世界500强企业名录，成为支撑国际产能合作的关键主体。

在制造业方面，陕西加快打造一批先进产业集群，既包括现代农业技术、能源矿产、工程承包等传统产业，又包含清洁能源、装备制造、集成电路等朝阳产业。陕西龙头企业通过持续深化与共建"一带一路"国家的务实合作，加快布局海外市场，形成了互利共赢的国际产能合作生态。

2. 共建园区搭建深化产能合作载体

中俄丝路创新园打造中俄产能合作平台。作为中俄两国政府战略层面的合作项目之一，中俄丝路创新园"一园两地"，两国联合组建中俄合作投资委员会统一管理与协调，由中俄双方共同开发，是两国产能合作的重要载体之一。中方园区位于西安西咸新区沣东新城，定位高新技术产业；俄方园区位于莫斯科格林伍德国际贸易中心，定位总部经济、信息技术等领域。目前中方园区已引入53家企业和机构，独联体科技成果库、中俄海洋联合实验室、外籍院士专家工作站等科技项目和科研平台相继落地，建成"一站式"国际企业服务窗口、俄罗斯国家对外语言等级考试中心。俄方园区致力打造陕西企业赴俄投资的大本营，目前已引入22家企业。

中欧合作产业园承载高端制造业。中欧合作产业园的目标是建设集科创研发、创业孵化和高端商务配套为一体的对外开放产业综合体，着力引进欧洲和国内掌握尖端技术的智能制造中心企业，高标准打造智能制造、机器人研发制造、科技服务等智能工厂。这一园区计划分两期、两区开发建设。一期高铁新城片区规划面积约800亩，于2023年建成运营，已引入德国博世、宝马，法国阿尔斯通、法国国家铁路、达能、瑞士布勒、欧瑞康等欧洲企业投资的9个项目；二期泾渭新城片区规划面积约1200亩，主要引进汽车、高端装备、新材料、消费品制造、军民融合、通用航空、金融与现代服务业，落地发展高铁新城起步区中孵化的优质科技型项目，形成相应的专业化科技制造工业园区。

3. 政策措施保障产能合作高效推进

十年来，陕西出台多项政策措施，为推进国际产能合作中心建设保驾护航。

2015年，陕西省政府相继出台《关于进一步做好境外投资工作的实施意见》《关于加快实施"走出去"的战略意见》，重点鼓励企业参与共建"一带一路"国家的基础设施建设。在农业合作上，以非洲、中亚和东欧为重点，扶持有条件的涉农企业在境外进行农作物种植、畜牧业养殖、农产品加工等领域的投资与项目合作。

2016年陕西省出台《关于推进国际产能和装备制造合作的实施意见》，明确支持在能源化工、有色冶金、建材等十大领域推进国际产能和装备制造合作，以此推动经济结构调整和产业优化升级。2017年，陕西省国资委出台《关于推进省属企业开展国际产能合作的意见》，从4个方面对省属企业参与"一带一路"建设进行引导和规范。

《陕西省"十四五"深度融入共建"一带一路"大格局、建设内陆开放高地规划》提出，"十四五"时期，通过提升产业链国际竞争力、推动合作园区建设、强化能源产业合作，提高国际产能合作中心发展水平。

在2023年"中国—中亚峰会"后陕西提出，将支持企业在中亚五国设立海外仓，进一步推动陕西省轻工日用消费品、石油钻井机械等出口，扩大重要能源资源、粮食、植物油、肉类等进口，推进与中亚五国经贸合作走深走实。

（二）"走出去"深度参与国际产业分工

十年来，陕西对外投资合作稳步推进，陕企积极"走出去"拓展海外市场，深度参与国际产业分工。隆基绿能在全球布局32个生产基地和150多个分支机构，隆基绿能马来西亚光伏组件生产项目在当地创造近 4000 个就业岗位；爱菊粮油集团在哈萨克斯坦发展 150 万亩"订单农业"，每年可压榨油料、加工面粉各 30 万吨，西安爱菊哈萨克斯坦粮油经贸合作区被列入"中哈产能与投资 55 个合作项目清单"；陕汽重卡远销全球 110 多个国家和地区；陕鼓系统解决方案和系统服务遍及全球 100 多个国家和地区；陕西建工集团承建的奥什医院项目是吉尔吉斯斯坦南部最大的现代化大型综合医院。

1. 传统优势产业"走出去"互利共赢

产能合作的核心是互利共赢。十年来，陕西的油气、农业、承包工程等传统优势领域积极"走出去"，与众多发展中国家加快工业化步伐的战略高度契合，成为双方合作共赢的最大交集。油气领域，延长石油已获得吉尔吉斯斯坦 1.13 万平方公里油气区块勘探开发权，并与哈萨克斯坦多个油气资源区块开发进行商谈合作。2017 年，陕煤集团下属中亚能源公司在吉尔吉斯斯坦投资的中大石油公司 80 万吨 / 年炼油项目正式投产运行，为保障吉尔吉斯斯坦市场各类成品油及液化气的供应发挥重要作用。

农业领域，陕西积极发挥农业领域的产业优势，在中亚及周边国家布局，铸就"一带一路"粮食进出口陆路通道，打造中国的海外粮仓。依托陕西杨凌上合组织农业技术交流培训示范基地平台，陕西持续开展农业科研交流合作、现代农业科技人才培养培训、国际农业产业园区建设，实现区域间互利共赢。

爱菊集团与哈萨克斯坦开展产能合作，建成"北哈州、新疆阿拉山口、西安"中外三位一体园区。目前，爱菊集团在哈萨克斯坦建成年加工30万吨的油脂厂，与当地农场主建立友好合作机制，签订150万亩"订单农业"协议，累计收购油料、小麦等近40万吨，直接和间接带动当地就业1000多人，为哈萨克斯坦创汇10000多万美元。

工程承包领域，陕西建工集团华山国际工程有限公司等一批企业"走出去"，在共建"一带一路"国家承建各类工程，为促进基础设施互联互通贡献陕企力量。十年来，华山国际工程公司加快"走出去"步伐，在阿联酋、巴基斯坦、马来西亚建立经营分支机构负责海外市场开发，业务涉及斯里兰卡、孟加拉国、沙特阿拉伯、乌兹别克斯坦、塔吉克斯坦等共建"一带一路"国家。

图5 2013—2022年陕西省对外承包工程营业额

数据来源：陕西省商务厅。

2. 现代高端装备制造业海外谱新篇

十年来，陕西高端制造企业持续加快海外市场的拓展步伐，在马来西亚、泰国等共建"一带一路"国家加大投入，不断取得项目及市场突破，逐步实现海外高水平发展。

陕鼓集团的节能环保产品、系统解决方案和系统服务方案覆盖印尼、马来西亚等数十个国家和地区。在越南，陕鼓集团与用户签订高炉EPC工程项目，确立了企业在世界范围冶金领域高炉风机设备的领先地位。

作为中国齿轮行业领军企业，法士特集团泰国工厂2014年建成投产，具备年产3万台变速器的生产能力。目前，法士特泰国工厂已为海外地区几十家汽车厂提供变速器，涉及高端化、智能化、自动化十多个系列、二十多个品种，配套范围和销量逐步攀升，助力法士特加速向战略全球化、定位高端化、市场细分化、品牌国际化的目标迈进。

3. 清洁能源为"一带一路"添绿色

当前，全球能源生产和消费格局面临深度调整，能源清洁低碳转型不断加速。陕鼓、隆基等企业持续创新，通过技术支持、能力建设、咨询服务等方式，参与到共建国家的清洁能源产业发展进程中，为"一带一路"添绿色。

作为分布式能源系统解决方案和节能环保技术提供商，陕鼓积极拓展共建国家的分布式能源市场，相继获得印尼OSS燃煤发电运维项目等合同。截至目前，陕鼓承建的海外工程遍及近百个国家，系统解决方案能力不断增强。

隆基绿能积极响应共建"一带一路"倡议，2016年在马来西亚古晋投资3.11亿美元，建设首个海外生产基地隆基（古晋）有限公司。隆基绿能在马来西亚大力发展光伏产业的同时，积极履行企业社会责任，改善当地学校条件、减少贫困人口、培训技术人才、增加就业机会、改善当地民生，让光伏更好地惠及当地群众。

（三）"引进来"着力打造特色产业集群

十年来，陕西利用陆空交通便利、人力资源丰富、产业基础较好的优势，加快外向型产业集聚发展，积极承接境内外加工贸易产业转移，吸引三星、美光、施耐德等跨国公司项目落户，比亚迪、

图6 2013—2021年陕西省实际利用外资情况

数据来源：陕西省统计局历年"经济与社会发展统计公报"。

康佳等显示器制造等企业在陕布局制造业基地，一批集成电路设计、制造、封装测试企业集聚发展，形成了芯片、高端制造及新能源汽车等产业集群。

数据显示，世界500强企业在陕投资设立144家外资企业。截至2022年底，陕西全省306家境外企业累计实现对外投资68.8亿美元，其中在共建"一带一路"国家投资18.2亿美元，占总额的26.5%。

1. 自贸试验区厚植企业发展沃土

陕西省自2017年4月1日正式成立自由贸易试验区以来，出台了多项政策支持其建设。2017年12月陕西公布实施《中国（陕西）自由贸易试验区管理办法》；同月，陕西省发展和改革委员会印发《进一步支持中国（陕西）自由贸易试验区建设的若干意见》；2018年9月发布《关于积极有效利用外资推动经济高质量发展的实施意见》；10月发布《陕西省人民政府关于支持中国（陕西）自由贸易试验区深化改革创新若干措施的意见》。

2021年陕西出台的《中国（陕西）自由贸易试验区条例》，对管理体制、投资促进、贸易便利、金融服务、"一带一路"经济合作与人文交流、推进西部大开发及服务与监管、法治保障等方面进行了规范和细化。这意味着陕西自贸试验区建设进一步规范，改革创新有法可依。

陕西自贸试验区改革创新持续提速，坚持以制度创新为核心，累计形成创新案例792项，其中36项改革创新成果在全国复制推广;"证照分离"改革持续深化,下放(委托)229项省级行政管理事项,开展外籍人才出入境便利创新创业试点,设立人才投资基金,出台金融服务自贸试验区建设36条等政策措施;不断提升投资贸易自由化、便利化水平,全面落实外资准入前国民待遇加负面清单管理制度,完善国际贸易"单一窗口"功能,设立RCEP企业服务中心,先后建成贸易金融、跨境电商等20多个功能性平台,吸引一大批外资企业落户;推动秦创原创新驱动平台和自贸试验区相互赋能,在全球设立22个离岸创新中心等平台,"科创自贸"建设能级不断提升,"农业自贸"示范作用不断强化。

通过一系列的制度创新探索,陕西自贸试验区各功能区逐步形成特色鲜明的产业集群。其中,中心片区重点发展战略性新兴产业和高新技术产业,具体包括高端制造、航空物流、贸易金融等产业,打造面向"一带一路"的高端产业高地。西安国际港务区片区探索以铁路运输为主导的国际多式联运物流运输规则,重点发展国际贸易、现代物流、金融服务、旅游会展、电子商务等产业。杨凌示范区片区以农业科技创新、示范推广为重点,加快生物科技、智慧农业等领域发展。

2. 集成电路产业集聚式发展

近年来陕西依托自身产业基础,引进集成电路设计业、晶圆制造、封装测试、支撑业等上下游产业,形成了从晶圆制造到封装测试的集成电路全产业链。

在上游 IC 设计环节，陕西西安聚集了中兴克瑞斯、华为、紫光国芯、拓尔微等 120 余家半导体设计企业；在 IC 制造中游环节，陕西西安拥有三星、西岳电子、卫光、派瑞等 8 家晶圆制造企业；而在 IC 封装下游环节，三星、华天、美光、力成、华羿等 13 家企业落户陕西。在支撑业中，陕西有奕斯伟、理工晶科、唐晶量子、吉利电子化工等 70 余家企业。

以三星项目为例，2014 年 5 月，韩国三星半导体一期投资项目竣工投产。2017—2020 年，三星电子又追加 150 亿美元建设储存芯片二期项目，累计投资达到 260 亿美元。三星半导体项目落户后，吸引了美国空气化工、日本住友、韩国东进世美肯、华讯微电子等一大批国内外企业的到来，直接或间接增加万余个就业岗位。三星半导体 2022 年产值突破 1000 亿元人民币，截至 2022 年，项目总投资高达 270 亿美元。

3. 现代服务业创新百花齐放

陕西依托国家加工贸易产业园和西安综合保税区，加快"陆港""空港"联动，聚集产业链上下游企业上百家，将实现年总产值 500 亿元，年纳税总额 10 亿元，吸纳就业约 2 万人。

"陆港"方面，截至 2023 年 2 月，"一带一路"临港产业园一期起步区已全部交付使用，出租率达 81%，入园企业 12 家，京虹科技、硕达视创、思达智、威码逊、德世美、华展科技等 9 家企业已正式投产运营，产品主要聚焦智能终端和显示面板两大类产业，出口欧洲、中亚、俄罗斯、北美、东南亚、非洲等地。

"空港"方面，从单一的保税物流逐渐拓展至以保税物流为保障，加工制造、检测维修、供应链服务、跨境电商等多元配套发展的产业格局。截至2022年底，累计引进企业88家，总从业人数约540余人，其中仓储物流约占80%，跨境电商约占10%，国际贸易约占5%，其他服务业约5%。

（四）纵深推进国际产能合作中心建设

当前，陕西省国际产能合作取得务实成效的同时，仍面临对外投资存量规模小、外资来源地单一、加工贸易质量效益不高等问题。

继续纵深推进国际产能合作中心建设，应充分发挥合作园区载体功能，重点推进西咸新区中俄丝路创新园、西安高新区三星城、西安经开区中欧合作产业园、咸阳中韩产业园、榆林陕煤集团中日国际合作材料产业园、杨凌"一带一路"现代农业国际合作中心、西咸新区空港中日生命科技园、汉中中日现代中医药产业园等园区建设，形成陕西对外开放合作优势载体。加大国际招商力度，积极开展线上线下专题招商、定向招商、投行思维招商，吸引产业发展新动能。

应着力推进国际合作重点项目建设。提升境外投资质量效益，以高端装备、输变电设备、汽车制造等优势产业为重点，支持陕鼓集团、西电集团、陕重汽、法士特等企业面向"一带一路"布局产业链、供应链。推进上海合作组织农业技术交流培训示范基地建设，鼓励对外设计咨询企业共同开拓市场，带动装备、技术、服务等出口，提升对外承包工程质效。

应继续深化协同创新推进自贸试验区建设。对标高标准经贸规则开展压力测试，推进投资贸易、人文交流、金融服务等领域系统性集成性制度创新。深化自贸试验区法律服务业改革创新，加快创新要素集聚、科技成果转化、产业链创新链融合，构建"科创自贸试验区"。建设第二批自贸试验区协同创新区，积极融入黄河流域自贸试验区发展联盟，加强与其他自贸试验区的协作，深化与共建"一带一路"国家的经贸投资合作。

应进一步畅通开放平台和贸易通道。推进西安高新综保区与西安关中综保区资源整合和优化升级，鼓励陕南各市和开发区申报设立综保区。推动综保区与自贸试验区、经开区等平台物理重组、功能整合、政策叠加，吸引企业集聚。充分发挥第五航权开放功能作用，支持延安、榆林、陕南航空口岸和西安铁路车站口岸正式开放。

应加大对优势产能"走出去"的支持力度。加快隆基马来西亚光伏产业合作区等重点项目建设。加强对国际贸易准则和行业规则的研究，聚焦产品服务、工程合作、投资合作、产融结合、战略合作等领域，加快构建合作平台，将陕西的优势产能、发达国家的先进技术和发展中国家的发展需求有效对接，共同推动积极拓展第三方市场合作，实现多方共赢。

主题篇

科技教育中心交流合作拓点扩面

十年来,陕西省依托各类科技创新主体、高校资源,不断强化与共建"一带一路"国家科技和教育合作交流,逐步形成了思路清晰、规划有度、重点突出、执行有力的陕西特色科技教育交流体系。"丝绸之路大学联盟"已汇聚37个国家和地区的150所高校;"鲁班工坊"建设深入推进,"秦岭工坊"自主品牌影响力不断提升;包括7家国家级和省级"一带一路"联合实验室,147家国际科技合作基地在内的对外科技创新合作平台体系形成;上海合作组织农业技术交流培训示范基地与60多个国家和地区开展了现代农业合作。

(一)搭建科技人文交流桥梁

为推进科技中心建设,陕西省注重顶层设计,制定出台了陕西省《实施创新驱动发展战略纲要》和《"十四五"科技创新发展规划》。在制度引领之下,陕西省大力打造科技人文交流通道,统筹国际科技资源，建设国际创新合作平台，拓展科技园区国际合作，加速科技成果转移转化，提升参与全球科技发展的竞争力。

1.建设高质量国际创新合作平台

推进秦创原创新驱动平台建设。秦创原是全省创新驱动发展的总源头和总平台，陕西省致力于将其打造成为立体联动"孵化器"、成果转化"加速器"和两链融合"促进器"，借此积极融入全球创新网络、打通国际科技交流合作"堵点"，打造市场化、共享式、开放型、综合性科技创新大平台。

秦创原创新驱动平台建设自2021年3月正式启动以来，以西咸新区和西部科技创新港为总窗口，加速两链融合，深入推进"三项改革"、"三器"建设，加快创新资源聚集，营造了良好创新生态。两年多来，秦创原在全国的品牌效应彰显，秦创原现象、秦创原生态、秦创原模式和秦创原板块初现，企业主体、人才主力、市场主导、政府主推的创新生态体系逐步完善，机床、光伏、氢能、储能等产业链规划布局，先进制造、新能源、新材料、生物医药等领域一大批中小企业落户聚集，一大批传统企业创新发展，一大批高校院所科技成果就地转化。

中俄丝路创新园是秦创原综合服务中心中的一个园区，相继在陕西省西咸新区东新城和俄罗斯莫斯科格林伍德开园运营，累计引入50余家机构企业。除了中俄丝路创新园，陕西省还重点推进中国西部科技创新港、西安高新区三星城、西安经开区中欧合作产业园、咸阳中韩产业园、榆林陕煤集团中日国际合作材料产业园、杨凌"一带一路"现代农业国际合作中心、西咸新区空港中日生命科技园、汉中中日现代中医药产业园等合作园区建设。

陕西省鼓励有条件的企业"走出去"建立有创新功能的示范园区。2022年，位于乌兹别克斯坦塔什干州的西北农林科技大学中乌节水农业海外示范园建成运行。示范园中的智能水肥一体化灌溉设备通过信息采集传输、远程控制，能够有效实现灌溉和施肥的信息化、精准化和自动化。

建设国际科技合作基地。陕西省于2014年出台《陕西省国际科技合作基地管理办法》，2020年出台《陕西省国际科技合作基地评估实施细则》。截至目前，陕西省与40多个国家和地区建立了全方位、多层次、宽领域的国际科技交流合作关系，有国家级国际科技合作基地23个、省级国际科技合作基地124家。

国际科技成果转移转化加速。近年来，陕西省产学研机构共承担实施国家级国际科技合作项目50余项、省级国际科技合作项目350余项，累计获支持经费近3亿元。2022年以来，陕西全省入库科技型企业1.59万家，同比增长42%；技术合同成交额3053亿元，同比增长30%以上。陕西已在现代农业、新材料、地球科学等领域开展国际合作，累计申请国际专利102项。

2.开展多层次对外科技合作交流

积极申建"一带一路"联合实验室。2021年西北大学"中国–

中亚人类与环境'一带一路'联合实验室"获批建设国家第三批"一带一路"联合实验室。该联合实验室与乌兹别克斯坦、吉尔吉斯斯坦、塔吉克斯坦等国高校和科研机构合作，以丝绸之路沿线文化遗产与地质环境为研究对象，聚焦"地质构造－环境变迁－人类发展－文明传承"，揭示丝绸之路地质构造与环境协同演化机理。目前，围绕航空航天、电子信息、精准医学、光子技术、生态水利技术等领域，陕西省布局并认定首批6家省级"一带一路"联合实验室，有力支持创新主体开展关键技术联合攻关、向国外示范推广先进技术，对推进陕西国际科技合作，提升对外开放水平具有重要的促进作用。

举办各类科技人文交流活动。近年来，陕西举办和参加海内外各类科技会展论坛等活动40余场次，其中"陕西国际科技创新创业博览会"逐渐成为具有较大影响力的区域性科技创新创业专业会展。陕西连续6年举办全球硬科技创新大会，连续多年举办全球程序员节、中国创新挑战赛（西安）硬科技发展专题赛、"一带一路"人工智能高峰论坛、新材料国际发展趋势高层论坛等活动。全国首个硬科技仲裁院于2022年全球硬科技创新大会正式成立。

积极推动医学合作交流。由陕西省中医研究院、西安中医脑病医院联合建设"中医药研究示范型国际科技合作基地""中医脑病诊疗示范型国际科技合作基地""中国－哈萨克斯坦传统医学中心"，推动中医诊疗技术和中医药文化在中亚国家传播。与捷克欧洲中医药中心、塞尔维亚诺维萨德大学医学院、马拉维驻华大使馆、赞比亚大学"一带一路"联合研究中心签署合作协议，致力于扩大中医药海外影响力，推动中医药"走出去"，培养"洋中医"，共计为16000余名境外患者提供中医药服务。

3. 推进多元化科技创新要素聚集

构建区域创新基地。加快西安科学城、西部科技创新港、杨凌农科城、榆林科创新城、宝鸡科技新城、汉中航空智慧新城等科技创新城建设。作为国家级农业高新技术产业示范区和我国唯一以农业发展为主要特色的自贸试验区，杨凌示范区以"一带一路"海外农业国际合作园区为载体，努力培育海外农业园区服务体系，先后与全球60多个国家在现代农业领域建立了合作关系，开展国际交流合作活动500余项。

持续增强CIC（中国以色列中心）中国西北国际科技创新中心优质科创资源的聚集作用。推进中亚科教合作中心、中德国际科创中心、上海合作组织农业技术实训基地建设。进一步发挥"一带一路"国家计量测试研究中心（陕西）作用，加快中亚标准化研究中心建设，促进标准"软联通"。

科技创新人才加速聚集。通过"人才+项目""松绑+赋权"等机制，陕西省吸引了诸多国内外人才留在西安创业、就业，截至2022年底，西安市有各类人才344万，其中专业技术人才达到104万，现代产业人才突破72万人。

西北农林科技大学2016年发起成立的"丝绸之路农业教育科

技创新联盟"，如今已有18个国家的96所涉农高校或研究机构入盟，在哈萨克斯坦、吉尔吉斯斯坦等5个国家建设了8个现代农业示范园区，成立海外人才培养基地，初步形成"大学—企业—政府—农民"合作新模式。借此平台，西北农林科技大学先后合作成立非洲研究中心、哈萨克斯坦研究中心、中俄农业科技发展政策研究中心、南南农业合作学院等一批国别研究中心，通过开办农业研修班、举办涉农国际会议、推进海外农业科技示范园建设等，为共建"一带一路"国家培养农业领域专业技术及管理人才。2020年10月22日，上海合作组织农业技术交流培训示范基地在杨凌揭牌。杨凌深化农业技术援外培训，为上合组织国家培训农业官员、技术人员1100多名，举办面向上合组织国家的农业技术专题讲座30余期，3.1万人次在线参与学习。

法律服务护航科技创新。自2021年陕西省"一带一路"国际商事法律服务示范区成立后，司法部"三中心一基地"、17家法律服务机构等各种涉外法治力量不断向示范区汇集。"一带一路"国际商事法律服务平台上线，提供集咨询、查询、申请、预约、办理于一体的全业务全过程服务。

（二）深化教育国际交流合作

陕西积极发挥高校资源富集的优势，以打造"一带一路"教育共同体为目标，以制度和平台建设、国际化人才培养、语言互通、国别区域研究和中外合作办学等工作为抓手,积极开展"一带一路"教育国际合作交流中心建设,使教育国际化水平实现质的飞跃。

1. 搭建优质教育交流合作平台

自 2014 年以来,陕西省连续举办 8 届丝绸之路教育合作交流会,先后有万余名国内外专家学者参与活动,签署合作协议 200 余项,成立丝绸之路大学联盟等有关联盟和教育研究机构 20 余个,举办中国传统文化展示、"一带一路"国际学生文化艺术季户外展演等活动近 50 场次,构建了全方位、多层次、宽领域的教育合作与交流平台,打造了与共建"一带一路"国家教育合作交流的新高地。

自 2020 年起,陕西省连续 3 年举办丝绸之路国际产学研用合作会议,累计来自 60 多个国家的 3000 余名中外专家围绕关键核心技术攻关、科技转化应用效率提升、国际化科技人才培养等重大问题进行研讨、交流。该会议为中外高校、科研机构、企业搭建了合作平台。

2015 年,西安交通大学发起成立"丝绸之路大学联盟",秉承"和平合作、开放包容、互学互鉴、互利共赢"的丝路精神。目前已有五大洲 37 个国家和地区的 150 所高校参与,围绕能源、化工、全球健康、法学等诸多方向,形成了 13 个学科子联盟。2018 年,"丝绸之路大学联盟推进区域合作发展项目"获第五届全国教育改革创新特别奖。该联盟的成立有效推动了中外高校在科技应用领域的合作,创新校企、校地合作新模式,促进共建"一带一路"国家校企之间的沟通合作。

2017年,陕西职业技术学院发起成立"一带一路"职教联盟,目前,已有来自17个国家的105所职业院校、行业、企业加入,为"一带一路"应用型人才培养、专业人员培训交流、边远地区教育帮扶等领域提供了支持。

同年,陕西师范大学牵头成立了"丝绸之路教师教育联盟""丝绸之路人文社会科学联盟""丝绸之路图书档案出版联盟",已有7个国家的27所高校和研究机构加入联盟,通过推进盟校间合作办学、学生交流、教师交流、学分互认、教育实践基地建设、科研合作、联合出版、资源共享等,促进成员单位人文交流与合作。

此外,西北工业大学发起成立"一带一路"文化遗产国际合作联盟;长安大学成立"中亚五国交通基础建设人才培养联盟";西北大学成立"丝绸之路文化遗产联盟保护与传承联盟";西安外国语大学成立"'一带一路'语言文化大学联盟";西北政法大学设立中国-中亚法律查明与研究中心,不断提升与中亚五国教育合作交流质量。

2. 优化陕西国际学生培养模式

共建"一带一路"倡议提出以来,陕西省国际学生学历生占总规模比例稳中有增,由2013年的46.6%提升至2022年的70%;国际学生中,共建"一带一路"国家学生占比逐年提高,由2013年的51.2%提升至2022年的71%。陕西省高校对共建国家尤其是中亚国家学生的吸引力逐步凸显。

陕西已成为中亚国家学生首选出国留学目的地之一。2013—2022年，全省共接收留学生约10.92万人。2019年在陕西的留学生人数比2013年增加了近一倍，2020—2022年受疫情影响留学生人数有小幅减少。

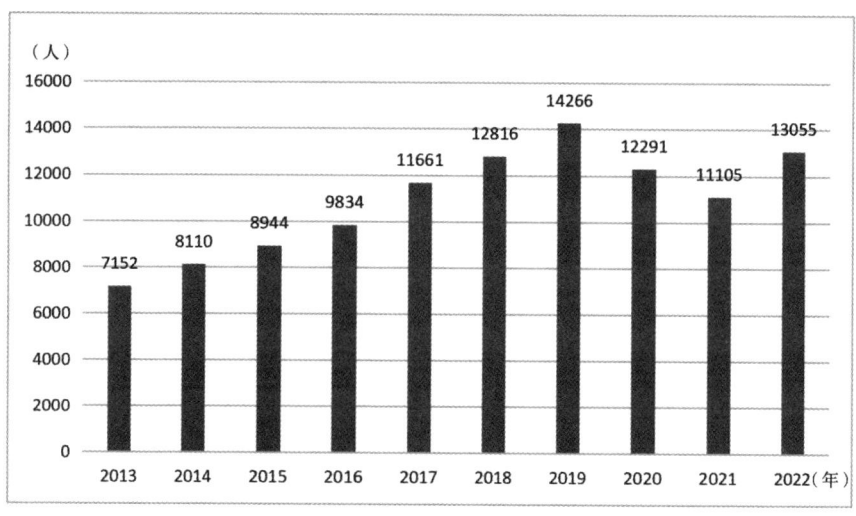

图7　2013—2022年在陕留学生人数

数据来源：陕西省教育厅。

为进一步提质增效，陕西创新国际学生培养模式，联合行业优势企业，加强校企合作及与海外院校和机构合作，建立国际学生联合培养基地，逐步形成校企联合、订单式、学术导向的来华留学培养模式，大力培养语言通、专业精的本土化、国际化复合型人才。

长安大学与中国土木工程集团合作培养尼日利亚籍学生累计

300余人,并于2020年9月签署协议共建尼日利亚交通大学,为尼日利亚以及非洲培养交通和基础设施建设行业专业技术和管理人才,为当地经济发展创造机遇。西北大学、西安石油大学以油气人才培养为支点,与企业合作,采用"订单班"的模式为吉尔吉斯斯坦、塔吉克斯坦等国培养近700名石油化工、油气管道建设运营专业人才。

不断扩大优质国际教育资源,加大中外合作办学规模。截至2023年8月,陕西共有27所高校与14个国家和地区的40所高校开展中外合作办学,合作办学机构与项目增至46个。其中,本科以上层次中外合作办学机构10个、项目30个,机构数量居西部前列;在读学生1.3万余人,430名学生被世界知名高校录取,超过640人次获得国家级和省部级创新奖励等。

3.加快对外交往语言互通服务

随着共建"一带一路"的持续推进,陕西的对外交往更加活跃,语言服务需求更加旺盛。陕西大力培养语言通、专业精的国际化复合型人才,积极推进共建"一带一路"国家非通用语种新专业和复语教育。截至目前,陕西省5所高校开设非通用语种20个,并指导西安中学启动高中俄语国际课程班,储备各类非通用语种国家语言人才。

西安外国语大学联合陕西省相关部门,共同开发建设了陕西省"一带一路"语言服务及大数据平台,满足陕西省乃至西部各省份对共建"一带一路"国家的语言需求,为促进陕西省乃至我国西部地区企业"走出去"打下坚实的基础。陕西省加快"一带一路"知识产权语言服务人才培养中心建设,重点围绕涉外知识产权人才培养、教育培训、企业合作和语言高端服务等方面开展工作,服务与促进对外交流合作。

依托相关高校开展国别区域研究。西北大学等8所高校12个国别与区域研究中心成功获批,设立了丝绸之路经济带法律政策协同创新中心、丝绸之路区域合作与发展法律研究院、中国(西安)丝绸之路研究院等研究机构,承担了对中亚和其他丝路国家的大量研究任务,推动教育部国别区域研究中心等智库建设,为开展与丝路国家的教育合作与交流提供政策建议。2022年,陕西省16个国别区域研究中心全年累计主持或参与省部级及以上课题70项,有力提升了陕西高校研究实力、声誉和影响力。

4. 推进国际职业教育人才培养

积极参与教育部"鲁班工坊"建设。陕西铁路工程职业技术学院—肯尼亚铁路培训中心获批全国首批鲁班工坊立项(全国共25个),陕西工业职业技术学院—中国-赞比亚职业技术学院获批全国有条件运营立项项目(全国共8个),陕西省进入鲁班工坊建设第一梯队。2019年,陕西工业职业技术学院成立"中国-赞比亚职业技术学院机械制造与自动化分院、陕西工业职业技术学院赞比亚分院",推动境外留学生职业技能培训及学历提升。

创新打造"秦岭工坊"自主品牌。2022年,陕西省创新设立了"秦岭工坊",以"优势互补、互惠互利、求实高效、共同发展"为原则,突出陕西地域特色和文化意蕴,培养适应国际市场的职业技能人才。目前,共有4所高职院校首次在希腊等4国开设"秦岭工坊",同时,还为坦桑尼亚研发9个国家级岗位职业标准和配套人才培养方案,助力当地企业拓展国际市场。

（三）继续提升科教开放水平

陕西积极承接国家"一带一路"教育合作和科技创新行动计划,不断推动科学教育高质量发展。推进"一带一路"科技创新以及教育交流合作是一项全新的探索实践,继续提升陕西科技教育对外开放水平,推进科技教育中心建设,加强国际科教合作,宜从以下几个方面重点发力。

1.加强科教合作的政策引导

应加强统一协调,组织专家开展顶层设计和统筹规划,制定陕西省"一带一路"科技教育中心建设中长期发展规划,明确省内高校、企业和研究院所的优势特长,强调政府部门在对接过程中的组织者、协调者和服务者定位,分阶段分重点地安排政府部门、高校、企业和研究院所,有层次、有计划地与共建国家开展科技及教育合作,确保互相配合、高质量高效率的协同发力。

2.整合资源扩大对外开放

统筹陕西省科技、教育、文化、旅游等资源，加强资源整合，可通过文化旅游交流为先手，通过政策倾斜，增强陕西与更多国家的科技教育交流合作，扩大陕西"一带一路"科技教育中心建设的国际影响力。加强创新人才国际化和合作研究，密切科技信息交流，促进科技能力提升，邀请国外专家进行深度科技交流合作，同时加强双向流动及海外研究工作。

3.拓展科教合作项目范围

大力拓展与共建国家和一些发展中国家开展科技教育的项目合作。设立鼓励科技教育合作的研究项目和科技人文交流的培养项目，引导国内外学者共同参与共建国家的科学研究与人才培养；设立"一带一路"科技教育中心建设基金，奖励在与共建国家合作中取得突出成绩的高校、企业、科研院所和研究团队，支持共建实验室和联合研究中心的人才培养与研究项目。

POINT 四

国际文化旅游中心活力与日俱增

十年来,陕西省着眼于推进国际旅游枢纽建设的战略目标,依托陕西厚重的历史文化、丰富的景观资源、优越的地理位置、庞大的旅游流量等天然优势,大力开拓国际人文交流渠道,创新"一带一路"相关文化资源和旅游产品,从不同维度推动陕西旅游的高质量发展,提升陕西文旅品牌影响力。十年间,陕西举办了九届丝绸之路国际艺术节、八届西安丝绸之路国际旅游博览会、三届世界文化旅游大会;"国风·秦韵"陕西文化周、非遗精品展等一批文化交流项目在海外引起强烈反响;已有41个国家的108个城市与陕西缔结友城关系,其中54个是共建"一带一路"国家城市。

(一)发挥优势打造文旅中心

作为古丝绸之路的起点、西部大开发的"桥头堡",陕西充分发掘千年古都、华夏之源的历史文化价值,弘扬丝绸之路精神,依托打造"国际文化旅游中心"方面的独特优势,积极唱响"丝绸之路起点旅游"品牌。

1. 强化文旅政策引领

《陕西省推进建设丝绸之路经济带和21世纪海上丝绸之路实施方案（2015—2020）》提出了打造"'一带一路'国际文化旅游中心"目标。《陕西丝绸之路经济带旅游行动纲要》，指导了国际旅游合作交流的务实有序推进，确立了丝绸之路起点旅游走廊建设方案。《陕西省"一带一路"建设规划》明确了"建成中华文明—丝绸之路旅游核心区，成为彰显华夏文明的历史文化首选地，全省文化产业增加值占生产总值比重达到3.5%以上，旅游总收入突破1万亿元，旅游总人次达到9亿人次"的发展目标。陕西省连续9年出台的推进共建"一带一路"建设年度行动计划或工作要点，将打造"国际文化旅游中心"作为重点之一明确了年度任务要求。

2. 依托文旅资源优势

文化是陕西最大的资源之一，是陕西形象的深厚底蕴。陕西的黄帝陵、兵马俑、延安宝塔、秦岭等是中华文明、中国革命、中华地理的精神标识和自然标识。省会西安古称"长安"，与古罗马、开罗、雅典并称世界四大文明古都，先后有周、秦、汉、唐等13个王朝在此建都，历时1180年，是人类历史不可缺少的重要组成部分和人类共同的宝贵财富。

陕西拥有3项9处世界遗产：一是秦始皇帝陵及兵马俑坑。二是"丝绸之路：长安–天山廊道路网"，包括汉长安城未央宫遗址、唐长安城大明宫遗址、大雁塔、小雁塔、兴教寺塔、彬县大佛寺石窟、张骞墓。三是长城（与其他省份共有）。

陕西的历史文化遗产浓缩了中华文明相当长一个时期的精华，体现了世界古代东方的先进文化，见证了东西方文明相互交融和碰撞的历史。西汉时期，张骞从长安出使西域，开拓出了举世闻名的"丝绸之路"。陕西省作为古丝绸之路的起点，丝路旅游资源富集，丝路遗产数量众多，面对新的历史机遇，陕西省紧抓丝路旅游资源的优势，彰显丝路旅游魅力。

3. 彰显交通区位亮点

陕西省是全国重要的交通枢纽，也是中国通往中亚、俄罗斯的通道。目前陇海、宝成铁路、西宝客运专线等穿境而过，西安咸阳机场累计开通国际客运航线83条。陕西省已被国家确定为重要的铁路枢纽和运营调度中心之一，成为八大航空枢纽之一和重要的公路枢纽。完善的陆、空网络为陕西省丝路旅游发展奠定了良好的基础。

（二）砥砺奋进谱写文旅新篇

文明因交流而精彩，文化因多样而丰富。陕西秉承"民心相通，文化先行"理念，不断加强与共建"一带一路"国家文化旅游领域的友好交流与务实合作，充分发挥文化和旅游在促进民心相通中的重要作用，作为国际文化旅游中心的活力与日俱增。

1. 打造和擦亮丝路品牌，持续提升交流平台

全面打造丝路文旅品牌。陕西省着力打造"国风秦韵""丝绸之路起点·兵马俑的故乡"等文化旅游品牌，发挥民心相通、交融共进的桥梁纽带作用。"国风秦韵"项目通过开展陕西优秀传统文化节目国际巡演交流、国内展演推广，推动陕西优秀传统文化"走出去"。"国风秦韵"的海外宣传推广力度不断加大，已先后在20多个国家和地区组织了"国风秦韵——陕西传统文化周"活动，在海外宣传推广中国民乐、陕西皮影、陕西秦腔、陕西剪纸、西安鼓乐、安塞腰鼓等非遗精品项目，取得较好效果。陕西省还不断做大做强"文学陕军""长安画派""西部影视""陕西戏曲"等知名品牌，继续打造"丝路春晚""丝绸之路万里行"重点品牌项目，谋划打造非物质文化遗产项目品牌。

扎实推进国际交流合作平台建设。十年以来，陕西成功举办了九届丝绸之路国际艺术节、八届西安丝绸之路国际旅游博览会、三届世界文化旅游大会。"国风·秦韵"陕西文化周、非遗精品展、"丝绸之路起点·兵马俑的故乡""一带一路"倡议10周年暨中哈商品展开幕式、丝绸之路国际电影节、西安文创系列展示活动等一系列文化交流活动，在海外引起强烈反响，全面彰显陕西"国际旅游中心的地位"。

西安丝博会举办以来，泰国、吉尔吉斯斯坦、格鲁吉亚等11个国家先后担任主宾国，共有来自全球190多个国家和地区的9000多

名境外客商参展参会，展销特色商品3万多种，观众人数超过60万人次。丝绸之路国际艺术节是首个以"丝绸之路"为主题的国家级综合性国际艺术节，第八届丝绸之路国际艺术节吸引了美国、日本、阿根廷等29个国家参与，共举办文化艺术活动58场（次），惠及观众399万余人次，有力推动了丝路文化交流、民心相通、文明互鉴。多年来，陕西多样化的国际交流平台搭建起艺术交流的纽带、商贸往来的通道、民心相通的桥梁，为高质量共建"一带一路"凝聚人文力量。

2. 互联和交流并进，不断深化文旅项目

文旅互联机制不断健全。陕西的国际"朋友圈"不断扩大，截至2023年5月，国际友城遍布全球五大洲41个国家，国际友城数量达108个，其中共建"一带一路"国家友城54个，陕西省10个设区市、杨凌示范区均有了国际友城。陕西联合北京和上海建立了国内首个入境旅游省际合作机制，实现旅游信息互通、客源互送、市场共建、产品共推。西安领事馆区加速建设，泰国、韩国、柬埔寨、马来西亚、哈萨克斯坦5个国家设立总领事馆，法国、英国、德国等32个国家设立签证中心，陕西对外交流更加便利。

西安咸阳国际机场口岸72小时过境免签政策，吸引国际旅客来陕旅游。2013—2019年，全省累计接待境内外游客33.57亿人次，平均增速16.34%，入境游客2536.19万人次，旅游总收入29495.01亿元，全省平均增速22.49%，其中国际旅游收入累计162.28亿美元，平均增速12.25%。

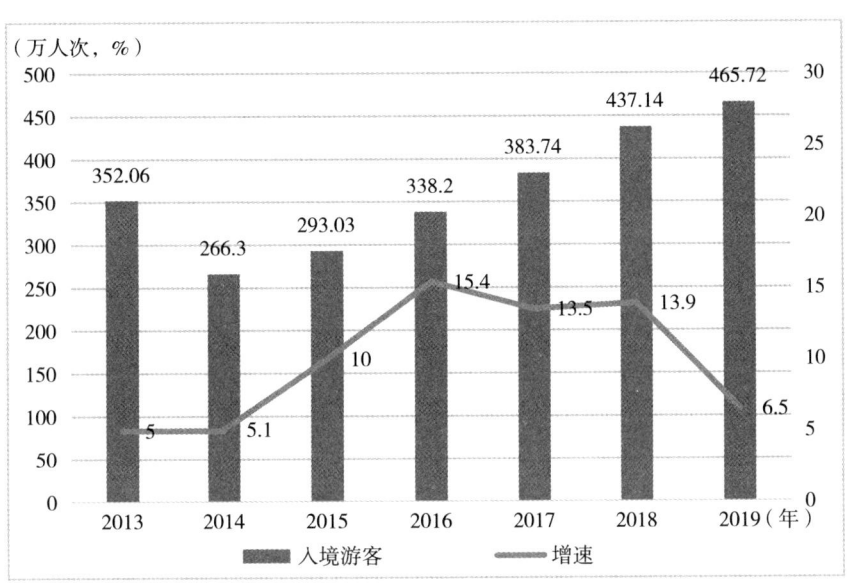

图8　2013—2019年陕西省入境游客及增速

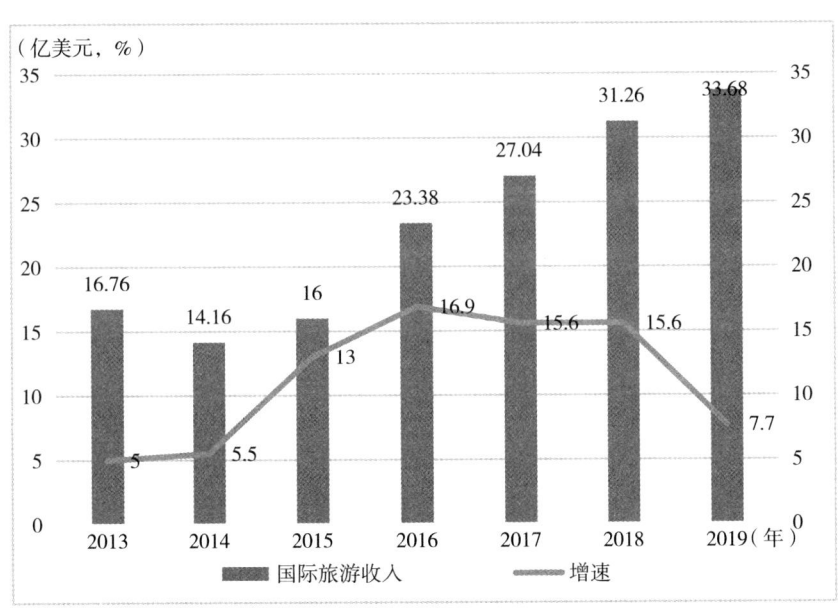

图9　2013—2019年陕西省国际旅游收入及增速

数据来源：陕西省文化和旅游厅、陕西一带一路网。

对外文化交流持续拓展。陕西省先后承办了丝绸之路旅游部长会议暨第七届联合国世界旅游组织丝绸之路旅游国际大会、中阿丝绸之路文化之旅——中国文化周等十余项重大文化和旅游交流活动。

承办青年汉学家研修计划,自2016年以来共有来自六大洲近60个国家的130名青年汉学家在陕西参与了研修活动,成为传播中华文化的使者。承办2022"一带一路"媒体合作论坛,来自40多个国家和国际组织的120多位中外媒体代表通过线上线下相结合的方式广泛交流沟通。

3. 合作与协作齐抓,积极推进各方参与

国际合作不断深化。陕西省先后与联合国世界旅游组织（UNWTO）、世界旅游联盟（WTA）、亚太旅游协会（PATA）、国际大会与会议协会（ICCA）等国际组织合作,通过加入会员、承办大型国际会议等方式,深化文化和旅游领域合作。西安市打造"一带一路"中华优秀文化传承示范区,当选2019"东亚文化之都",并开展百余场文化交流活动。2021年,世界城地组织亚太区旅游委员会组织亚洲首个地方行动港——青年教育与对话港落户西安。西安市还入选首批澜湄旅游城市合作联盟,组建丝绸之路国际旅游城市联盟,持续扩大西安旅游国际影响力,增强国际旅游话语权。陕西省图书馆加入"丝绸之路国际图书馆联盟"并参加首届丝绸之路国际图书馆联盟大会,提升了陕西在共建"一带一路"国家的文化和

旅游影响力。

文化遗产领域合作持续加强。陕西省成立"一带一路"文化遗产国际合作联盟，将文化遗产保护与研究力量联动形成合力，创新文化遗产保护利用研究。"丝绸之路：长安—天山廊道的路网"成为首例跨国合作、成功申遗的世界文化遗产项目。西北大学考古队在全国率先走出国门赴中亚国家开展境外考古发掘研究，出色地完成了乌兹别克斯坦拉巴特遗址、塔吉克斯坦贝希肯特谷联合考古发掘和调查工作，找到了月氏人西迁后的踪迹，廓清了他们在中亚地区的分布范围，更验证了中国历史文献上的记载，建立起中国的丝路考古话语体系，用文物和遗迹还原丝绸之路真实历史。继建立陕西省丝绸之路考古中心后，2023年4月，丝绸之路考古合作研究中心的成立，面向中亚、西亚、南亚开展联合考古工作，研究丝绸之路历史和古代东西方文明交往互动历程，中国与共建国家在文化遗产领域的国际合作进入崭新阶段。

充分发挥陕西文物"外交使者"作用。2022年，"兵马俑与古代中国——秦汉文明的遗产展览"赴日展出。陕西省文保单位联合体承担实施的中国政府援助缅甸蒲甘他冰瑜佛塔修复项目正式启动，彰显陕西文保国际担当，为增进民心相通发挥了重要作用。"公输堂彩绘保护"入围法国"中法合作团队创新奖"，"秦兵马俑史密森尼数字教育项目"入选联合国教科文组织亚太遗产中心"全球世界遗产教育创新优秀推荐案例"，《西京故事》入选2021—2022年度国家文化出口重点项目。

4. 线下和线上发力，广泛拓展传播渠道

推动文艺作品"走出去"。陕西省积极参加澳门旅博会等国际旅展及境外知名艺术节活动，持续在悉尼、巴黎等城市举办"欢乐春节"活动，"古法新作"陕西文化艺术展在巴黎成功举行，舞剧《门》、杂技剧《如梦长安》在韩国海比奇艺术节上精彩亮相，"秦丨QIN——兵马俑的前世今生现代艺术展"、舞剧《青铜》等线上展播通过巴黎中国文化中心官网、微信公众号，以及脸书、推特等海外社交媒体平台同步播出，受到海外网友的好评。

对内对外传播声量不断提升。西安广播电视台"丝路频道"，是全国唯一经国家广播电视总局正式批准以"丝路"命名的电视频道，已开播六年。六年来，西安广播电视台"丝路频道"以弘扬丝路精神、传播丝路文化为宗旨，致力于打造共建"一带一路"成果的展示平台，先后打造了《行走丝路》《从长安到罗马》等一批栏目、节目，举办"丝路城市春晚"等文化活动，以媒体力量助力打造丝路文化高地。

自 2014 年起，陕西省相继在 Fackbook、Twitter、Instagram 等 8 个国际知名平台开通"游陕西"英、日、韩三个语种共 14 个官方账号；并采用贴近不同区域、不同国家、不同群体受众的精准传播方式，策划实施了数百场线上线下推广活动，全力构建陕西文旅境外传播融媒体矩阵，汇聚起传播陕西声音的强大力量。截至 2023 年 5 月，陕西境外社交媒体账号粉丝总量近 110 万人，累计发帖

2万余篇，曝光超 2.55 亿次，互动超 1280 万次，综合传播力跻身陕西省各级行政机构和全国省级文旅机构国际新媒体账号前列。

5.创作和质量共进，精心发展文旅产业

文化产业蓬勃发展。西安高新区于 2018 年列入首批国家文化出口基地，重点发展数字出版、动漫游戏、创意设计、互联网服务等高附加值文化产业，聚集了 4000 多家文化企业。2021 年，西安高新区在首批国家文化出口基地绩效评价中综合排名第二。西安曲江新区于 2021 年获批国家文化出口基地，重点发展影视制作、演艺演出、文创设计、电竞体育服务等文化产业，规上文化企业 207 家。西安曲江文化旅游股份有限公司等优秀文化企业不断涌现，打造了大唐不夜城、大唐芙蓉园等旅游地标和景区，以及"丝路印记""唐文化"等一系列旅游品牌。

积极实施文化旅游项目带动战略。陕西旅游集团与意大利都市设计工程公司签署《马可·波罗》水上实景演艺合作协议，有力促进了中欧文化交流。华夏文旅城项目、兴汉生态旅游示范区汉文化项目、张骞文化园、丝绸之路风情城等重点项目进展顺利。

（三）多管齐下讲好陕西故事

十年来，陕西的国际文化旅游中心建设取得丰硕成果的同时，面临资源零散、品牌核心竞争力有待提升、对外交流合作还需深入等困难。为更好地发挥固本强基的基础性作用，搭建起中外人文交流的桥梁，将陕西的独特文化旅游资源，更有效地转化为继续推动"一带一路"文旅高质量合作的动力，陕西宜加强区域协作，用好独特资源，从服务外交大局的高度提升交流合作水平，通过基地建设做大文旅投资贸易的"蛋糕"，以进一步推动国际文化旅游中心建设。

1. 加强区域协作，打好丝路文旅"资源牌"

加强与共建国家合作，整合具有鲜明丝路标识的文化旅游资源，共建秦岭、黄河等文化旅游带和西北五省、川陕甘等旅游协作区，加强与京津冀、长三角、粤港澳大湾区、成渝等地区的合作，培育精品旅游线路，强化一体营销和推广，共建丝绸之路国际文化和旅游带。

拓展文化遗产保护、文化旅游、非物质文化遗产等领域对外人文交流合作，积极参与亚洲文化遗产保护行动，持续提升陕西省丝绸之路考古中心和丝绸之路考古合作研究中心影响力，推动非物质文化遗产项目、优秀艺术剧目"走出去"。

2. 服务外交大局，提升国际交流合作水平

持续用好对外交流平台和驻外机构，加强文化和旅游对外交流合作机制建设。继续推进会庆旅游经济，通过办好一系列高规格重点节庆、会展等活动，把陕西建成"一带一路"国际会展中心和国

际游客集散中心。加强与国家相关部委的沟通对接，积极申办"一带一路"国际合作高峰论坛框架下的高级别会议，争取将丝博会纳入国家机制性涉外展会范畴，进一步提升国际影响力。

推动与共建"一带一路"国家友城务实合作，提升友城合作水平。依托各类国际交流合作机制和平台加强文旅交流合作，加强与我国驻外机构及联合国世界组织、世界旅游联盟等国际组织开展相关合作。

3. 推动基地建设，做大文旅投资贸易"蛋糕"

推动陕西建设国家第四个对外文化贸易基地，助力陕西加快形成面向中亚、南亚、西亚国家的重要产业和人文交流基地，构筑内陆地区独具特色的国际贸易通道。围绕影视制作、出版发行、文艺演出等重点领域，培育一批具有竞争力的外向型文化企业，构建政府引导与市场运作相结合，国有文化企业主导和民营文化企业联动"走出去"的对外文化贸易和投资新格局。

着眼发展入境旅游，完善用好京沪陕中国入境旅游枢纽合作机制，进一步探索发挥过境免签政策的作用，吸引更多国际旅客。支持陕西实行更加便利的签注政策，扩大人员往来，持续为打造国际文化旅游中心创造良好条件。

POINT 五

丝绸之路金融中心探索试点创新

围绕丝绸之路金融中心建设,《陕西省"十四五"深度融入共建"一带一路"大格局、建设内陆开放高地规划》明确提出,成为具有重要影响、特色鲜明、辐射西部和欧亚国家的区域性金融中心,金融业增加值占地区生产总值比重达到8%左右。针对这一目标,陕西从促进金融要素集聚、创新金融产品服务以及推动金融改革试点等方面提出了具体举措。

十年来,陕西通过持续深化金融改革,鼓励金融业态创新,着力打造丝绸之路金融中心,在创新探索中不断积累符合共建"一带一路"倡议需求的金融产品和创新服务,金融业的服务支撑能力不断提升。

(一)以要素集聚打造区域金融中心

1. 金融组织体系趋于完善

在《陕西省推进建设丝绸之路经济带和21世纪海上丝绸之路

实施方案（2015—2020）》等整体规划设计的基础上，陕西相继出台了《西安丝绸之路金融中心发展行动计划（2020—2022年）》《西安丝绸之路金融中心发展规划》《关于金融支持中欧班列（西安）集结中心暨中国（陕西）自由贸易试验区高质量发展的意见》等丝绸之路金融中心建设的政策措施。十年来，陕西通过招商与新设金融机构并举，发挥区位、科技、人才优势，金融组织体系趋于完善。

吸引境内外各类金融机构落户。平安银行、广发银行、渤海银行在陕西开设分支机构，全国12家股份制银行全部完成在陕布局；新加坡星展银行、韩国韩亚银行、三星财险以及台资富邦华一银行落户陕西；组建全国第6家省级农商行——秦农银行；西北地区首家汽车金融公司——比亚迪汽车金融有限公司、首家消费金融公司——长银消费金融公司、首家法人健康险公司——瑞华健康险股份有限公司、首家公募基金公司——朱雀基金管理有限公司相继开业，填补金融牌照空白；陕西投资集团财务公司开业；筹建丝绸之路农商银行发展联盟，为全国成员机构数量最多的农商银行联盟组织。

引进全国性金融机构总部型功能性机构。国家开发银行西安数据中心及开发测试基地、农业发展银行金融科技中心、中国银行西安客服中心、工商银行、浙商银行全国制卡中心等全国性金融机构中后台落户陕西，初步形成金融产业聚集地。

2. 金融业支柱产业地位持续巩固

十年来，陕西金融业平稳快速发展，金融业增加值从 2013 年的 791.1 亿元增加到 2022 年的 2109.7 亿元，10 年增长了 2.7 倍，年均增长率 11.5%，比同期 GDP 年均增长率高出 3.1 个百分点。其中，2014 年全省金融业增加值首次突破 1000 亿元，金融业增加值占 GDP 比重首次超过 5%，跻身支柱产业之列。

十年间，陕西金融业增加值占 GDP 平均比重从 2013 年末的 5.0% 上升到 6.4%，金融业支柱产业地位持续巩固，已经成为第三产业中排位第二的生产性服务业。

截至 2022 年，陕西累计实现人民币跨境收付金额 4536.99 亿元，辐射 148 个国家和地区，其中覆盖 96 个共建"一带一路"国

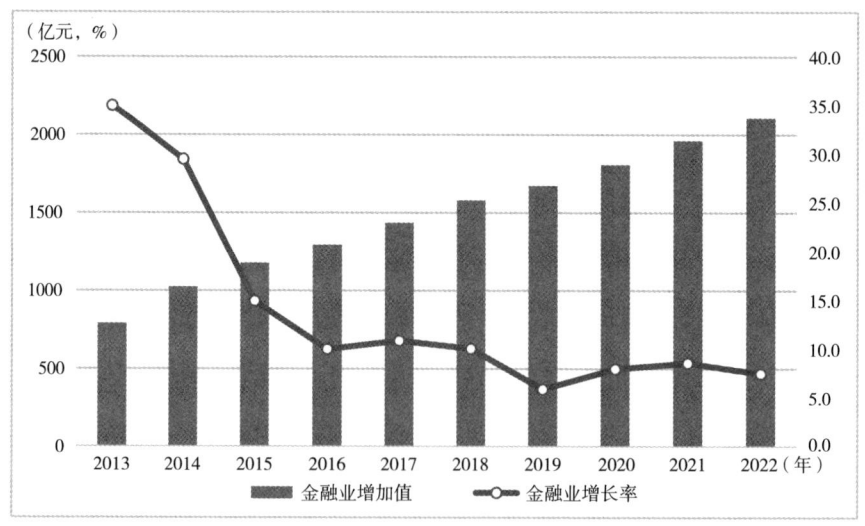

图 10　2013—2022 年陕西金融业增加值及增长率

数据来源：中国人民银行西安分行。

家，累计实现人民币跨境收付金额1813.17亿元，超全国平均水平约20个百分点。

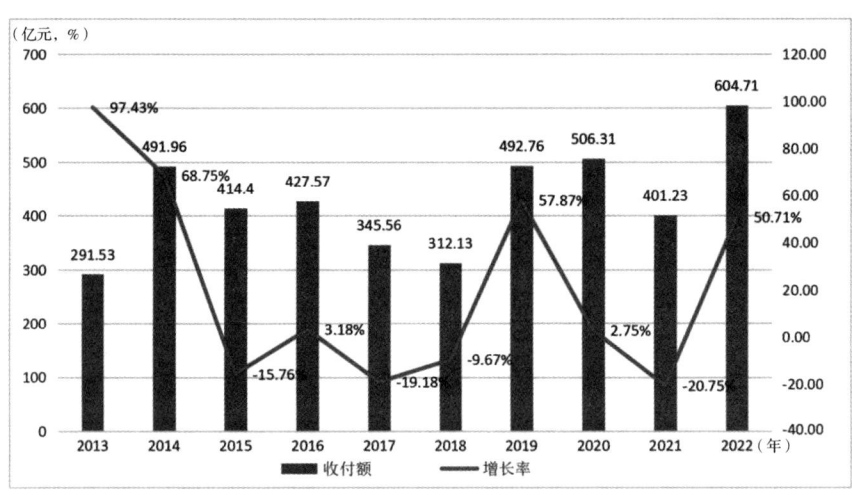

图11　2013—2022年陕西省跨境人民币收付金额

数据来源：中国人民银行西安分行。

（二）以服务创新强化金融支撑功能

1. 主动作为，开展金融改革开放试点

通过主动谋划、积极争取，陕西省先后被中央金融管理部门确定为全国13个金融科技试点、8个区域性股权交易市场"科技创新专板"试点、6个跨境业务区块链服务平台试点、3个商业车险自主定价试点省份之一，西安市获批数字人民币试点城市，铜川市被国务院确定为国家级普惠金融改革试验区，陕西股权交易中心获批区域性股权市场区块链建设试点。

围绕自贸试验区改革创新,开展资本项目收入支付和贸易外汇收支便利化试点,推动本外币合一银行结算账户体系试点,积极开展合格境外有限合伙人资金汇出入管理及企业外债便利化额度试点。

"通丝路"陕西跨境电子商务人民币业务服务平台是陕西探索金融服务共建"一带一路"倡议的代表性案例。通过这个平台,为小微企业和贫困农户将陕西特色产品推向全球市场搭建了一条便捷的"人民币网上丝绸之路"。"通丝路"平台荣获2019年全国自贸试验区第三批"最佳实践案例",还入选了"2022年西安市数字人民币跨境支付结算试点"。

2021年8月,"通丝路"平台成功接入人民币跨境支付系统(CIPS),成为西北地区首家部署CIPS标准收发器的电商平台,为平台精准支持跨境电商企业海外发展提供便利,进一步提升了入驻企业跨境人民币收付体验及支付效率,节省了跨境支付费用。目前,"通丝路"平台入驻的外贸认证企业达300余家,涉及装备制造、工业品、农产品等200余种品类,覆盖陕西80%的县域地区,出口地覆盖多个共建"一带一路"国家和地区。截至2023年5月,"通丝路"平台累计交易额已突破5000万元人民币。

中国一印度尼西亚双边本币结算机制(LCS)业务落地,是另一个陕西探索金融创新取得实效的代表性案例。为解决西安某企业中印度尼西亚双边本币不能直接兑换、无法完全规避汇率风险的困难,中国人民银行西安分行推动中行雅加达分行通过中国一印度尼西亚双边本币结算机制为企业实现结算,并且完成首笔1230.51万元人民币的结算业务。这也是LCS业务在试点地区外的首次尝试。

LCS最早是印度尼西亚央行在资本不能自由流动背景下提出的本币结算机制,主要应用于经常项目和直接投资项下跨境结算。中国—印度尼西亚双边本币结算机制的框架设计采取非对称合作模式。印度尼西亚卢比使用严格限于两国贸易投资往来,中国企业不将印度尼西亚卢比用于与第三国主体间的结算,而印度尼西亚企业可以将人民币自由用于与第三国主体间的结算。在人民币/印度尼西亚卢比区域市场引入多家印度尼西亚当地银行,更好地匹配供需两端,畅通清算平盘渠道,提升了交易活跃度。允许区域市场参加行将被动持有的人民币或印度尼西亚卢比头寸在市场中平盘,并首次在区域市场中支持远期、掉期等衍生交易,实现外汇产品全覆盖,充分满足流动性和汇率风险管理需要。

2. 探索创新,增强金融发挥支撑功能

十年来,陕西通过开展资本项目收入支付便利化试点和跨境金融服务平台试点,创建了中欧班列长安号数字化综合金融服务平台,推出"央行·长安号票运通""涌金出口池""中欧班列贷"等金融创新产品,着力解决涉外企业"融资难、融资贵"等问题。首创的"通丝路"平台被评选为第三批全国自贸试验区最佳实践案例,并成功接入人民币跨境支付系统(CIPS)标准收发器。

"央行·长安号票运通"是中国人民银行在全国范围内首次为

中欧班列打造的专属融资产品,为全国首创的跨境贸易金融产品。该产品的具体操作方式为:西安自贸港建设运营有限公司取得的银行授信,将平台公司银行授信额度反向分享给中欧班列长安号相关的物流和商贸企业,物流和商贸企业再向平台公司开具带利息的商业承兑票据,平台公司将收到的商业承兑汇票向合作银行申请贴现后,合作银行就将运费打给平台公司,物流和商贸企业只需要在票据贴现时先行向银行支付运费利息,在还款期限内将运费偿还给银行。

这一创新产品构建了"再贴现定向引导+财政政策资金防控风险+核心企业优质信用让渡+商业银行主动授信保贴"多方机制,有效缓解了物流或出口企业运费垫付压力。例如,2019年10月,陕西众联豪运物流公司、西安飞盛国际货运代理公司和陕西益万家农副产品有限公司向西安自贸港建设运营公司签发商业承兑汇票84万元,用于支付中欧班列长安号运费。

中欧班列长安号数字金融综合服务平台是陕西省探索金融服务创新的重要实践。这一平台通过"班列+数字金融"模式,为企业提供"铁路提单融资"等系列金融服务,旨在解决企业融资流程难、融资效率低、融资周期长等问题。截至2022年末,长安号场景吸引入驻企业484家,13家试点银行通过该场景为43家中欧班列产业链相关企业提供资金支持57.24亿元人民币。

国家外汇管理局陕西省分局推动金融机构依托中欧班列应用场景优势,开发更加契合中欧班列长安号产业链企业的金融产品服务创新，不少全国"首单"业务率先落地实施。中国银行陕西省分行落地全国首笔国际铁路联运提单贷110万元人民币，被评为2021年陕西自贸试验区"最佳实践案例"；浦发银行西安分行落地全国首单中欧班列长安号产业链企业便利化外债105万美元；建设银行陕西省分行落地首笔线上纯信用运费贷730万元人民币，有效缓解了企业融资难题。

（三）以开放合作打破未来发展瓶颈

金融不仅是现代经济的核心，也是实体经济的血脉。陕西相较于沿海地区存在创新力度小、金融服务模式落后、与共建"一带一路"国家和地区的资金互联互通较少等问题。未来，陕西宜深化金融开放合作，打破当前发展瓶颈，继续推动丝绸之路金融中心建设向既定目标前行。

1. 促进资金互联互通

大力发挥共建国家货币市场、资本市场和保险市场的作用，提高共建国家金融资源的整合能力和配置效率。加快共建国家和地区之间在金融发展理念、法律法规、金融监管等各个方面达成共识，努力打造公开透明、高效和谐的"一带一路"融资机制。鼓励社会资本参与，积极解放企业及个人思想，主动开拓融资渠道，借助资本市场的发展壮大实现各个产业与金融业共生共荣。

继续推进多边金融机构如亚洲基础设施投资银行和丝路基金等多边融资合作机制的发展、加快推进陕西省丝绸之路经济带产业发展基金的设立，以便为国家基础设施建设以及生产协作发展等提供资金支持。加强贸易数字化、跨境融资、保险等领域合作。加大招商引资的政策支持，通过吸引外资来进一步提升陕西经济社会发展。

2. 创新金融服务模式

为加快陕西融入共建"一带一路"大格局，金融业需要加强创新意识，紧密结合经济主体的金融服务需求，不断改革创新，构建贸易投资便利化的金融服务体系。

金融机构应通力合作，不断探索跨国企业集团跨境人民币资金集中运营管理新模式，探索制定与陕西自贸试验区相适应的人民币跨境使用、人民币资本项目可兑换、利率市场化和外汇管理等重点领域的改革创新措施，对接"走出去"企业，满足企业跨境金融业务需求，在贸易融资、跨境资金管理等方面提供资金支持，切实促进资金融通。

3. 搭建金融国际合作平台

引导金融机构调剂资金需求，结合《西安丝绸之路金融中心建设规划》及行动方案，搭建金融国际合作平台，建设金融市场规则标准、跨境结算清算等体系，倡导绿色金融理念，推动跨境金融风险防范机制建设，营造稳定、可持续的金融环境，成为一个互利共赢和专业高效的金融平台。

发挥金融对"一带一路"经济合作的推动作用，充分利用资本市场多种方式进行融资，助力陕西成为"一带一路"区域性金融中心、欧亚大陆贸易核心枢纽、东西双向互济的重要门户。利用宏观审慎监管等方法多角度、全方位分析"一带一路"相关国家和地区与陕西签订战略协议所带来的机遇与挑战，进一步推动相关产业的发展。

专题篇

2021年11月，习近平总书记在第三次"一带一路"建设座谈会上强调，"要稳妥开展健康、绿色、数字、创新等新领域合作，培育合作新增长点"。

《陕西省"十四五"深度融入共建"一带一路"大格局、建设内陆开放高地规划》提出，"深化多领域创新合作，拓展互补发展空间，加强'一带一路'数字、健康、绿色领域共建，深入培育开放合作新领域、新方向、新优势"。

新的领域，新的方向，新的成果。陕西立足自身特点，围绕健康、绿色、数字领域进行深入工作、广泛合作，正在形成一批陕西实践、陕西探索、陕西经验，为新时代新征程高质量共建"一带一路"贡献陕西力量。

健康新领域共筑卫生健康共同体

陕西是科技大省，又是医药大省。依托医药资源、文化、气候、交通、科研人才、园区和龙头企业等众多优势，近年来生物医药产业成为陕西重点打造的新支柱产业之一。其中中医药产业发展较为突出，早在2002年，以西安中医脑病医院为代表的医疗机构开始尝试以针灸带动中医，开启"走出去"篇章，并取得了初步进展。

卫生领域合作是"一带一路"建设的重要内容。以增进各国人民健康福祉为宗旨的健康丝绸之路成为共建"一带一路"国家民心相通的重要纽带。2016年，习近平总书记提出携手打造健康丝绸之路。陕西依托自身医药产业优势，在"一带一路"机遇下乘风起航，产业不断升级，中医药海内外全方位合作格局形成，跨境卫生合作稳步推进。

（一）陕西迎来医疗产业升级

立足当前国内外发展新形势、新要求，陕西集医、研、政、企、资各方资源于一体,共建产业创新生态、共谋高质量发展之道,通过对接海内外资源,为医药健康行业"走出去""引进来"提供平台,使国际交流合作更加便利。

1. 生物医药成为新支柱产业

制度型开放为医药健康行业"引进来"创造了良好的营商环境,大幅提升了全球先进医疗力量寻求与陕西合作、实现融合发展的动力。

1985年10月,西安杨森制药有限公司成立;2014年,强生全球供应链生产基地项目在陕西破土动工,现已成为美国强生全球产能最大的供应链生产基地、全球制药企业4.0无人化工厂的典型代表……在龙头企业的带动下,人才、企业、技术加速聚集,产业集群效应显现。

如今,生物医药产业成为陕西重点打造的六大新支柱产业和《〈中国制造2025〉陕西实施意见》着力培育的14个重点产业之一,已形成集产品研发、生产制造和临床应用为一体的完整产业链条:既有清华德人、金花制药、碑林药业、世纪盛康等中药龙头,也有杨森、力邦、嘉禾生物、巨子生物等化学药、生物药龙头,还有天隆科技、康拓医疗、大医集团等医疗器械龙头,以新通药物、康龙化成为代表的产业应用基础平台,以及佰美基因、华大基因等生物诊断、生物芯片研发企业。

2. "引进来"重大项目加速落地

生物医药产业的临空指向性相对较强,需要高端人才和冷链航空物流的全球联通。借助西安咸阳国际机场高效、快捷的航空运输体系,空港新城发挥"临空+自贸+保税+跨境+口岸+航权"六大功能叠加优势,推动重大项目加速落地。

2021年7月,西咸新区国睿一诺药物安全评价研究有限公司获国家药监局颁发的国家药物GLP认证,填补了陕西GLP实验室的空白。在此基础上,年产1.4亿头份口蹄疫疫苗的梅里众诚动物疫苗项目建设提速,以生物医药、国际诊疗、医疗器械等为核心的欧亚(陕西)自贸试验区健康医药城也签约落地。其中,欧亚(陕西)自贸试验区健康医药城项目围绕"国际化国家级健康医疗医药产业基地"目标,坚持"医疗、医药、医保、医养、医院"五医联动理念,依托空港新城国家临空经济示范区政策优势,引进国内外优质资源,打造集陕西自贸试验区生物医药、丝绸之路全球会诊、医疗器械创新、保健品跨境电商等四大特色创新平台。预计到2030年,该项目将形成技工贸年产值500亿元以上,年利税10亿元以上的经济体。

3. 医药外贸转型升级加速

陕西通过建立药品流通企业机构、深化健康医疗大数据安全共享,助力加快健康产业开放发展。

优化营商环境，提升口岸便利度。2022年5月，陕西省政府发布"推动开展跨境电商零售进口部分药品及医疗器械试点"措施，支持具备条件的自贸试验区片区开展跨境电商零售进口部分药品及医疗器械业务。鼓励符合条件的自贸试验区片区申请设立首次进口药品和生物制品口岸。这是陕西借助五大中心建设的一次尝试和创新，也是陕西不断优化营商环境、提升出口便利的又一举措，市场活力加速迸发。提升"互联网＋医疗健康"，搭建跨境合作平台。依托陕西医药企业龙头、产业发展园区等，陕西先后成立了跨境电商子品牌大健康（保税）跨境购、欧亚国际（陕西）健康产业集团公司、自贸蓝湾一号产业园、秦创原陕西国际生物医药创新中心、陕西省临床医学示范型国际科技合作基地等国际合作平台。

（二）中医药国际合作格局基本形成

中医理论是系统观下对生命健康的全面认知，《黄帝内经》中"不治已病治未病""平人者不病"的观念对于指导现代生命健康建设具有重要意义。近年来，中医药交流合作已经成为共建"一带一路"高质量发展的新亮点，在服务人类卫生健康、促进民心相通等方面发挥了重大战略作用。《推进中医药高质量融入共建"一带一路"发展规划（2021—2025年）》提出，"十四五"时期，中国将与共建"一带一路"国家合作建设30个高质量中医药海外中心，颁布30项中医药国际标准，打造10个中医药文化海外传播品牌项目，建设50个中医药国际合作基地，建设一批国家中医药服务出口基地。中医药文化正沿着"一带一路"阔步走向世界，为促进世界文明交流互鉴、助力构建人类卫生健康共同体提供强劲动力。

近年来，陕西省为响应国家"推动中医药走向世界"的号召，促进中医药在共建"一带一路"国家推广，确立"文化先行、医药跟进、贸易合作"的思路，通过组织申报国家中医药管理局中医药国际合作项目，充分发挥陕西中医药大学、陕西省中医药研究院、西安中医脑病医院等中医医疗机构作用，实施中医药"走出去"战略，积极推进与共建"一带一路"国家医疗卫生领域合作交流，取得了一定成效。陕西中医药"一带一路"全方位合作新格局基本形成，与共建"一带一路"国家合作建设九个中医药海外中心、一个丝绸之路中医药国际合作基地、一个国家中医药服务出口基地，并组织制定了一项中医药国际标准。

1. 陕西中医药影响力持续扩大

陕西是中医药的重要发源地，自古名医辈出，诞生了神农氏、扁鹊、孙思邈、王焘等历代大医，留下了"大医精诚"的医学人文思想，在中国医药史上有举足轻重的地位。

陕西也是中医药"天然药库"。全国第三次中药资源普查数据显示，陕西省中药资源目录共计3291味，12种中药材产品获国家地理标志保护产品认证。在全国中药材资源重点普查的364个品种中，陕西省拥有283种，占比77.7%。截至目前，陕西有中药饮片加工、中药提取和中成药制造企业近200家，中药生产批准文号3000多个，中药工业产业年产值约433亿元，年产值过亿元的中成药大品种80余个。陕西正把中医药资源优势转化为产业优势和发展优势，不断提升"秦药"品牌影响力，推进全省中医药产业实现高质量发展，为中医药"走出去"提供强势动能。

陕西积极实施"请进来""走出去"的中医药对外交流战略。近年来，陕西踊跃邀请和接待40余个国家和地区的专家学者来陕中医药机构进行中医药诊疗及文化交流。组建陕西省中医药代表团出访俄罗斯、匈牙利、哈萨克斯坦、乌兹别克斯坦等国，共同探讨交流合作途径，促进了中医药在共建"一带一路"国家传播与推广。

陕西连续举办孙思邈中医药文化节，进行中医药发展新技术、新理念交流合作平台建设。在2023年文化节上，来自英国、土库曼斯坦、乌兹别克斯坦等15个国家的来宾，以及韩国、马来西亚、泰国驻西安总领事等共计520名嘉宾齐聚铜川，共同探究孙思邈中医药文化资源和时代价值，促进中医药国际交流合作，推动中医药走向世界。

2. 对外合作机制平台不断增加

陕西利用现有政府间合作机制，通过加强传统医学政策法规、人员资质、产品注册、市场准入、质量监管等方面的交流沟通和经验分享,为有条件的中医药机构"走出去"搭建平台,为中医药对外合作提供政策支持。

陕西已先后举办欧亚经济论坛多届国际中医药交流合作论坛,承办了"世界中医药大会第五届夏季峰会""陕西省丝绸之路青年学者论坛医疗分论坛""中国-中亚五国民间友好论坛传统医学与健康分论坛"等,就中医药产业发展政策、中医药标准化与国际化、中医药文化等进行交流研讨,进一步扩大了陕西中医药的国际影响力。

拓展医疗机构合作与医学人才培养也是重要方面。目前,陕西中医药大学、省市级中医医疗机构与俄罗斯、哈萨克斯坦、匈牙利、捷克等国传统医学院、研究院、医科大学等医疗、科研及教育机构建立了合作关系,签订19个中医药双边战略合作协议、中医药人才培养合作协议及备忘录。作为我国最早具备条件对外国留学生和港澳台地区学生开展中医药教育的高等院校之一,陕西中医药大学现有16个国家的留学生,其中来自巴基斯坦、哈萨克斯坦、吉尔吉斯斯坦、乌兹别克斯坦、白俄罗斯、缅甸、孟加拉国等共建"一带一路"国家的学生占全校留学生的90%以上。该校先后同美国、加拿大、韩国等高校建立校际合作交流关系,为全球30多个国家和地区培养了3000多名中医药人才。

3.中医药产品和服务贸易逐步扩大

陕西在医疗卫生与健康产业发展方面开展了多项合作,包括传统医药、医院援建、中国制造医疗设备推广应用等。

延长中医药产业链条。陕西利用全球183个国家和地区承认中医针灸合法资格的有利条件，构建"以针带医、以医带药、以医带培、以医带销、以医带游"的"五带"中医药服务链。该模式得到广泛认可，并成功入选全国服务贸易"最佳实践案例"。通过中医针灸带动中医医疗服务"走出去"，再通过中医诊疗服务带动中医药饮片、中成药等药品的出口，相继带动中医药诊疗技术培训、中医药诊疗设备与医疗器械的销售、中医药健康旅游等产业链对外发展，着力深化医疗卫生合作，增强中国制造医疗设备推广应用。陕西省部分中医医疗机构先后在国（境）外开办中医医院、连锁诊所等国际分支机构，提供中医医疗、养生保健和康复服务。在瑞士（日内瓦）、俄罗斯、哈萨克斯坦等共建"一带一路"国家建立了九个国际中医药诊疗（康复、传统医学）中心。作为全国首批国家中医药服务出口基地的西安中医脑病医院，自2002年起，先后接诊了来自哈萨克斯坦、塔吉克斯坦、俄罗斯、土耳其、巴基斯坦等20余个国家和地区的约1.2万人（次）患者。积极搭建"互联网+中医药"平台。利用国际智慧医院、中医药产品研发、技术研发服务三大平台，为俄罗斯、哈萨克斯坦等用户提供线上问诊、会诊等服务，实现双方医疗机构远程会诊、远程教育等功能；通过西北现代医药物流中心、中欧物流班列为中医药产品出口提供便利，推动中医药产品和服务贸易发展。

（三）跨境医疗卫生合作稳步推进

1. 国际卫生医疗援助巩固发展

近年来，陕西发挥所长，派遣联合工作组赴塔吉克斯坦助力抗疫合作，帮助塔方建立疫情防控机制，向塔政府等捐赠价值500万元抗疫医疗物资；配合中非团结抗疫特别峰会，向几内亚捐赠价值830万元抗疫医疗物资；并累计向22个国际友城、26个陕籍海外侨社团组织、15个国家的陕籍海外留学生组织、驻外使领馆以及四个友好组织等捐赠价值686万元的各类抗疫医疗物资。省内医疗机构先后与40余个国家开展网络视频学术交流，向国际社会分享抗疫经验。

在合作推进产学研用融合新体系方面，西安天隆科技有限公司与西安交通大学、清华大学等国内外高校及科研院所通力合作，建立产学研用融合新体系。创新的产学研用一体化模式吸引了白俄罗斯、斯里兰卡、阿曼等20多个共建"一带一路"国家医疗卫生代表团访问和交流；公司产品如核酸提取仪等已取得150余项海外注册及认证，产品进入全球市场，出口至北美、欧洲、亚太、中东等地100余个国家和地区的医疗机构、疾控中心、科研院所、食品企业等单位。

2. 信息共享架起民心相通桥梁

陕西持续推进健康丝绸之路建设，全面启动丝路卫生健康命运共同体行动计划,加快推进国际人才培养。

为增强医疗健康国际学术交流,陕西先后举办四届"一带一路"全球健康国际研讨会、三届国际中医药对外交流合作论坛,以及东北亚地区传统医药合作研讨会、杨凌示范区大健康产业推介会、国际医学大会、首届"一带一路"中医药发展论坛、中国—捷克—尼泊尔多边医学学术会议等多项交流活动,加深了各国之间在医疗卫生领域的互动交流。

陕西对外合作开展医疗健康课程设计体系,依托西安交通大学第一附属医院与新加坡、日本、比利时、英国等国大学开展交流合作,承担中非对口合作医院机制项目三个,上线"丝路卫生健康命运共同体国际大讲堂"系列课程,架设起民心相通的桥梁。

(四)提质"走出去"还需协同发力

在日益严峻的国际局势下,基于国内经济循环的需求和共建"一带一路"国家的比较优势,继续深化陕西与共建国家的双边、多边医疗合作,鼓励陕西企业因势利导,"各施所长,取长补短",推进更大范围、更宽领域、更深层次的区域分工与医疗健康产业合作,是更好地推动健康丝绸之路建设的重要举措。为实现陕西从医药大省向医药强省的转变,仍需进一步做好顶层设计,统筹施策,为陕西医疗健康产业"走出去"提供持续的激励与支持。

1. 打造高质量的健康丝绸之路品牌

健康丝绸之路是一项复杂和系统的实践性工程，需要政府、企业和民众的多方发力、各司其职、共同合作。展望未来，陕西要实现多方协同发力的大健康工作格局，在制度层面进行统筹谋划，从战略性高度制定全面系统的合作方案；同时做到因国施策，因地施策，充分考虑共建"一带一路"国家的差异，切实推动务实的健康合作项目建设，打造陕西高质量健康丝绸之路品牌。

2. 发挥体制机制创新的先行示范作用

从区域层面来看，需要积极建设"一带一路"海外医疗中心与国际科技合作基地，为共建"一带一路"国家医疗可持续发展贡献力量。更加积极深入地参与全球公共卫生治理，通过支持共建重大公共卫生设施，鼓励跨国学术交流及科技成果转化落地等措施，加快医药学人才培育，发挥体制机制创新的先行示范作用，提升陕西在健康丝绸之路中的影响力和全球救治能力。

3. 加快陕西中医药"走出去"步伐

陕西在健康丝绸之路建设中应充分发挥中医药产业的独特优势和作用。要加强与共建"一带一路"国家在中医药领域的交流与合作，拓宽合作领域、拓展项目范围。要打造高水平医疗服务平台，推动国家中医药服务出口基地、中医药海外（诊疗）中心项目等国际合作"窗口"建设。支持有能力的教育机构与国外高校联合办学,指导相关中医药机构以线上、线下相结合形式,为共建"一带一路"国家从业人员提供中医药学历教育和短期培训,吸引更多人员来华学习中医药知识,加强海外中医药从业人员培养。推进中医药产业合作,做强秦药品牌。鼓励省内中医药企业入驻中外产业园,提供优质中医药产品,增加中药类产品海外注册数量;鼓励合作建立中药材海外基地;推动与共建国家联合开展药用植物保护、开发与利用,加强专家和技术人员交流合作。

4. 筑牢健康丝绸之路数字化基础

加强数字化在全球医疗卫生与生命健康领域中的运用是推进陕西健康丝绸之路快速发展的重要着力点。开展 5G 智慧医疗系统等基础设施建设,搭建 5G 智慧医疗示范服务平台,加快疫情预警、院前急救、远程诊疗、智能影像辅助诊断等互联网医疗应用推广。加快生物医疗等领域科技成果转化。筑牢数字化和信息化基础,让健康丝绸之路不断惠及陕西与共建"一带一路"国家国民健康。

绿色新领域探索生态环境治理样本

陕西地质复杂、生态环境多样，在生态文明建设方面积累了丰富的经验。2018年出台的《陕西省推进绿色"一带一路"建设实施意见》明确提出，要以"提升绿色发展水平，把陕西建成西部重要的生态环境屏障"为总体目标，落实"提升绿色发展水平，保障生态环境安全；加强宣传和交流平台建设，推动生态环保政策沟通；完善政策措施，促进绿色发展；开展生态环保领域合作，加快'走出去'步伐"的四大任务。

近年来，陕西不断筑牢生态安全屏障，同时，加快产业结构绿色低碳转型，不断提升绿色发展水平。陕西还不断扩展在生态环保领域的国际合作，积极参与全球绿色治理和生态文明建设，为全球生态环境治理提供了陕西范例。

（一）逐步构建生态安全新屏障

陕西是国家"两屏三带"生态安全战略格局的重要组成部分，

是国家第一批低碳试点省份,全国荒漠化综合防治、"三北"等重点生态工程建设的重点省份之一,也是我国生物物种资源丰富、珍稀濒危野生动植物分布密集的重要区域之一。特殊的地缘环境赋予了陕西在"一带一路"绿色发展中"西部重要的生态环境屏障"定位。为此,陕西不断挖掘绿色发展潜能,逐步构建起国家生态安全新屏障。

1.统筹规划打造生态名片

在生态环境保护方面,陕西坚持"重在保护、要在治理"的思路,协调推进问题整治、节水控水、保护修复等各项工作,对生态保护提出了系统规划和任务目标,重点打造了一批生态环境典范和生态名片。

秦岭和合南北、泽被天下,是我国的中央水塔,在涵养水源、保持水土、调节气候等方面发挥着重要的作用。黄河流域是中华文明的发源地,也是我国重要的生态安全屏障。陕西以秦岭生态环境保护和黄河流域生态保护为高质量发展的基准线,不断构建生态安全屏障。

陕西系统推进生态环境保护修复,全面推行林长制,开展生态环境保护纵向综合补偿。同时,不断提升信息化监管水平,搭建"网格化""信息化"平台,初步构建生态环境保护"空天地网一体化"监测监管体系,探索出智慧管护的模式。

2. 精准施策守护蓝天碧水

在守护蓝天碧水净土方面，陕西多举措精准施策。推进关中区域"一市一策"精准治霾，加强多污染物协同控制，强化重污染天气预警应对，积极推进企业绩效分级管控；建立"两大流域—三个板块—25个重点河流控制单元—111个国控断面"管控体系；严格重点建设用地环境准入，加强优先监管地块管理。数据显示，2015—2022年，陕西省环境空气质量优良率整体实现攀升，2013—2022年，河流Ⅰ-Ⅲ类水质断面比例稳步上涨。

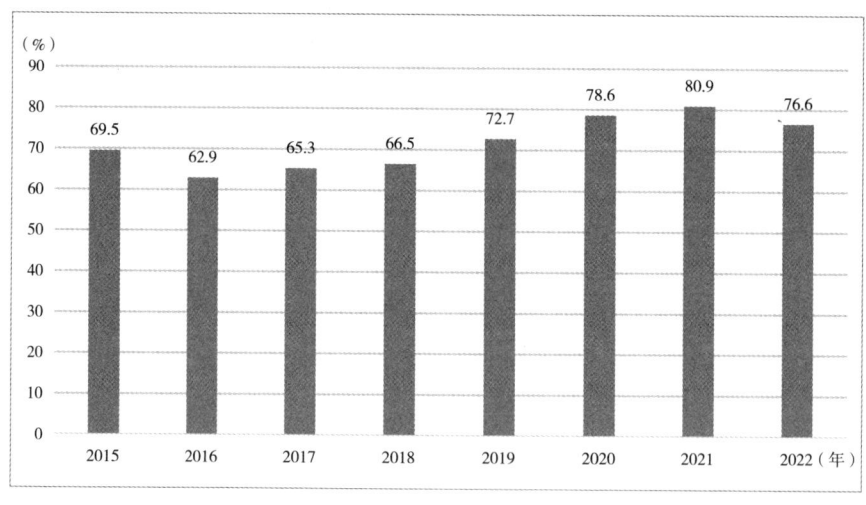

图12 陕西省2015—2022年环境空气质量优良率

注：2015年以后统计口径发生变化。

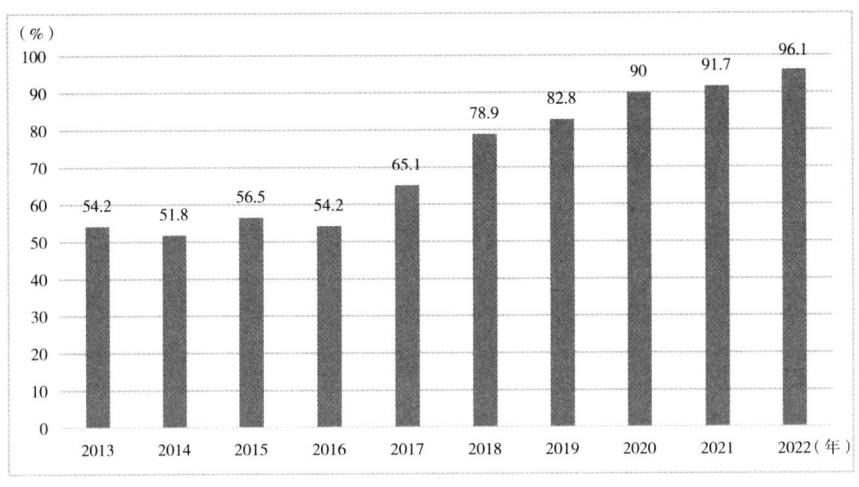

图13　陕西省2013—2022年河流Ⅰ~Ⅲ类水质断面比例

数据来源：历年陕西省生态环境状况公报。

（二）不断拓展绿色领域国际合作

陕西筑牢生态安全屏障的同时，还借助"一带一路"开放理念，不断加强系统治理，推动经济发展全面绿色转型，在发展清洁能源、履行国际义务等方面成效显著。其生态治理经验和产业绿色转型成效通过国际交流、产能合作等方式"加速出海"，为我国向世界展示大国形象和担当作出贡献。

1.清洁能源国际合作加速

清洁能源合作是高质量共建"一带一路"的重点领域之一。作为能源资源大省，陕西在"四个革命、一个合作"能源安全新战略和"双碳"目标的指引下，大力发展新能源产业并积极开展国际合作。

2021年，陕西省能源局出台《关于进一步加强可再生能源项目建设管理的通知》，鼓励引导地方政府和企业优先发展光伏、风电等新能源。2022年7月，陕西出台氢能产业发展规划，提出将氢能产业打造为推动全省能源绿色低碳转型的新引擎。在多重利好政策的支持下，截至2022年底，陕西可再生能源累计装机达到3111万千瓦，占全部电力装机的8.5%。同时合理控制化石能源消费，实施770万千瓦煤电机组节能降碳改造、灵活性改造、供热改造"三改联动"。

随着清洁能源的快速发展，陕西企业"走出去"的步伐也在加快。近年来，陕西大力推广风电、光伏、水电、智能电网等清洁能源，建成了马尔代夫马累环网（一期）工程项目，满足了居民用电需求，提高了当地供电能力、供电可靠性，持续促进当地经济社会发展；积极推动巴基斯坦达沃风电、埃塞俄比亚阿达玛风电、南非OYA混合能源等风电、光伏、储能项目建设，稳妥审慎推动马来西亚巴莱水电站、赞比亚下凯富峡水电站、印尼佳蒂格德水电站等重大水电项目，带动所在国能源绿色低碳发展；通过咨询、设计、EPC总承包等多种方式，参与沙特阿尔舒巴赫2.6GW光伏电站等项目建设，厚植绿色发展底色。

隆基绿能是陕西新能源企业"走出去"的代表之一。在哈萨克斯坦，隆基绿能为巴尔喀什电站一期项目提供P型PERC高效率高功率的单晶组件,为用户带来每年减少二氧化碳排放 70000 吨的环境效益。在乌兹别克斯坦,隆基绿能参与了多个政府主导的工商业项目,包括税务局大楼 2.3 兆瓦工商业分布式光伏项目、阿尔马雷克矿山冶金联合体 750 千瓦项目、国立世界语言大学 120 千瓦项目、国家电网大楼 550 千瓦工商业分布式光伏项目、塔什干行政大楼 300 千瓦项目、地区电网股份公司 260 千瓦项目等。

2. 与世界共享绿色发展经验

陕西乘着共建"一带一路"倡议的东风,主动举办国际论坛、参与国际会议,与国际社会分享陕西在绿色发展方面的实践经验,共同探讨绿色发展的未来路径。

十来年,陕西先后参加联合国《生物多样性公约》第十五次缔约方大会,举办第五届丝博会碳中和(西安)国际论坛,参加美国驻华大使馆和蒙古国大呼拉尔民主党来陕考察座谈和第三届中国阿拉伯城市论坛,开展应对气候变化和生物多样性等重点领域的国际对话交流。

第五届丝博会碳中和(西安)国际论坛以"两链融合发展迈向碳中和"为主题,汇聚了"政产学研金服用"各界专家学者,共同探讨了当前形势下我国积极应对气候变化、实现碳达峰碳中和的策略和途径,为我国绿色低碳发展,抢占新的战略制高点,切实迈向生态文明贡献陕西力量。

陕西利用"环保技术国际智汇平台"省级合作基地、陕韩环保合作事务委员会平台，开展产业技术交流，召开2021年中国（陕西）—韩国环保产业合作论坛暨企业线上洽谈会，参加东北亚地区自治团体联盟视频会议和首届中国（青海）国际生态博览会，推动产业技术交流与合作。

陕西积极主动承担商务部和生态环境部"2019年发展中国家固体废物管理与环境保护官员研修班"的学习交流任务，与来自汤加、塞舌尔、南非、朝鲜等11个国家的24位环境官员对陕西省生态文明建设、重要生态环境保护和固体废物处理处置等工作的总体情况、举措及成效进行了交流分享，并进行了实地考察。

3. 积极履行国际生态环保义务

在融入共建"一带一路"大格局的过程中，陕西认真履行生态环境保护相关国际公约明确的义务。实施《关于汞的水俣公约》能力建设项目，推进履行《关于持久性有机污染物的斯德哥尔摩公约》，禁止六溴环十二烷生产及使用工作，开展全省持久性有机污染物（POPs）情况调查；不断壮大绿色环保战略性新兴产业，将大型环保及资源综合利用装备列入陕西省首套重大技术装备产品项目重点支持领域，为向世界展现守信践诺、积极参与全球治理的中国形象作出陕西贡献。

（三）"一盘棋"布局绿色开放合作

近年来，陕西生态环境质量虽持续改善，但推动共建绿色"一带一路"的基础还不扎实。下一步，要把陕西生态环境保护放到全国生态环境保护和推动共建"一带一路"的大局中谋划推进。

1. 深化优化生态环境领域政策体系

陕西是能源大省，生态环保任务重。需要严守生态环境保护底线，继续弥补短板，筑牢共建绿色丝绸之路的生态安全屏障。在绿色发展的政策体系上，需要更加有效地发挥生态环境保护对经济发展的引领、优化和倒逼作用。在生产环节，加快产业用能、交通运输用地结构调整，加强煤炭清洁高效利用，大力发展新能源和清洁能源。在消费环节，大力倡导绿色消费，推进资源节约集约利用，逐步形成绿色节能降碳的生活方式，推动经济社会全面绿色转型，打牢共建绿色丝绸之路的社会经济基础。

2. 全面提升生态环境治理能力和治理水平

以应对气候变化和生物多样性保护为牵引，着力推动生态环境科技创新、成果转化和工程技术迭代升级，不断壮大环保产业，打造更多亮点示范工程项目，夯实共建绿色丝绸之路的工作基础。完善绿色发展支撑体系，推动绿色基建、绿色能源、绿色交通、绿色金融、绿色贸易、绿色科技等领域务实合作，有效服务生态环境治理体系和治理能力现代化。

3.以绿色理念引领打造陕西绿色丝绸之路建设高地

将绿色丝绸之路建设理念体现在陕西生态环境工作的谋划实践中。发挥中国—中亚峰会重大主场外交活动的引领带动作用和欧亚经济论坛平台作用，坚持"引进来"和"走出去"相结合，共享治理成果和经验。不断激发陕西绿色发展新动能，形成共建绿色丝绸之路的新格局，打造陕西绿色丝绸之路建设高地。

数字新领域面向未来推动国际合作

数字丝绸之路是数字基础设施、数字技术等与共建"一带一路"的有机结合,是中国在数字经济时代提出的推动全球共同发展的重要举措,正在成为推动新型全球化的数字桥梁。

近年来,陕西主动拓展数字经济合作领域,推动在物联网、大数据、人工智能、5G、工业互联网、区块链等数字技术领域与共建"一带一路"国家和地区的合作,数字经济成为陕西共建"一带一路"的重要主题之一。

(一)筑牢数字经济发展的制度基础

1. 完善发展数字经济顶层设计

《陕西省"十四五"深度融入共建"一带一路"大格局、建设内陆开放高地规划》《陕西省"十四五"数字经济发展规划》的出台,从顶层设计到实施路径,为陕西省数字丝绸之路建设制定框架。

《陕西省"十四五"深度融入共建"一带一路"大格局、建设内陆开放高地规划》提出，加大数字技术应用及基础设施建设，大力推动科技创新，搭建国际数字合作平台，不断推动数字领域合作，高质量共建数字丝绸之路。从提升数字化建设水平、创新合作机制以及深化数字经济合作三个方面提出一系列具体举措。《陕西省"十四五"数字经济发展规划》《数字经济发展规划》提出要打造数字丝绸之路建设示范区，在扩大与共建"一带一路"国家和地区开展数字经济交流合作等方面作出具体部署。

陕西省2023年政府工作报告提出，坚持数字产业化、产业数字化两手抓。突出网络、信息服务、科技创新、信息化应用等重点，加强关键数字技术研究攻关，推动物联网、大数据等数字技术融合应用，建设国家新一代人工智能创新发展试验区，加快推进大数据、软件信息服务等千亿级产业集群建设，力争数字经济核心产业增加值占比超过8%。

2.紧抓数字化发展机遇建立项目库示范区

2020年以来，陕西省连续两年明确要持续推进数字丝绸之路建设，并在当年的"一带一路"建设行动计划中明确具体任务及分工部署。2022年，陕西省发展改革委发布通知征集数字经济重点建设项目，开始建立陕西省数字经济重点建设项目库，包括数字基础设施建设项目、数字产业化重点项目、行业数字化基础公共服务平台项目、行业数字化示范应用项目等。

陕西省政府以及各地市政府均在抢抓数字化发展机遇，大力促进数字技术和数字经济建设。2021年,陕西省委网信办会同陕西省发展改革委、陕西省工信厅发出《关于公布我省首批省级数字经济试点示范名单的通知》,认定首批省级数字经济示范区5家,宝鸡市省级数字经济示范区(渭滨区)、铜川市省级数字经济示范区(耀州区含新区)、延安市省级数字经济示范区(宝塔区)、榆林市省级数字经济示范区(神木市)和西安市省级数字经济示范区,西安市省级数字经济示范区包含西安高新区、经开区、国家民用航天产业基地、阎良国家航空高技术产业基地、浐灞生态区等。

(二)数字经济助力共建"一带一路"

近年来,陕西信息丝绸之路、数字经济试点示范区建设得到了有序推进,华为、京东等一批数字经济龙头企业陆续在陕落地,一批具有创新活力的本土数字经济产业加速成长。数字经济正在成为推进陕西省经济高质量发展和推动共建"一带一路"的强劲引擎。

1. 陕西数字经济增速位居全国前列

近年来,陕西统筹推进网络强省、数字陕西、智慧社会、数字丝绸之路建设,为高质量发展提供了有力的信息化支撑。截至2023年5月,陕西省累计建成4G基站总数超过19.6万座,5G基站6.3万座。大数据产业加快集聚发展。比亚迪智能终端、长安鲲鹏产业基地等一批重点项目建成投产,各地因地制宜打造数字经济聚集区，建成一大批数字经济示范园区、数字经济示范平台。据测算，陕西省数字经济总量占生产总值比重超过30%。

2022年，陕西数字经济规模首次超过1万亿元，增速达13.9%，位列全国第五。大数据、半导体、网络安全等数字经济核心产业增长较快，产业增加值占GDP比重为7%。其中，半导体产业规模超过1700亿元，位列全国第四。数字经济产业成为推动陕西经济社会高质量发展的重要引擎。

与此同时，陕西数字经济核心产业快速发展，能级不断提升。美林数据位列全国工业大数据企业排行榜第一，中煤航测、陕西天润等企业位列全国地理信息大数据百强企业，陕煤集团等企业位列全国工业互联网百强企业，交大捷普等企业位列全国网络安全百强企业。

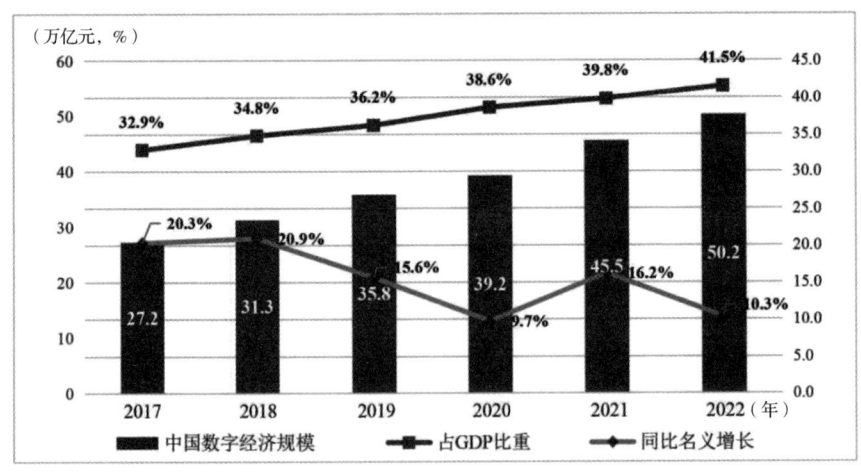

图14 2013—2022年中国数字经济规模及增速

数据来源：新华财经、中国一带一路网。

2. 推动实现数据链与产业链耦合发展

陕西把发展数字经济作为推动经济发展质量变革、效率变革和动力变革的"加速器",充分把握数字经济和实体经济融合发展的趋势,大力推动产业数字化和数字产业化,形成数字与实体经济共促高质量发展的新合力。

以陕西省大数据集团为例,该集团以"经营政府数据,盘活社会数据,带动产业发展"为方向,立足陕西、面向全国,打造了多个城市智慧政务平台,推出陕西省疫情防控码平台、云上丝博数字化平台、全运一掌通APP、全运会大数据统一平台等,为推动陕西大数据产业和数字经济发展贡献了智慧和力量。

陕西工业体系完整,创新资源丰富,在发展数字经济上具有显著的创新研发优势和丰富的应用场景优势。通过链圈结合的发展方式,陕西重点培育发展数字技术应用业,以数据管理能力成熟度评估模型为标准牵引,由点扩线至面,逐步构建大数据产业"生态圈"。2022年,陕西成为企业开展数据管理国家标准试点地区,首批确定60户试点企业,覆盖乘用车、重卡、输变电装备、煤制烯烃等制造业重点产业链"链主"企业和龙头企业17户,初步实现了数据链与产业链耦合。

3. 数字经济融入"一带一路"大格局

陕西紧抓数字经济发展机遇,以数字产业化为重点、产业数字化为根本,打造"一带一路"数字枢纽,建设数字经济产业聚集区,夯实数字经济发展基础,促进数字资源要素加快流动,向全球数字经济第一方阵迈进。

西安高新区是陕西乃至全国的创新驱动发展引领区。数字经济成为西安高新区培育新动能、实现新跨越的核心抓手。西安高新区重点突破人工智能、大数据与云计算、网络信息安全、边缘计算等变革技术,聚焦发展集成电路、智能终端、数字创意,西安高新区数字经济发展正进入全国第一方阵,成为"一带一路"数字产业创新高地、全国数字经济先行示范区。

数字经济也成为陕西"一带一路"国际盛会的重要主题。2017年以来,西安高新区连续举办四届全球硬科技创新大会和全球程序员节,为西安打造"全球硬科技之都"和"数字丝路明珠"提供重要支撑。2023年6月,以"共享数字成果,共创数字未来"为主题的首届"数字丝路"先进科技发展论坛在西安举办,旨在促进和推动我国互联网及先进制造领域科技企业与上海合作组织国家在工业互联网领域的务实合作,扩大对外开放。

(三)跨境电商产业链和生态圈初步形成

1.跨境电商综试区加速跨境电商产业形成

目前,陕西省跨境电商产业链和生态圈已初步形成。2018年7月24日,国务院正式批复同意设立中国(西安)跨境电子商务综合试验区，自此西安市先后设立了空港新城、国际港务区、曲江新区、高新区、经开区、碑林区等三批共 9 个创新示范先行区，基本形成了跨境电商产业发展格局。引进考拉海购、菜鸟等国内知名跨境电商相关企业，全市跨境电商及相关企业 1300 余家，从业人员 3 万余人。截至 2022 年底，西安市拥有跨境电商及相关企业 1800 余家，跨境电商交易额 144.27 亿元，同比增长 46.4%，跨境电商增势强劲，已成为拉动外向型经济发展的新动能。

2. 多个平台通道共同推动跨境电商集聚增长

西安市依托航空、铁路口岸及综保区等平台通道，共同推进西安跨境电商产业的集聚增长。2021 年以来，西安市重点打造中欧班列长安号跨境电商全国集结中心，实行跨境电商散货"先报关，后装箱"新模式，提高货物通关时效 2—3 天。2022 年，西安市累计开行跨境电商班列 198 列，实现跨境电商交易额 35.1 亿元，同比增长 40%。

发展数字经济是加快产业转型升级和增强自主创新的重要抓手，数字丝绸之路建设有利于共建"一带一路"国家加速提升国际竞争力和影响力。陕西推进数字丝绸之路建设将不断促进开放力度，与共建国家形成"利益共同体"，进而形成"命运共同体"。

（四）"一带一路"高质量发展需要数字动能

面向新征程，陕西以数字基础设施互联互通为抓手，以促进数字经济与实体经济深度融合为核心，以关键核心技术攻关为关键，着力推进跨境电商和数字贸易健康发展，为高质量共建"一带一路"提供数字动能。

1. 协同推进陕西数字产业化与产业数字化

大力推动数字经济与实体经济融合发展，推进5G、物联网、人工智能、工业互联网等新型基建投资。以数字政府建设全面引领驱动数字化发展。立足秦创原创新驱动平台建设，发挥陕西科教优势和产业优势，推动数字要素产业化，促进电子信息制造、软件和信息服务业高水平发展，促进物联网、大数据、云计算、人工智能等产业发展，打造具备国际竞争力的新一代信息技术产业集群，引导数字经济高水平集聚发展，形成具有特色的数字产业生态。

2. 以国际交流互动提升陕西数字经济话语权

积极搭建国际数字合作平台，发挥全球程序员节、全球硬科技大会、"数字丝路"先进科技发展论坛等国际数字经济盛会作用，扩大陕西在"一带一路"数字经济发展中的话语权。鼓励相关企业"走出去"，推动基础设施建设、数字经济发展、网络安全保障等方面的国际交流合作，持续探索开展数据要素跨境流通、数字贸易等试点。

3. 构建数字丝绸之路标准规则体系

发挥中国国际经济贸易仲裁委员会丝绸之路仲裁中心和中国（西安）知识产权保护中心作用，组建"一带一路"产业知识产权联盟，探索建设"一带一路"知识产权保护示范区，为数字经济高质量发展提供知识产权支撑。通过标准和规则体系的逐渐建立，助力数字丝绸之路建设。

展望篇

2023年5月,首届中国—中亚峰会在陕西西安召开。共建"一带一路"倡议提出10周年之际,世界的目光再次聚焦古丝绸之路起点,陕西迎来推进共建"一带一路"新机遇。

习近平总书记在中国—中亚峰会召开前夕专门听取了陕西省委和省政府工作汇报。他指出,陕西"要着力扩大对内对外开放,打造内陆改革开放高地。更加主动融入和服务构建新发展格局,更加深度融入共建'一带一路'大格局,在扩大对内对外开放中强动力、增活力,打开发展新天地。"

蓝图绘就,号角吹响。面对新形势下推动共建"一带一路"高质量发展的更高要求,陕西将着眼全国大局、发挥自身优势、明确主攻方向,更加深度融入共建"一带一路"大格局、更高质量打造内陆开放新高地,着力推动中国—中亚峰会涉陕成果落地落实,持续放大峰会效应,积极拓宽合作领域,努力培育更多新增长点,树牢开放理念、增强开放自觉,更加主动融入和服务构建新发展格局,高水平推进对内对外开放,不断增强发展动力和活力,努力打开发展新天地。

POINT 一

明确主攻方向补齐开放不足最大短板

开放不足是制约陕西发展的最大短板。陕西对外开放起点相对偏低，经济发展基础偏弱，虽经十年追赶，与改革开放前沿地区相比仍有不小差距。2022年，陕西进出口额仅占全国的1.1%，实际利用外资和对外直接投资分别占全国的0.8%和0.4%，人均GDP仅为全国平均水平的一半。

在高质量共建"一带一路"的新征程上，陕西将不断加强顶层设计，进一步完善规划体系、责任体系、安全体系、考核体系，强化协同配合，凝聚工作合力，明确主攻方向，发挥纵横汇通的枢纽作用，明确面向中亚、南亚、西亚的重点方向，不断补足开放不足这一最大短板，使得打造"内陆改革开放高地"更具成效，推动共建"一带一路"高质量发展迈出更大步伐。

（一）纵横汇通的交通物流枢纽作用更突出

持续聚焦基础设施"硬联通"，位于东西走向亚欧陆海贸易大通道重要区域的陕西，连接向西南的西部陆海新通道，将不断提升陕西的国际交通枢纽能级。未来，陕西将积极参与西部陆海新通道建设，充分发挥中欧班列西安集结中心作用，不断增强辐射带动作用，深入推进港产、港贸、港城融合，加快形成面向中亚、南亚、西亚国家的重要对外开放通道，在促进国内国际双循环中发挥更大作用。

（二）面向中亚、南亚、西亚的重点方向更明确

立足陕西区位特点，打造中国向西开放前沿。陕西地处亚欧大陆桥的主通道，原先不靠海不沿边的劣势将逐渐转化为贯通东西、连接南北的优势。面向中亚、南亚、西亚开放合作将成为陕西新阶段的使命，也是陕西构建以国内大循环为主体、国内国际双循环相互促进的新发展格局的必备条件。

新形势下，陕西成为面向中亚开放的重要区域之一。首届中国—中亚峰会发表的《中国—中亚峰会西安宣言》、达成的一系列重要共识和实现的一系列制度安排，为陕西促进中亚区域在经贸、文化等方面形成更加紧密的联系打下了坚实基础。面向中亚，实现共同繁荣发展，成为陕西融入"一带一路"大格局的主要方向之一。

区域经济协助也将成为陕西开放发展的重要途径。2023年6月，《区域全面经济伙伴关系协定》（RCEP）对菲律宾正式生效，标志着全球人口最多、经贸规模最大、最具发展潜力的自由贸易区

进入全面实施新阶段。陕西积极参与践行协定，与贸易伙伴进出口与利用投资稳步增长。随着《区域全面经济伙伴关系协定》全面生效，陕西也将不断提升与东南亚区域国家合作的水平。

（三）打造"内陆改革开放高地"更主动

共建"一带一路"以开放为导向，坚持普惠共赢，打造开放型合作平台，推动形成开放型经济。对于处于内陆地区的陕西来说，参与共建"一带一路"正是向外开放与向内改革一体推进的重要方式，为陕西破解开放不足这一制约发展的突出短板，为打造内陆改革开放高地提供了抓手。

高质量共建"一带一路"与区域高质量发展互为前提。通过推进基于规则且开放、透明、包容的"一带一路"多边贸易体制，促进贸易投资自由化、便利化，共建高标准自由贸易区，陕西将不断强化高质量项目支撑、营商环境突破，提高治理体系和治理能力现代化水平。

发挥自身特色实现重点领域新的突破

依托陕西自身特色,实现重点领域新突破,既是未来陕西推进共建"一带一路"责任,也是更好地发挥陕西作用的坦途。陕西将发挥历史悠久、文化多元丰富的特色以及在农业、健康、绿色等领域积累的独特优势,打造文明互鉴的"区域窗口",以进一步发挥自身特色实现多领域多层次新突破。

(一)"一带一路"农业领域合作更务实

陕西是中国重要的农业省份,在"一带一路"农业合作中具有重要示范引领作用。随着上海合作组织农业技术交流培训示范基地在杨凌示范区揭牌和中国杨凌农业高新科技成果博览会的连续成功举办,陕西已经成为中国与世界各国在农业领域深入合作交流的重要代表。

展望未来,作为农业大省的陕西将继续发挥自身优势,主动在惠及民生最基本福祉的农业上与共建"一带一路"国家开展更加务实的合作，推动合作向国际化、市场化、专业化的高水平迈进，带动共建国家共同发展农业，推广农业种植技术、品种、模式，让优质农业造福共建国家乃至全球各国的民众。

（二）健康绿色等新领域合作更深入

陕西拥有丰富的中医药文化，也是中医药和生物制药的重要省份。围绕前期已经开展的中医药等领域的国际合作，陕西还将进一步扩大陕西中医药"走出去"，同时吸引更多留学生、医护人员来陕学习，推动传承创新中医药、弘扬中医药传统文化，促进与共建"一带一路"国家民心相通，更好地推动中医药国际化，为共建人类卫生健康共同体贡献陕西中医药力量。

打造美丽中国的"陕西样本"，参与全球绿色治理，正成为陕西的重要特征之一。随着秦岭生态环境保护和黄河流域生态保护常态化长效化机制的建立，产业结构绿色低碳转型升级，绿色新能源龙头企业提质增效，绿色发展水平不断提升，陕西将逐渐成为全球生态文明建设的重要参与者、贡献者、引领者，为共建"一带一路"国家生态环境治理注入更为鲜明的绿色力量。

（三）实现文明互鉴的"区域窗口"更清晰

共建"一带一路"为各国之间的文化交流、文明互鉴提供了平台。作为古丝绸之路起点的西安,是中华优秀传统文化传承示范的主要区域之一。面向未来,陕西将以探索建设西安"一带一路"综合试验区为契机,实施中华文明标识保护工程,打造中华文明根脉城市和"天然历史博物馆"之城,守护千年古都风貌,彰显世界历史文化名城独特魅力。西安将不断深化与共建"一带一路"国家在文化旅游、文物考古、历史研究等领域交流合作,持续提升西安国际知名度和影响力。

一花独放不是春,百花齐放春满园。陕西历史文化资源遍及三秦大地。陕北地区的红色文化、草原文化,关中地区的周秦汉唐文化,陕南地区的汉文化、巴文化等都是中华优秀传统文化的重要承载体,具有超越地理位置的重要影响力,是中国与世界其他国家文化交流、文明互鉴的重要渠道。未来,陕西将充分发挥各地优势,强化与"一带一路"国家的对话交流,成为具有特色、务实深入的对外交流"区域窗口"。

文化交流、文明互鉴从来都是双向的,"走出去"学习交流同等重要。陕西将充分发挥文化与旅游资源大省优势,坚定文化自信,积极搭建平台、扩充渠道、创新机制,与共建"一带一路"国家加强合作,探索中欧班列(西安)人文班列等新的文化交流模式与载体,实现共建"一带一路"国家与陕西多层次交流交往,深化了解。

深化创新驱动、释放高质量发展内生动力

共建"一带一路"已经成为共建国家创新发展的新平台,实现跨越式发展的驱动力,也成为世界经济发展的新动能。陕西将统筹改革、开放、创新三大动力,进一步深化改革,深度融入共建"一带一路"大格局,推动创新驱动发展,坚决破除制约高质量发展的难点、堵点,持续释放内在潜力。

(一)西安"双中心"辐射作用更明显

2023年,西安获批建设综合性科学中心和科技创新中心(以下简称"双中心"),成为继北京、上海以及粤港澳大湾区后第四个获批建设"双中心"的城市,标志着西安科技创新迈向高质量发展新阶段。推进"双中心"建设,将实现打造具有全球影响力的硬科技创新策源地、具有前沿引领性的新兴产业衍生地和"一带一路"顶尖人才首选地。

西安综合性科学中心由"一核两翼"构成,"一核"位于丝路科学城(西安科学园),"两翼"分别位于中国西部创新港和长安大学城。西安科技创新中心将构建"一核一圈一带"空间布局,"一核"即西安综合性科学中心核心区,"一圈"即以西安都市圈为中心的协同创新生态圈,"一带"即面向"一带一路"的丝路科技创新合作带。"双中心"将打造具有全球影响力的硬科技创新策源地,具有前沿引领性的新兴产业衍生地和"一带一路"顶尖人才聚集地,成为陕西继续推进"一带一路"建设的一大优势。

(二)"秦创原"科技成果转化能效更强大

共建"一带一路"需要建好用好综合开放平台,实现创新驱动发展。秦创原是陕西于2021年设立的创新驱动平台,该平台致力于打造立体联动"孵化器"、科技成果转化"加速器"和两链融合"促进器",助推区域经济高质量发展。

陕西已构建起"一中心一平台一公司"科创服务体系,打造了一批"立体联动孵化器、成果转化加速器、两链融合促进器"的示范样板,推行了"科学家+工程师"队伍建设等改革,引进了各类金融机构和服务机构,有效地促进了科技、经济、金融的融合。

随着各类要素资源在共建"一带一路"国家之间共享、流动和重新组合,秦创原创新驱动平台将利用自身优势,在科技成果转化等方面与共建"一带一路"国家合作共享，深化创新驱动发展，巩固陕西省作为科教创新先导区的地位。

（三）数字化牵引作用更强劲

数字经济符合共建"一带一路"国家经济和社会现代化的优先发展方向，将成为支撑各国经济发展的新动能。中国数字经济发展迅速，陕西省内大数据企业、人工智能企业、各类软件及信息服务企业众多，正逐渐成为经济社会发展的强劲引擎。

蓬勃发展的数字经济形态是经济驱动的重要方式之一。共建"一带一路"要坚持推动大数据、云计算、智慧城市建设，陕西将不断加强新技术、新业态、新模式的国际交流合作，助力共建"一带一路"国家数字化转型，实现新的增长动能和发展路径。

锚定目标推进高质量共建"一带一路"

面向未来,陕西将锚定高标准、可持续、惠民生的发展目标,实现政府、企业、社会多方联动,创办高品质的国际活动,积极拓宽合作领域,高质量推动共建"一带一路"。

(一)高标准、可持续、惠民生的目标更可期

陕西将积极打造市场化、法治化、国际化的营商环境,提高招商引资的质量和水平。凭借坚实的工业基础、雄厚的科教实力等优势,吸引全球各国企业和企业家来陕投资兴业、交流合作,吸引海内外人才来陕就业创业、实现理想。同时,陕西将抓住国际产能合作这一新机遇,将本土优势产业、企业的持续发展与共建"一带一路"国家经济发展壮大的需求结合起来,实现共赢、多赢。

陕西将继续深化同共建国家的互利合作,助力越来越多的国家与区域加快经济发展。通过着力推进自贸试验区建设,聚焦推动区

域内创新链、产业链、价值链协同升级和加速国内外物资流、资金流、人才流、技术流和信息流集聚转化，积极布局发展现代产业，加快制度集成创新，全力打造更高能级的开放平台。与此同时，陕西的全方位联动开放布局也将得以逐步实施。

（二）能盈利促双赢的外向型经济更多元

"引进来""走出去"不仅帮助企业开拓了国际市场，更重要的是加速陕西经济转型升级，以更大力度、更开放的形态推动陕西经济向高质量发展，提升竞争力。

继续高水平"引进来"，三星、美光等外资巨头投资和产能有望持续扩大，中欧合作产业园起步区、中俄丝路创新园内的外资企业也有望加大投资、扩大产能。

加速高水平"走出去"，陕西省围绕23条重点产业链优势产品，聚焦共建"一带一路"国家、RCEP国家和欧美传统市场，拓展非洲等新兴市场，推动省内企业抱团出海，提升陕西产品的国际市场份额。陕汽、隆基、爱菊等一批本土龙头企业在共建"一带一路"国家设立生产基地、物流园区和分销网络，将持续提高市场能力、盈利能力。一些传统和新型产业企业也将陆续走进共建国家，形成更加多元的"走出去"企业矩阵和服务体系，外资合资企业将更加便利地进入陕西。

（三）高层次、高品质的论坛活动更丰富

国际高端平台是实现开放的重要载体，高层次、高规格、高品质的论坛活动，是区域对外交往的重要载体和重要象征。来自全球超过120个国家和地区的180位政要、8000名客商参会参展的丝绸之路国际博览会暨中国东西部合作与投资贸易洽谈会，已成为推动共建"一带一路"、促进东中西部地区联动发展的重要平台。

随着中国—中亚峰会的成功举办，以丝绸之路博览会、欧亚经济论坛等为代表的高层次、高规格、高品质论坛活动将有望持续提升规格和水平，成为"一带一路"国际合作交流的重要平台。

未来，陕西将高层次推动自贸试验区、综合保税区、临空经济示范区、跨境电商综试区、杨凌上合组织农业技术交流培训示范基地等各类开放平台协同发力，通过高水平对外交往，推动高质量共建"一带一路"。

结　语

　　历史的发展波澜壮阔，前进的道路无比宽广。陕西主动深度融入共建"一带一路"大格局，是历史发展的必然，也是发展机遇的垂青。这是一条和平、繁荣、开放、绿色、创新、文明、廉洁之路，是共建"一带一路"国家人民与陕西人民共享发展机遇、创造美好生活的"各美其美、美人之美、美美与共"之路，是实践中华优秀传统文化"民胞物与、协和万邦、天下大同"理念，构建人类命运共同体之路。

　　时间与空间交汇在新时代的三秦大地。从古丝绸之路起点的西安到出使西域张骞的故里汉中，从出土"宅兹中国"的宝鸡到发现丝路象征"鎏金铜蚕"的安康，从红色圣地延安到丝路驼城榆林，从中医药大家孙思邈的故乡铜川到中国最早撰述"西域"的司马迁故里渭南，从丝路名都咸阳再到盛产传自欧亚大陆的核桃的商洛，陕西各地市无不与"一带一路"相关，又都在以新的方式、新的面貌在新的时代与共建"一带一路"国家展开新的合作。

　　在共建"一带一路"新征程上，陕西将紧紧围绕高质量发展这个首要任务，拿出争当时代弄潮儿的志向和气魄，扩大高水平对外开放，在推进中国式现代化建设中勇立潮头、奋力追赶、敢于超越，在西部地区发挥示范作用，奋力谱写中国式现代化建设的陕西篇章。

陕西推进"一带一路"建设大事记
（2013—2023年）

2013年

9月7日，习近平主席访问哈萨克斯坦时提出共同建设"丝绸之路经济带"。

9月27日，在第五届欧亚经济论坛上，来自丝绸之路经济带的中外城市代表共同倡议发布《共建丝绸之路经济带西安宣言》。

10月3日，习近平主席在印度尼西亚国会发表演讲时提出共同建设21世纪"海上丝绸之路"。

11月28日，陕西省首趟国际货运班列中欧班列长安号列车发车。

2014年

3月19日，海关总署正式批复西安为国家跨境贸易电子商务服务试点城市。

5月23—26日，第十八届中国东西部合作与投资贸易洽谈会暨丝绸之路国际博览会在西安举行，16个共建"一带一路"国家设立展览馆。

5月24日，陕西与吉尔吉斯斯坦楚河州正式缔结友好省州关系，签字仪式在西安举行。

6月18日,首列丝绸之路旅游专列首发仪式在西安火车站举行。

6月22日,"丝绸之路:长安-天山廊道的路网"成功申报世界文化遗产。

9月12—27日,首届"丝绸之路国际艺术节"在西安举办。

9月19—21日,首届"中国西安丝绸之路国际旅游博览会"在西安开幕,成为丝绸之路旅游国际营销平台。

10月,陕西省推进丝绸之路经济带新起点建设工作领导小组成立。

10月12—16日,在中俄两国总理见证下,陕西省政府与俄罗斯直接投资基金、中俄投资基金、俄罗斯斯科尔科沃创新中心代表签署《关于合作开发建设中俄丝绸之路高科技产业园的合作备忘录》。

10月20—26日,首届"丝绸之路国际电影节"在西安举行。

10月27日,国家四部委联合发文,批复设立陕西西咸空港保税物流中心。

12月19日,"西安港"国际代码(CNXAG)、国内代码(61900100)正式启用。

2015年

2月13—16日,习近平总书记来陕考察调研时指出,陕西是"向西开放的前沿位置""陕西要找准定位,主动融入'一带一路'大格局"。

3月28日,《推动共建丝绸之路经济带和21世纪海上丝绸之路的愿景与行动》发布，其中明确提出要打造西安内陆型改革开放新高地。

4月1日，陕西省人民政府办公厅下发关于成立"一带一路"金融合作推进领导小组的通知。

5月6日，"一带一路"国家企业高峰论坛在西安举办。

6月17日，《陕西省"一带一路"建设2015年行动计划》发布，自此陕西连年发布年度行动计划，部署全年重点任务。

6月18—19日，丝绸之路旅游部长会议暨第七届联合国世界旅游组织丝绸之路旅游国际大会在西安举行。

10月22日，陕西省与中国银行签署全面支持陕西"一带一路"建设合作备忘录。

12月15日，陕西电子口岸综合服务平台上线，标志着陕西省电子口岸"单一窗口"运营正式启动。

12月25日，西咸保税物流中心通过正式验收。

12月29日，西安国际港务区的西安铁路临时开放口岸通过考核验收，成为陕西唯一的进境粮食指定口岸。

2016 年

3月，《陕西省推进建设丝绸之路经济带和21世纪海上丝绸之路实施方案（2015—2020年）》印发。

3月1日，隆基股份在海上丝绸之路重要节点马来西亚古晋投资3.11亿美元建设首个海外生产基地隆基（古晋）有限公司。

5月13日，2016丝绸之路国际博览会暨第二十届中国东西部合作与投资贸易洽谈会在西安开幕，规模为历届最大。

8月31日，陕西获批国家第三批自由贸易试验区。

9月6日，"丝绸之路工商领导人（西安）峰会、丝绸之路国际总商会合作发展大会"在西安举办。

10月18日，陕西省与中国建设银行签订"丝路"系列基金战略合作协议。

12月12日，西安至阿姆斯特丹（长安号）国际货运航班开航。

2017年

4月1日，中国（陕西）自由贸易试验区在西安揭牌，陕西自贸试验区正式成立。

5月18日，海航现代物流集团在西安举行成立大会"西安—阿姆斯特丹""西安—上海—安克雷奇—芝加哥"两条货运洲际航线开通。

5月22日，京东集团与西安航天基地签订了京东全球物流总部、京东无人系统产业中心、京东云运营中心合作协议，五年内计划投资205亿元。

6月30日，中国（陕西）国际贸易"单一窗口"正式上线运行。

7月6日，陕西省推进丝绸之路经济带新起点建设工作领导小组调整为陕西省推进"一带一路"建设工作领导小组。

8月19—20日，首届世界西商大会在西安举办。

9月22日，首届"一带一路"中医药发展论坛举行。

9月25日，"一带一路"全球健康国际研讨会举行。

9月27日，国家"一带一路"领导小组办公室到陕西督导调研"一带一路"建设工作。

9月30日，《陕西省人民政府关于积极有效利用外资推动经济高质量发展的实施意见》印发。

10月，陕西省国资委出台《关于推进省属企业开展国际产能合作的意见》，从4个方面对省属企业参与"一带一路"建设进行引导和规范。

10月13日，"一带一路"国家计量测试研究中心（陕西）获批。

11月27日，全省推进"一带一路"建设工作领导小组全体会议召开，会上举行陕西"一带一路"网上线仪式。

12月12日，第十二届全球孔子学院大会在西安举行。

12月14日，陕西省人民政府发布《中国（陕西）自由贸易试验区管理办法》。

12月29日，《进一步支持中国（陕西）自由贸易试验区建设的若干意见》印发。

2018年

1月2日，国家外汇管理局陕西省分局印发《进一步推进中国（陕西）自由贸易试验区外汇管理改革试点实施细则》。

1月29日，陕西省环保厅、陕西省外事办、陕西省发展改革委、陕西省商务厅联合出台《陕西省推进绿色"一带一路"建设实施意见》。

4月9日,陕西省与德国莱法州签署发展友好省州关系意向书。

4月9日,首届上海合作组织人民论坛在西安开幕。

4月10日,陕西省与乌兹别克斯坦撒马尔罕州签署友好合作备忘录。

4月16日,"通丝路"陕西跨境电子商务人民币结算服务平台上线仪式举行。

5月12—13日,中国、俄罗斯、哈萨克斯坦等国学者发表《国际"丝绸之路"考古与文化遗产保护西安共识》。

5月25日,陕西省制定《关于推动交通物流融合发展的实施方案》,提出到2020年,陕西在"一带一路"沿线综合枢纽地位得到强化,西安"国际航空枢纽"功能明显提升。

5月31日,首届"一带一路"汽车产业发展国际论坛在西安召开。

6月29日,最高人民法院第二国际商事法庭在西安揭牌。

7月19日,京沪陕三地建立入境旅游省际合作机制。

7月24日,国务院批复同意在西安等22个城市设立跨境电子商务综合试验区。

8月14日,《陕西省标准联通共建"一带一路"行动计划(2018—2020年)》发布。

8月15日,中国(陕西)—俄罗斯经贸合作推介会在莫斯科举行。

9月17日，第三届中法文化论坛在西安开幕。

9月17日，第二届中德历史文化名城对话会在西安开幕。

9月21日，首场"陕西'一带一路'建设五年成就"主题系列新闻发布会召开。

10月9日，2018世界文化旅游大会峰会在西安浐灞生态区开幕。

10月30日，中欧班列长安号2018年开行首超千列活动在西安国际港务区举行。

11月2日，第25届杨凌农高会国际合作周拉开序幕。

11月5—10日，首届中国国际进口博览会在上海举行，3000余名企业人员组成的陕西交易团参会。

12月4日，陕西省政府和泰国农业与合作社部共同主办的2018"一带一路"陕西经贸文化推介洽谈会在曼谷举行。

12月5日，陕西省推进"一带一路"建设工作领导小组会议召开。

12月5日，《中国（西安）跨境电子商务综合试验区实施方案》印发。

2019年

1月11日，国家发展改革委批复西安咸阳国际机场三期扩建工程项目建议书。

1月14日，陕西省推进"一带一路"建设工作领导小组印发《西安建设"一带一路"综合改革开放试验区总体方案》。

1月15日，西咸新区秦汉新城管委会和新疆博州阿拉山口市政府签订战略合作协议。

2月22日，西安国际粮油论坛召开。

3月11日，2019意大利国际合作博览会暨"一带一路"展会西安市推介会举行。

3月25日，中欧班列（西安）集结中心合作论坛暨共建陆海联运大通道倡议发布仪式举办，发布《共建"一带一路"（西安）陆海联运大通道倡议》。

3月27日，中国（陕西）—白俄罗斯经贸合作暨中白工业园推介会在西安召开。

4月2日，西安市印发《积极有效利用外资推动经济高质量发展的实施意见》。

4月8日，陕西首单跨境电商网购保税进口商品在西咸保税物流中心正式通关。

4月9日，第9届中国西部国际物流产业博览会在西安开幕。

4月9日，陕西"一带一路"律师学院在西北政法大学成立。

4月10日，2019"一带一路"国际物流交流合作大会在西安举行。

4月18日，陕西自贸试验区西安经开功能区两周年建设情况发布会暨"一带一路"国际产能合作与民营企业发展论坛举办。

4月20日，"一带一路"陕西西安（三星）·2019城墙国际马拉松赛开赛。

4月22日，西安市与英国克罗伊登市签署发展友好城市关系意向书。

4月24日，陕西省与北哈萨克斯坦州签署发展友好省州关系意向书。

4月25日，"2019中俄丝路工业与科技创新论坛"成功举办。

5月13日，陕西首条第五航权航线"首尔—西安—河内"成功首航。

5月20日，丝路（西安）前海园项目签约。

5月28日，中欧班列长安号西安—明斯克跨境电商出口专列首列发车。

6月4日，隆基股份宣布，拟在马来西亚砂捞越州古晋市投资9.57亿元建设年产1.25GW单晶电池项目。

6月11日，中巴农业生物资源研究中心在西北农林科技大学成立。

6月14日，习近平主席在上海合作组织成员国元首理事会第十九次会议上提出，"中方愿在陕西省设立上海合作组织农业技术交流培训示范基地，加强同地区国家现代农业领域合作"。

6月18日，西安咸阳国际机场获批进口肉类指定监管场地。

7月2日，法士特马兹公司在中国—白俄罗斯巨石工业园奠基。

7月27日，丝路文化发展论坛在曲江国际会议中心举行。

8月15日，西安咸阳国际机场南三指廊及站坪工程正式启用。

9月3日，施耐德电气全球两大设计中心落地陕西。

9月29日，全国首批"央行·长安号票运通"供应链金融新模式在西安国际港务区正式启动。

10月18日，深交所陕西资本市场服务基地正式揭牌。

11月1日，陕西首开多式联运中欧班列，首次使用统一运单，实现"一单到底"。

12月9日，陕西省与中国科学院签署共创榆林能源革命创新示范区战略合作协议。

12月17日，陕西首个"国家中医药服务出口基地"获批。

12月26日，宝鸡综合保税区正式获得国务院批复。

2020年

1月15日，陕西省侨联海外科技成果转化研究院揭牌。

1月22日，陕西西咸空港综合保税区（一期）正式封关运行。

3月20日，国家分子医学转化科学中心建设正式启动。

3月25日，《西安丝绸之路金融中心发展规划》《西安丝绸之路金融中心发展行动计划（2020—2022年）》发布。

3月27日，《支持中欧班列长安号高质量发展的若干措施》发布。

3月30日，西安咸阳国际机场首架搭载防疫物资的飞机飞往欧洲的德国。

4月23日，习近平总书记在陕西考察时指出，"对陕西而言，开放不足是制约发展的突出短板""要深度融入共建'一带一路'大格局"。

5月8日，陕西省政府和中国民航局联合印发的《西安国际航空枢纽战略规划》正式公布。

6月9日，陕西省丝绸之路考古中心揭牌。

6月30日，苏宁物流产业园项目奠基仪式在西安国际港务区举行。

7月2日，现代农业国际合作多语种翻译中心在杨凌揭牌。

7月6日，中欧班列西安集结中心纳入国家示范工程，获中央预算内投资。

7月10—12日，"2020陕西国际科技创新创业博览会"在西安举办。

7月22日，西安咸阳国际机场三期工程开工。

8月1日，申通国际西安口岸转运中心在空港新城揭牌。

8月8日，"一带一路"文化传播与经济发展论坛在西安举行。

8月14日，西安海关签发全省首份电子化《入境货物检验检疫证明》。

8月27日，中国西部国际采购展览会线上展会在西安举办。

9月14—15日，"2020全球汽车物流大会"首次在西安举行。

9月16日，陕西省政府与中国出口信用保险公司在西安签署战略合作协议。

10月10日，中国人民银行西安分行、国家外汇管理局陕西省分局出台《关于金融支持中欧班列（西安）集结中心暨中国（陕西）自由贸易试验区高质量发展的意见》。

10月22日，上合组织农业技术交流培训示范基地正式揭牌。

10月23日，全省首个"国际航材超市"西安国际航材供应链管理中心在西咸新区空港新城揭牌。

11月18日，陕西省首笔服务贸易对外支付税务备案信息网上核验业务落地。

12月13日，全国人工智能职业教育产教协同创新联盟在西安成立。

12月28日，西安航天基地通用机场正式取证运营。

2021年

1月27日，陕西省进口物品口岸流转信息管理平台上线运行。

1月27日，"一带一路"国际多式联运智慧物流枢纽平台——"陆港云码头"正式进入试运营阶段。

2月3—4日，"2021丝路嘉年华·和美之约——丝路云春晚"联动五大洲。

2月18日，世界最大航空级钛合金棒材生产线在陕贯通。

3月18日，宝鸡入选全国跨境电商零售进口试点城市。

3月19日，西安咸阳国际机场荣获国际机场协会（ACI）健康机场认证。

3月19日，陕西自贸试验区能源金贸区功能区与中国银行陕西省分行签订《自贸试验区金融协同创新合作协议》。

3月24日，西安国际港务区举行"中欧人才班列"首发仪式。

3月30日，丝路国际水务科创园项目在西咸新区泾河新城奠基

4月9日，中国（陕西）赴塔吉克斯坦联合工作组被授予"国际友谊贡献奖"。

4月21日，西安国际陆港集团分别与比利时北海港集团、奥斯坦德－布鲁日国际机场签署战略合作谅解备忘录。

4月25日,《陕西省推进"一带一路"建设2021年工作要点》印发。

5月1日,《中国(陕西)自由贸易试验区条例》正式施行。

5月12日,中国(陕西)—韩国经贸合作洽谈会在西安举办。

5月13日,2021中欧—榆林经济合作论坛在西安举行。

5月20日,西部陆海新通道国际货运榆林班列正式开通运营。

6月16日,宝鸡综合保税区首个跨境商品展示交易中心——陕果集团跨境体验店开业。

6月18日,在国家外汇管理局的大力支持和精准指导下,跨境金融区块链服务平台中欧班列长安号应用场景正式上线。

7月1日,农业农村部、外交部、科技部、陕西省人民政府联合印发《上海合作组织农业技术交流培训示范基地建设方案》。

7月5日,"秦丨QIN—兵马俑的前世今生现代艺术展"在尼泊尔正式上线。

7月7日,陕建安装集团承建马来西亚综合磷化工EPCC项目投产。

7月15日,空港新城设立海外人才服务窗口。

8月20日,"中俄商企资源云推荐会"举办。

8月12日,世界城地组织地方行动港高级别青年对话论坛在西交大成功举办。

8月22日,西北大学"中国-中亚人类与环境'一带一路'联合实验室"获科技部批准建设。

8月23日,"通丝路"陕西跨境电子商务人民币结算服务平台接入人民币跨境支付系统。

9月30日,陕西首条面向共建"一带一路"国家第五航权货运航线开通。

10月23日《陕西省"十四五"深度融入共建"一带一路"大格局、建设内陆开放高地规划》印发。

10月23日,上合组织农业技术交流培训示范基地实训基地揭牌。

10月28日,2021丝绸之路国际产学研用合作会议在西安开幕。

12月29日,陕西省商务厅、西安海关、国家税务总局陕西省税务局、人民银行西安分行联合印发《全面对接RCEP经贸新规则扎实推进高水平对外开放行动方案》,全面对接RCEP经贸新规则,深化陕西省与RCEP成员国经贸合作。

2022年

3月31日,第十一届APEC中小企业技术交流暨展览会主论坛举行。

4月18日,全国首趟享受陆路启运港退税政策的中欧班列从西安国际港站驶出,西安港成为全国首个陆路启运港退税政策试点内陆港。

5月18日,陕西省政府发布"推动开展跨境电商零售进口部分药品及医疗器械试点"措施。

6月8日,第十二届金砖国家农业部长会议暨金砖国家农村发展和减贫研讨会召开。

6月21日,中欧班列长安号(海防—西安—阿拉木图)班列从西安国际港站首发,标志着中欧班列长安号与陆海新通道首次实现通道互联互通。

7月7日,上合组织农业基地建设方案出炉。

8月9日,2022"一带一路"媒体合作论坛在西安开幕。

8月14日,中国(陕西)—乌兹别克斯坦经贸合作及文化旅游推介会在西安举行。

8月15日,"一带一路"农业贸易与乡村振兴论坛在西安召开。

8月15日,"一带一路"智能制造高峰论坛在西安举办。

8月16日,首届"一带一路"商事法律合作高峰论坛在西安举办。

9月7日,陕西首份RCEP原产地自主声明落地。

9月15日,2022上合组织现代农业发展圆桌会议在杨凌示范区召开。

9月27日,第五届中国—中亚地方合作论坛在西安举办。

10月13日,陕西省中医药管理局、陕西省发展和改革委员会印发《陕西省"十四五"中医药发展规划》。

10月26日,全国首趟境内外全程时刻表中欧班列从西安出发。

11月29—30日,首届亚欧青年领导人交流营暨亚欧青年绿色发展论坛在西安举办。

12月21日，上合组织农业基地中国（陕西）商品交易中心启用。

12月23日"中国—哈萨克斯坦传统医学中心"在哈挂牌成立。

2023年

2月21日，陕西省与乌兹别克斯坦锡尔河州签署发展友好合作关系备忘录。

3月22日，陕西省社会组织国际交流促进会成立大会在西安召开。

3月27日，陕西省工商联国际合作工作委员会在西安成立。

4月24—26日，亚洲文化遗产保护联盟大会在西安召开，这是亚洲文化遗产保护联盟发起以来首次于线下召开的大范围、高级别国际会议。

5月17日，习近平总书记在听取陕西省委和省政府工作汇报时强调，"要着力扩大对内对外开放，打造内陆改革开放高地。更加主动融入和服务构建新发展格局，更加深度融入共建'一带一路'大格局，在扩大对内对外开放中强动力、增活力，打开发展新天地"。

5月18—19日，中国—中亚峰会在西安举办。峰会期间，中国同中亚五国达成系列合作共识。

6月27日至7月1日，陕西省省长赵刚率陕西省代表团对土库曼斯坦进行友好访问，积极落实两国元首达成的重要共识和中国–中亚峰会涉陕成果。

8月1日,陕西召开全省推进"一带一路"建设工作领导小组和中国(陕西)自贸试验区工作领导小组会议。

9月1日至9月8日,陕西省委书记、省人大常委会主任赵一德率陕西代表团对乌兹别克斯坦、哈萨克斯坦、吉尔吉斯斯坦进行友好访问,积极落实国家元首达成的重要共识和中国-中亚峰会涉陕成果。

10月10日,陕西省人民政府新闻办公室举办共建"一带一路"倡议十周年系列发布会(第一场)。

Panorama

Overview

Over 2,100 years ago, Zhang Qian, a Han Dynasty envoy, was commissioned with extraordinary powers and made his journey twice to the Western Regions from Chang'an, capital of China then. Over a period of more than 20 years, Zhang's pioneering expedition opened up an overland route linking China, Central Asia and West Asia. Afterwards, this east-west channel further extended westward to Europe and became a prosperous path for economic and trade interactions and people-to-people exchanges among the BRI countries and regions, which was hence named the "Silk Road," contributing to a millennia-old miracle.

On September 7, 2013, Chinese General Secretary Xi Jinping delivered a speech at Nazarbayev University, Kazakhstan, during his visit to Central Asia, proposing the initiative of jointly building the "Silk Road Economic Belt," which aims to inject vitality into the ancient Silk Road and bring mutually beneficial cooperation between China and other Asian and European countries to a new high. "Shaanxi, my home province, is right at the starting point of the ancient Silk Road. Today, as I stand here and look back at history, I seem to hear the camel bells echoing in the mountains and see the wisps of smoke rising from the desert." recalled Xi. On October 3,

2013, Xi raised the initiative of jointly building the "21st Century Maritime Silk Road" when addressing the Indonesian Parliament during his visit to Southeast Asia. The initiative helps to maintain closer economic ties and deeper cooperation among the BRI countries, offers broader development space for them and brings benefit to their people.

Proposed by China, the Belt and Road Initiative (BRI) brings benefits and opportunities for the whole world and has been widely recognized by the international community. Over the past decade, China had signed over 200 BRI cooperation agreements with more than 150 countries and 30 international organizations across five continents, delivering a number of signature projects and small-scale yet impactful projects. The BRI has become an important bond for strengthening economic and trade interactions, industrial cooperation and people-to-people exchanges among the BRI countries, an important mechanism for promoting policy coordination, facilities connectivity, unimpeded trade, financial integration and people-to-people bond among these countries, as well as a major practice for achieving common development, improving global governance and building a community with a shared future for mankind.

As the starting point of the ancient Silk Road, Shaanxi has once again become a key node for jointly building the BRI in the 21st century. In the month when Xi proposed the initiative of jointly building the "Silk Road Economic Belt," Xi'an and 12 other cities signed the *Xi'an Declaration on Jointly Building the Silk Road Economic Belt*. In October 2014, Shaanxi set up a Leading Group for Building the New Starting Point of the Silk Road

Economic Belt headed by the provincial governor. Over the past decade, Shaanxi has earnestly acted on the important ideas of President Xi Jinping in jointly building the BRI and his important speeches delivered during his visit to Shaanxi, worked to develop the inland province into a highland for the reform and opening up, and made an all-out effort to build the province into a major center of the BRI for transportation, commerce and logistics, international industrial capacity cooperation, scientific and educational cooperation, international cultural tourism and Silk Road finance. Shaanxi has smoothed the channel, improved logistics efficiency, promoted economy and trade, attracted industries, and gathered talent to deeply integrate itself into the joint efforts in building the BRI, and achieved a host of remarkable achievements with Shaanxi characteristics.

Breakthroughs have been made in building a center for transportation, trade and logistics. The development of the Chang'an China-Europe freight train has been accelerated, with its operational quality and efficiency continuing to be enhanced. As of September 2023, the Chang'an China-Europe freight trains have conducted more than 20,000 trips. At present, the freight train service has launched 17 international transport routes, covering 45 countries and regions across the Eurasian continent, and 21 "+ Western Europe" assembly lines have been opened in China, which radiates into all major sourcing destinations nationwide. It is the freight train service with the highest transport efficiency, most wide-ranging lines, most complete functions, lowest overall costs and highest level of intelligence in China, providing a "golden channel" for international trade with high efficiency, low cost and excellent services. Xi'an Xianyang International Airport has operated an increasingly strong "Air Silk Road" network with a total of 386 international air passenger and cargo routes, including 83 international air passenger routes, 45 all-cargo routes, and four fifth-freedom freight air routes. All these accelerate the construction of an air route network that makes the Silk Road directly accessible to Europe and the United States, and connects five continents. Xi'an has achieved full coverage of passenger routes to "six cities in five countries" in Central Asia. The Airport New City of Xian New Area has become the largest airline cluster in northwestern China and the most functional airport-type national logistics hub.

Remarkable achievements have been made in building the international industrial capacity cooperation center. High-quality "bringing in" has promoted the optimization and upgrading of industrial structures in Shaanxi, bringing about emerging industrial clusters such as electronic information and new energy vehicles. High-level "go global" has helped the BRI countries and regions improve the level of development and achieve win-win outcomes in their cooperation in agriculture, energy, minerals and other fields. From 2013 to 2022, Shaanxi invested 1.24 billion US dollars in the BRI countries, accounting for 23.8 percent of the province's outbound investment during the same period. The turnover of Shaanxi's contracted projects in the BRI countries reached 13.57 billion US dollars, accounting for 52.6 percent of the province's turnover of overseas contracted projects during the same period. Meanwhile, the China (Shaanxi)

Pilot Free Trade Zone has carried out trials to improve the business environment, and attracted Samsung, BYD, Konka and other industry-leading enterprises to map out their production bases in Shaanxi on the basis of the China-Russia and China-Europe international industrial cooperation parks, to cultivate the special industrial clusters with global competitiveness.

The drive of the science education center continues to advance. Shaanxi has increased the frequency of international exchanges and cooperation, nurtured new growth areas for cooperation, and expanded the scope of cooperation. More than 150 universities in China and abroad have joined the "University Alliance of the Silk Road", and more than 100,000 foreign students have come to study in Shaanxi. Shaanxi has established 19 state-level and 64 provincial-level bases for international cooperation on science and technology, and set up the Shaanxi International Base Alliance for Cooperation on Science and Technology. It has also conducted multi-level cooperation with over 400 institutions from more than 40 countries and regions. The SCO Demonstration Base for Agricultural Technology Exchange and Training was officially unveiled in Yangling, Shaanxi, which has successfully carried out cooperation in modern agriculture with more than 60 countries. Over 30 SCO Modern Agriculture Development Roundtables and other exchange activities have been held successfully, and more than 28,000 participants from SCO countries participated in the skills training.

The international cultural tourism center becomes a bright spot. A number of cultural exchange programs such as the "Regional Songs ·

Qin Rhythm" Shaanxi Cultural Week and the Intangible Cultural Heritage Exhibition have aroused strong responses overseas, and the vigor and international influence of Shaanxi's cultural and tourism industry have been enhanced. Over the past decade, Shaanxi has newly established international friendship with 48 cities. In total, it has established international friendship with 108 cities in 41 countries, including 54 cities in the BRI countries. In addition, Shaanxi has successfully held eight Silk Road International Arts Festivals, three World Culture and Tourism Forums and seven Xi'an Silk Road International Tourism Expos.

Innovation activities have been carried out in building the Silk Road financial center. Shaanxi has deepened reform and opening-up in the financial sector, increased the efficiency of financial and foreign exchange services, and launched more financial products and innovative services that meet the demand of building the BRI, to advance the high-quality development of the Belt and Road cooperation through high-level opening-up. The added value of Shaanxi's financial industry increased from 79.11 billion yuan in 2013 to 210.97 billion yuan in 2022, a 2.7-fold increase over the past decade, with a compound annual growth rate (CAGR) of 11.5 percent. The total amount of cross-border RMB receipts and payments in Shaanxi reached 453.699 billion yuan, radiating into 148 countries and regions which include 96 BRI countries. The cross-border RMB receipts and payments between Shaanxi and the BRI countries achieved 181.317 billion yuan, about 20 percentage points higher than the national average.

Building five major centers serves as a lever for Shaanxi to further deepen and substantiate the Belt and Road cooperation. Over the past decade, Shaanxi has played a coordinating role. It has formulated guideline documents such as the implementation plan and special program for promoting the Belt and Road cooperation, released annual work plans for nine consecutive years, continued to specify and expand the roles of the five major centers, and developed a series of distinctive practices and experience: the China-Europe freight train (Xi'an) has become a vanguard of the China-Europe freight trains around China; the SCO Demonstration Base for Agricultural Technology Exchange and Training has set a model for modern agriculture; the University Alliance of the Silk Road has become a new paradigm of international cooperation in education; joint archaeological efforts between Shaanxi and Central Asia has become a great name card of the Silk Road; Qin physicians and Qin medicine go global have taken deeper roots in the heart of the people from BRI countries; Shaanxi enterprises represented by Longi Green Energy Technology Co., Ltd.(Longi) have become the pioneers of the green Silk Road. These practices have strongly supported the building of the five major centers, accelerated the formation of new advantages of all-round opening-up in Shaanxi, and played an increasingly prominent role in the Belt and Road cooperation.

Over the past ten years, Shaanxi has always followed and served the unified arrangements of the Central People's Government, and completed various tasks assigned by the Communist Party of China (CPC) Central Committee and the State Council.

In serving the country's overall diplomacy, Shaanxi stands ready to shoulder its responsibilities. Shaanxi has cooperated with state ministries and commissions to successfully greet more than 30 heads of state and government, and established sister-state ties with the hometowns of the heads of state of Kazakhstan, Kyrgyzstan, Uzbekistan and other countries. The "Belt and Road" has played an ever more prominent role driven by the head-of-state diplomacy. Shaanxi's capability of serving the country's overall diplomatic situation has been enhanced significantly, as demonstrated by its successful hosting of major diplomatic events such as the China-Central Asia Summit, and the second and fourth "China + Central Asia" (C + C5) Foreign Ministers' Meetings, and major foreign affairs such as the General Assembly of the Alliance for Cultural Heritage in Asia (ACHA), the Belt and Road Media Community Summit Forum.

In undertaking major strategic missions, Shaanxi has made much a difference. Taking the opportunity of getting approved to implement the demonstration project of the China-Europe freight train assembly center, Shaanxi has built the China-Europe freight train (Xi'an) assembly center against high standards, set up the Xi'an Guojigang Railway Station, launched the digital financial integrated service platform for the Chang'an China-Europe freight trains, and achieved strategic convergence with the New Western China Land-Sea Corridor, to accelerate the creation of an efficient and cost effective Eurasian Land-Sea Trade Corridor that provide optimal services. In order to carry out the instructions about "strengthening cooperation in modern agriculture with other countries in the region", Shaanxi has given full play to Yangling's role as a "national team" in developing modern agriculture, promoted the substantive operation of the SCO Demonstration Base for Agricultural Technology Exchange and Training at a high level, and cooperated with more than 60 countries in modern agriculture, to fulfill its exemplary role in international agricultural technology cooperation.

In building an international exchange platform, Shaanxi has shown its own characteristics. Shaanxi has tapped into the China (Shaanxi) Pilot Free Trade Zone's role as a pilot platform for comprehensive reform and opening-up, steadily expanded institutional opening up, and carried out a series of innovative practices in economy, trade, culture, people-to-people exchanges and other fields with the BRI countries, and 36 of the above typical experience have been promoted nationwide. Relying on important platforms such as the Second International Commercial Court and the Sixth Circuit Court of the Supreme People's Court, and the "three centers and one base" of the Ministry of Justice, the building of the Belt and Road Demonstration Zone for International Commercial Legal Services (BRDZ-ICLS) has been accelerated, to provide high-quality legal services and supports for international economic and trade cooperation. The service mechanism of the Silk Road International Exposition and the Eurasian Economic Forum has been improved, to build an international exchange platform for deepening cooperation among the BRI countries.

The joint building of the BRI has created a major historic opportunity for the inland provinces in Western China to become a highland for reform and opening up. In the process, Shaanxi has seized the opportunity to foster a new pattern of opening up and development and push its socioeconomic development to a higher level. With major advances in foreign trade, total imports and exports in Shaanxi has continuously surpassed the marks of 200 billion yuan, 300 billion yuan and 400 billion yuan, registering an annual growth rate of 14.7 percent; Shaanxi's trade volume with the BRI countries has quadrupled, with an annual growth rate of 18.4 percent, and exceeded 100 billion yuan for the first time in 2022, up 41 percent year-on-year. Considerable progress has been made in investment attraction. The fixed-asset investment in strategic emerging industries and high-tech industries has doubled since 2014, and Shaanxi's actual use of foreign investment since the 13th Five-Year Plan (2016-2020) has doubled compared with that during the 12th Five-Year Plan period (2011-2015). Industrial structures have been optimized. Over the past five years, the added value of the high-tech manufacturing sector has grown at an average annual rate of 13.1 percent, 7 percentage points higher than that of the value-added industrial output. Business efficiency has been significantly enhanced, with industrial revenues and profits in 2022 doubling compared with those in 2013. The level of economic growth has been improved across the board, with the per capita GDP of Shaanxi in 2022 nearly doubling compared with that in 2013.

Chang'an is working together again toe regain tis preaous treasune. In May 2023, the China-Central Asia Summit, which is China's first major diplomatic event after the COVID-19 pandemic, was successfully held. Leaders of China and Central Asia gathered in Xi'an to pursue their dreams with one heart and seek common development. Central Asia is where the

BRI was initiated and a demonstration zone for jointly building the BRI. Ahead of the 10th anniversary of the BRI, the China-Central Asia Summit further built consensus. The *Xi'an Declaration* issued at the Summit once again expressed the determination and confidence of all countries to jointly build the BRI, to inject new impetus into the Belt and Road cooperation, and bring more development opportunities to Shaanxi.

Evenything that is past is a preamble. Over the past ten years, Shaanxi has always kept in mind the important instructions on Shaanxi's opening up and development given by General Secretary Xi Jinping. It has insisted on top-down planning, enhancing coordination, leveraging strengths, and highlighting characteristics, to create a central node of the domestic market and a strategic link of China's new development paradigm of "dual circulation," and move toward nationwide opening-up that coordinates the coastal and inland areas and connects the eastern and western regions. In the future, in accordance with Xi's instructions on urging Shaanxi to strive toward writing a new chapter in advancing Chinese modernization, Shaanxi will deeply integrate into the BRI, support the China (Shaanxi) Pilot Free Trade Zone in leading the endeavor, further expand institutional opening-up with regard to rules, regulations, management codes and standards, and create a high-level open platform; it will pay more attention to the scientific and technological innovation-driven development, make greater efforts to create the Qinchuangyuan innovation-driven platform, pool innovation resources, and support the incubation and commercialization of scientific and technological achievements, to make innovation a powerful engine for the development of Shaanxi; it will further promote the high-quality building of the BRI that is high-standard, sustainable and people-centered, as well as digital, green and healthy development of the Silk Road; it will deeply integrate into the BRI, develop the inland province into a highland for reform and opening up, and increase dynamics and vitality in wider opening up both internally and externally, to open up a new horizon for development.

I. Shaanxi's Vision and Goals of Building the Belt and Road Initiative(BRI)

General Secretary Xi Jinping expected Shaanxi to be fully integrated into the BRI, and to position itself as an important node in jointly building the BRI. The major missions entrusted to Shaanxi by the state include serving as a crucial channel and node, exploring the building of Xi'an Belt and Road Comprehensive Pilot Zone, and creating a highland for reform and opening up and a hub of development and opening up for inland regions.

(i) Specifying Goals and Positioning and Drawing up the Blueprint

Over the past decade, General Secretary Xi Jinping has repeatedly made explicit instructions on the building of the BRI in Shaanxi, and numerous national policy documents have laid down specific requirements for Shaanxi to participate in the BRI, which have provided important guidelines for Shaanxi to make plans in this regard.

1. Firmly Grasping the Spirit of the Instructions

During his visit to Shaanxi in February 2015, General Secretary Xi Jinping pointed out that "Shaanxi is at the forefront of the country's westward opening up" and "it should accurately position itself and actively integrate into the BRI".

In April 2020, General Secretary Xi Jinping pointed out during his visit to Shaanxi that inadequate opening up is an apparent weakness that hinders development. Shaanxi should deeply integrate into the BRI, bring into play the leading role of the (Shaanxi) pilot free trade zone, properly leverage the platforms such as the Silk Road International Exposition, the Eurasian Economic Forum and the China Yangling Agricultural Hi-tech Fair, and establish the China-Europe freight train (Xi'an) assembly center, so as to speed up the creation of economic corridors, commercial logistics hubs, and bases for key industries and people-to-people exchanges that connect countries in Central Asia, South Asia and West Asia, as well as efficient and cost-effective international trade channels that provide better services.

In May 2023, while being briefed about the work of the CPC Shaanxi Provincial Committee and the People's Government of Shaanxi Province, General Secretary Xi Jinping stressed that Shaanxi should open up wider and develop the inland province into a highland for reform and opening up, integrate and serve the new development pattern more proactively, and be more deeply integrated into the overall pattern of jointly building the BRI, so as to strengthen Shaanxi's momentum and vitality in expanding opening up and open a new development landscape. It should steadily expand institutional opening-up with regard to rules, regulations, management codes and standards, promote the high-quality development of the pilot free trade zone, and create a high-level open platform. It should also actively participate in the building of the New Western China Land-Sea Corridor, give full play to the role of the China-Europe freight train (Xi'an) assembly center, speed up the creation of corridors connecting countries in Central Asia, South Asia and West Asia and play a bigger role in connecting the domestic and international markets. It should focus on creating a market-oriented, rule-of-law-based, and first-class international business environment, to improve the quality and level of investment attraction.

2. Fully Integrating into Opening-up Structure

According to the *Vision and Actions on Jointly Building the Silk Road Economic Belt and 21st Century Maritime Silk Road* issued by the National Development and Reform Commission, the Ministry of Foreign Affairs and the Ministry of Commerce in March 2015, in advancing the BRI, China will fully leverage the comparative advantages of its various regions, adopt a proactive strategy of further opening-up, strengthen interactions and cooperation among the eastern, western and central regions, and comprehensively improve the openness of the Chinese economy. In addition, the document explicitly requires that "building Xi'an into a new highland of reform and opening-up in China's interior…with the goal of creating strategic channels, trade and logistics hubs and key bases for industrial and cultural exchanges that connect Central, South and West Asian countries".

In May 2020, the CPC Central Committee and the State Council released a guideline on advancing the development of western regions in new era. The document proposes that "we should support Shaanxi in giving full play to its comprehensive strengths, and developing itself into a highland for reform and opening up and a hub of development and opening up; we should explore the establishment of the Belt and Road comprehensive pilot zones in key cities such as Xi'an, support Shaanxi in exploiting its historical and cultural advantages and playing an important role as an important channel and node of the Silk Road Economic Belt, and encourage Xi'an and other key cities to accelerate their development as international gateway and hub cities".

In October 2020, the CPC Central Committee and the State Council jointly issued the *Outline of the Yellow River Basin's Ecological Protection and High-quality Development Plan*. The document said that "we encourage Xi'an, Zhengzhou, Jinan and other major cities along the Yellow River to establish institutions and mechanisms that align with international rules and standards, accelerate investment and trade facilitation, attract high-quality factors around the world, strengthen their roles for promoting international exchanges, and create a gateway for opening up in the Yellow River Basin. In addition, we should foster Xi'an, Zhengzhou and other hub cities of China-Europe freight trains to develop export-oriented economy relying on the China-Europe freight trains, and set up a number of agricultural opening-up and cooperation pilot zones in the provinces and regions along the Yellow

River, deepen the cooperation in farming and animal husbandry with BRI countries and support capable enterprises to build overseas production and processing bases".

3. Carefully Planning the Blueprint

Following General Secretary Xi Jinping's instructions, Shaanxi issued the *Implementation Plan for Promoting the Building of Silk Road Economic Belt and 21st Century Maritime Silk Road (2015-2020)* in line with national overall plans in 2016. The document initiated the building of five major centers of the BRI, namely, the centers for transportation, commerce and logistics, international industrial capacity cooperation, science education, international tourism and regional finance. The *14th Five-Year Plan for Shaanxi Province to Deeply Integrate into Belt and Road Cooperation and Develop into Highland for Reform and Opening Up* issued in 2021 proposes the fostering of an opening-up pattern comprising "one core, two wings, four channels, five centers and multiple platforms". These two top-level design documents set out the agenda, timetable, and road map for pursuing the BRI in the whole province.

According to these plans, the more immediate goal of the Belt and Road initiative in Shaanxi is to cement the foundation and highlight the advantages in about 3-5 years. By 2020, the cooperation and exchange mechanism and the cooperation platform between Shaanxi and other BRI countries would further improve, Shaanxi would become more outward-looking in its economy, initial progress in the creation of five major centers would have been made, and a new pattern of all-round opening up that is wide-ranging, multi-tiered and high-level would have basically taken shape. The mid-term goal is, by 2025, to build a convenient and efficient sea-land-air international integrated corridor that connects the coastal and inland areas, a modern industrial system with Shaanxi characteristics, an innovative development system with Shaanxi characteristics and strengths, a Silk Road experience tourism core area and a financial cluster area on the Silk Road Economic Belt. The long-term goal is that by the middle of this century, a cooperation and exchange network between Shaanxi and other BRI countries will be established, with more frequent economic and trade exchanges, closer people-to-people exchanges and more extensive cooperation in energy; the overall economic competitiveness and cultural soft power of Shaanxi will be improved; the strategic objectives of building the five major centers of the BRI will be realized, and Shaanxi will develop into a highland for reform and opening up.

(ii) Strengthening Overall Planning and Coordination, and Optimizing Service Guarantee

On the basis of accurate positioning and clearly defined goals, Shaanxi has broken down the key tasks, established the working mechanism, strengthened policy guidance through overall planning and coordination, improved service support, and worked persistently to promote the building of the BRI.

1. Defining Goals and Breaking Down Key Tasks

Breaking down key tasks is an integral step for implementing the blueprint. Shaanxi has made it clear that during the "14th Five-Year Plan" period, its key task of the "Belt and Road" initiative is to build five centers, promote a digital, green and healthy Silk Road and carry out nine major projects, thus fostering an opening-up pattern consisting "one core, two wings, four channels, five centers and multiple platforms".

The pattern of "one core, two wings, four channels, five centers and multiple platforms" is a strategic layout in space. "One core" includes the main urban areas of Xi'an and Xianyang as well as the Xixian New Area; "two wings" refer to the base of energy and chemical industry in Northern Shaanxi and the ecological product supply area in Southern Shaanxi; "four channels" include the Asia-Europe trunk line "New Eurasian Land Bridge", the north-south trunk line "Mongolia & Russia-ASEAN Corridor", the South Asian branch line "China-Pakistan Economic Corridor", and the West Asian branch line that goes straight to the Mediterranean coast; five centers refer to the centers for transportation, commerce and logistics, international industrial capacity cooperation, scientific and educational cooperation, international cultural tourism and Silk Road finance; multiple platforms refer to open platforms such as pilot free trade zones, economic development zones, bonded zones, and the SCO Demonstration Base for Agricultural Technology Exchange and Training.

Specifically, the Five Center vision aims at building Shaanxi into a center for the operation and organization of the international trade and logistics hub and international land-sea trade corridor; building an industrial base with global competitiveness, to form a strong open industrial cluster and constructs a modern industrial system that places equal importance on both internal and external demand; establishing an innovation and development system with Shaanxi characteristics and advantages, to make Shaanxi a core region for innovation and start-up in China; establishing the Chinese civilization-Silk Road core tourism area, to make Shaanxi the first choice to showcase the history and culture of the Chinese civilization; building a financial cluster area on the Silk Road Economic Belt, to make Shaanxi a key regional financial center with distinctive characteristics which radiates into Western China regions and Eurasian countries.

In fostering and expanding new strengths, new directions and new areas of openness and cooperation, Shaanxi should strengthen the building of the digital Silk Road, build the infrastructure for the application of big digital technologies, advance scientific and technological innovation, and build an international platform for digital cooperation; it should strengthen the building of the Health Silk Road, promote the internationalization of traditional Chinese medicine (TCM), expand medical and healthcare cooperation and participate in global public health governance; it should also support the green development of the BRI, deepen international cooperation in ecological and environmental protection, improve the capacity for ecological conservation and environmental protection, and participate in global governance in ecological conservation and environmental protection.

The Nine Major Project vision refers to the building of numerous cooperation bases, centers and platforms that are open to the world: exploring the establishment of Xi'an Belt and Road Comprehensive Pilot Zone, improving the Asia-Europe land-sea trade corridor, building the China-Europe freight train (Xi'an) assembly center against high standards, developing the China (Shaanxi) Pilot Free Trade Zone in an innovative way, building the SCO Demonstration Base for Agricultural Technology Exchange and Training against high standards, accelerating the development of Xi'an Airport Economic Demonstration Zone, creating the Belt and Road Commodities Trading Center, focusing on the creation of the Xi'an Silk Road Sci-tech Innovation Center, and promoting the development of the Belt and Road Cultural Trade Exhibition Center.

2. Strengthening Policy Guidance Through Overall Planning and Coordination

An efficient working mechanism is an important basis for advancing key tasks and realizing the blueprint.

In October 2014, in response to the initiative of jointly building the "Silk Road Economic Belt", Shaanxi established the Leading Group for Building the New Starting Point of the Silk Road Economic Belt (now renamed the Leading Group for Promoting the Belt and Road Initiative), which was led by the provincial governor and joined by the heads of relevant functional departments and key cities. The provincial leading group office has convened plenary sessions several times to coordinate the province's BRI programs and provide key guidance for the province to promote the BRI at each significant moment.

Shortly after the establishment of the provincial leading group, the *Implementation Plan for the Key Tasks of Building the New Starting Point of the Silk Road Economic Belt* was issued, which proposed 40 measures for the work. Over the past ten years, the provincial leading group has guided relevant provincial departments to release a number of policies and measures about specific work, such as the *Implementation Plan for Promoting Integrated Development of Transportation and Logistics, Several Measures of Coordinating Epidemic Control and High-quality Belt and Road Cooperation, Several Measures of Supporting High-quality Development of Chang'an China-Europe Freight Trains*, and *Action Plan for Development of Xi'an Silk Road Financial Center (2020-2022)*.

Since 2015, the provincial leading group office has issued annual action plans for nine consecutive years, clarifying the key points of the year and assigning duties to responsible departments; relevant provincial departments, units and municipalities (districts) have pushed forward work according to the division of labor, and timely reported the progress of key tasks and major projects to the provincial leading group office; the office has reported the work progress to the provincial government every six months, reviewed and sorted out the implementation and completion of the tasks at the end of the year, and made plans for the next year.

Over the past ten years, the provincial leading group office has established rules for annual key task record, the liaison officer of group member units, information reporting and the "Belt and Road" risk prevention mechanism, and regularly reported the progress to the Office of the National Leading Group for Promoting the Belt and Road Initiative. The National Leading Group Office has visited Shaanxi several times to investigate and supervise the BRI programs.

3. Upgrading Services to Support the Implementation of Projects

Overall planning and coordination is essential for the implementation of key tasks. In order to strengthen coordination and gather strength, the provincial leading group office has organized member units to negotiate key work points of the year, scheduled key tasks on a monthly basis, established a mechanism of coordinating and promoting major projects, and availed policy opportunities such as additional local government bonds to promote the important channels and major platform projects of the BRI.

Shaanxi has continuously improved its support system in professional services: building a major project library of the BRI, improving the information database of foreign economic and trade activity, optimizing the comprehensive service platform for enterprises to go global, expanding business and trade service agencies stationed abroad, carrying out multi-level personnel training, supporting social professional service agencies, and improving the capability and level of supporting the BRI in every respect.

In terms of risk prevention and control, Shaanxi has improved the risk tracking, monitoring and early-warning system in key areas at the provincial level, strengthened the risk management of major projects, enhanced the emergency response capacity of enterprises through training, standardized the overseas investment activities of enterprises, and strengthened the guidance and supervision on overseas investment projects.

In terms of publicity and dissemination, Shaanxi has taken the lead in establishing the provincial-level network publicity platform "Shaanxi Belt and Road Portal", meticulously launched various major publicity activities, organized related forums and exhibitions, facilitated information exchanges among the government, enterprises, think tanks and the public, told wonderful stories of the BRI, promoted the sharing of BRI building experience, and created cooperation opportunities for all parties to jointly build the BRI.

II. Practical Achievements of BRI Building in Shaanxi

At the third symposium on the development of the Belt and Road Initiative (BRI), General Secretary Xi Jinping pointed out that for the joint building of the BRI, we should work at "hard connectivity" in infrastructure, support "soft connectivity" in rules and standards, and encourage "people-to-people connectivity" across the country to promote the high-quality development of the BRI and achieve solid and rich achievements.

Over the past decade, Shaanxi has carried out General Secretary Xi Jinping's instructions, seized the historic opportunity of jointly building the BRI to push the western region toward the forefront of the country's opening-up through "hard connectivity" "soft connectivity" and "people-to-people connectivity". Great efforts have been made to promote the development of the Center for Transportation, Trade and Logistics, Center for International Industrial Cooperation, Center for Technology and Education, Center for International Cultural Tourism, and Center for Regional Finance to build an important fulcrum of domestic circulation, a strategic link of dual circulation, and an opening-up pattern that builds connections with other countries over land and sea while creating synergy between eastern and western regions in China. With all these efforts, Shaanxi has deeply integrated into the overall pattern of jointly building the BRI and brought its social and economic development to a new level.

(i) Smoothing Auess to Achieve Hard Connectivity

Transportation comes first and foremost. Located in the geographic center of China, Shaanxi connects east to west, and north to south. Leveraging its geographical advantages, Shaanxi Province takes the China-Europe Railway Express (Xi'an) as the first step in the BRI, developing core hubs including an international land port and an international airport, and building a land-sea trade corridor as a major trade channel between Asia and Europe featuring sea-land-air multimodal transport. The carrying capacity and radiation level of the international transportation hub in Xi'an have been significantly improved.

1. High-quality Development of the Chang'an China-Europe Freight Trains

Over the past decade, Shaanxi has developed high-quality China-Europe freight trains and promoted the transformation of Chang'an China-Europe freight trains operating from "point-to-point" to "hub-to-hub". As of September 2023, the Chang'an China-Europe freight trains have conducted more than 20,000 trips. Currently, 17 Chang'an international routes have been opened, basically covering the whole Eurasian continent, and 21 "+ Western Europe" assembly lines have been opened radiating the major source of goods in China. As part of the global shipping system, to the east, Shaanxi has launched five scheduled freight train service through international sea-rail intermodal routes from Xi'an to Qingdao and Ningbo on a regular basis to meet the demands of cross-border transport of maritime cargo in East Asia. To the south, the China-Laos and China-Vietnam international freight train service and road-rail intermodal routes from Xi'an to Nepal and Pakistan have been launched. The North-South and East-West international logistics channels gather and integrate in Xi'an, effectively meeting the distribution needs of the national supply of goods and imported goods.

To enhance the aggregation and radiation effect of Chang'an China-Europe freight trains, Shaanxi has kept expanding and strengthening the China-Europe freight train assembly center in Xi'an. In 2020, the demonstration project of China-Europe freight train assembly center in Xi'an was approved by the National Development and Reform Commission. In 2022, the Chang'an China-Europe freight train assembly center was officially approved by the General Administration of Customs of the People's Republic of China (GACC). In 2022, about 70% of the goods from outside Shaanxi were transported by Chang'an China-Europe freight trains, and more than 65% of the imported goods were sent from Xi'an Guojigang Railway Station to various places in China. Containers designed by ITL Group have an annual throughput of 3.1 million TEU and a transport capacity of 38.5 million tons, which can support the operation of tens of thousands of freight trains.

In the process of developing the China-Europe Railway Express, Shaanxi has adhered to the government-led and market-oriented operation model, and introduced a number of policies to continuously optimize the operational organization of Chang'an China-Europe freight trains. In October 2016, Xi'an International Inland Port Multimodal Transport Co., Ltd. was established to schedule Chang'an freight trains in a unified manner. In July 2018, Xi'an Free Trade Port Construction and Operation Co., Ltd. was established to further strengthen the connection between the freight trains and the assembly center. At the same time, Shaanxi Province has made great efforts to enhance the function of Xi'an Port as a hub of distribution, and successively introduced leading domestic and foreign enterprises in logistics and related service industries, such as China Ocean Shipping Company, China Forestry Group Corporation, Shandong Port Group Co., Ltd, China Minmetals Corporation, Shanxi Forestry Group Co., Ltd, Shanxi Investment Group, etc., to develop a port function zone of the assembly center integrating container transport, cold chain logistics, futures delivery, bulk commodities, and vehicle transport. Shaanxi Province has also strived to improve the comprehensive service functions of the assembly center, build a comprehensive service platform of digital finance for Chang'an China-Europe freight trains, develop digital application scenarios and functions such as space booking, container leasing, shipping, customs declaration, logistics and transportation, container dynamics, digital finance, and cross-border settlement, so as to realize the "Integrated Online Platform" for space booking and financing services. Chang'an China-Europe freight trains and the assembly center in Xi'an have become the exemplary projects of the Belt and Road construction in Shaanxi.

2. Accelerating the Development of an International Aviation Hub

As an important carrier of the BRI, air logistics channel plays an important role in fostering a new development pattern. Over the past decade, Shaanxi has accelerated the development of Xi'an Airport Economic Demonstration Zone, continued to expand its air route network and foster the Air Silk Road, achieving remarkable results in the development of international aviation hubs.

In 2015, with the initiation of the Xi'an aviation hub program, the annual passenger throughput of Xi'an Xianyang International Airport surpassed 32.97 million person-times, and the cargo and mail throughput hit 208,000 tons, ranking eighth and 21st in China, respectively. According to a statistical report released by the Civil Aviation Administration of China, in 2020, Xi'an Xianyang International Airport overcame the difficulties brought by the Covid-19 pandemic and achieved a cargo and mail throughput of 376,000 tons, ranking among the top 10 in China for the first time both in cargo and mail throughput and passenger throughput. As a result, the situation of "more passengers than goods" has been initially reversed.

In November 2021, Xi'an Airport became the only approved airport-type national logistics hub in Northwest China. According to the data from the Management Committee of Airport New City of Xixian New Area, 386 passenger and freight routes have been opened in Xi'an Airport, including 83 international passenger routes and 45 all-cargo routes. In May 2019, Shaanxi opened the fifth freedom (i.e., the third-country right to transportation) air cargo route among Seoul, Xi'an and Hanoi, making Xi'an the second city in China to obtain and use the fifth freedom air full-cargo route. As of September 2023, Shaanxi has opened three fifth freedom air cargo routes and one fifth freedom passenger route.

In addition, the third phase of the expansion project of Xi'an Xianyang International Airport was launched, which gained project approval and feasibility study approval by the National Development and Reform Commission in January 2019 and January 2020 respectively. The airport entered the phase of construction in July 2021, and is planned to be fully completed and put into operation in 2025. By then, Xi'an Xianyang International Airport will have become a super-large international aviation hub which can support 83 million trips and 1 million tons of cargo and mail per year.

3. Exploring New Multimodal Transport Modes

Over the past decade, the high-speed railway, expressway and air transportation network connecting the rest of China has been improved in Shaanxi. Among them, Shaanxi's high-speed railway operation mileage has reached 1,019 kilometers, with a crisscrossing high-speed railway network directly accessible from Xi'an to Beijing, Zhengzhou, Chengdu, Lanzhou,

Yinchuan and other cities. The expressway operation mileage reached 6,696 kilometers, with a network of expressways including Lianyungang-Khorgos Expressway, Beijing-Kunming Expressway, Baotou-Maoming Expressway, Fuzhou-Yinchuan Expressway and Shanghai-Xi'an Expressway. Connecting with the China-Europe freight trains, the land-sea freight trains, the new land-sea corridor in Western China, and the domestic and foreign air routes, the maritime-land-air Silk Road and international logistics hubs have been taking shape.

Multimodal transport is an important support for the development of a comprehensive transportation system and the creation of efficient and cost-effective international trade channels that deliver optimal service. The shipper can complete the entire transport through one document as long as he/she signs a contract with the carrier and makes payments in full. While consolidating the transportation infrastructure, Shaanxi has actively explored the efficient integration of various transport modes such as rail, road, water and air, and taken the initiative to carry out pilot projects of air-rail, sea-rail and road-rail multimodal transport.

At present, the Belt and Road inland transit hub in Xi'an railway station and the CRINTERMODAL intelligent backbone network of containers featuring "land-sea linkage and multi-point coordination" have become national demonstration projects, and Xi'an Airport has also been selected as one of the first 29 National Demonstration Logistics Parks. The container distribution system for the joint development of inland port and airport in Shaanxi has initially taken shape. Xi'an, Baoji and Yan'an have been selected to support the national logistics hubs, and the total number of A-level logistics enterprises in the province has exceeded 230.

(ii) Improving Service to Promote Soft Connectivity

It's necessary to remove the barriers of "soft connectivity" to give full play to the roles of "hard connectivity". Shaanxi has taken an active role in promoting "soft connectivity" by exploring rules in such fields as land trade regulation and air transport traffic rights for China-Europe Railway Express, expanding the institutional opening-up in rules, regulations, management codes and standards, and accelerating engagement with high-standard international economic and trade rules such as the Regional Comprehensive Economic Partnership (RCEP) and the China-EU Investment Agreement. Since the approval of establishment of China (Shaanxi) Pilot Free Trade Zone in August 2016, a total of 620 innovation cases have come into being.

1. Facilitating Customs Clearance to Improve Cross-border Freight Efficiency

Shaanxi has taken the lead in the reform of customs clearance facilitation to promote "soft connectivity", making trade clearance more convenient. The "single window" interface has been adopted for 100% of main business functions, and the experience in 31 pilot reforms, including the new mode of railway transport manifest consolidation and the new mechanism of coordination of large airport operations, has been promoted across China.

To improve the clearance efficiency of imports through China-Europe freight trains, Xi'an International Inland Port and the Customs pioneered the "manifest consolidation and combined declaration" practice for imported goods transported by railway to replace the original import declaration mode of "one manifest for one container". Specifically, bulk imported goods of the same company, trade name, specification and batch under the same contract were consolidated into one manifest. Therefore, enterprises only need to fill in one customs declaration form, which can save over 90% of the costs and time of customs clearance. Approved by the General Administration of Customs, Xi'an International Trade and Logistic Park has launched the "express customs clearance service for the inbound and outbound railway transport". As required, the Customs of Xi'an Railway Station reviews, releases and writes off the electronic data on railway manifests, and completes all clearance procedures for the inbound and outbound goods at the station, so that these goods can pass directly at border ports such as Alashankou Port and Khorgos Port, without the need to make declarations and go through transit procedures. Such new practices help reduce the clearance time by half and greatly shorten the duration of delays at the border port. In addition, Xi'an has been the first in China to trial the "tax rebate policy at the inland port of departure". Based on the arrangements, enterprises can apply for tax rebates for exports in containers as soon as they clear the goods at the port of departure in Railway Station. Compared with general mode in which taxes are refunded after the goods leave the border, the tax refund time has been cut down from an average of 30 days to a minimum of two days, greatly shortening the period when enterprise funds are being tied up.

Xi'an Airport introduced the reform of 24-hour "direct loading" of international cargo upon arrival, unlike the previous process in which international goods arriving at the airport must be transported to the airport cargo warehouse for inspection before picking up. Enterprises can apply for cargo clearance procedures before the aircraft enters the destination country, and the Customs can conduct the non-unpacking inspection of goods from enterprises who have paid taxes or possess the tax guarantee qualification before arrival at the port, and release the arrival-and-release permit. Direct loading upon arrival service allows the 24-hour "instant picking up and loading" of international goods, thus reducing the time for picking up goods from warehouse by 2-3 days. This can meet the urgent requirements of enterprises for logistics timeliness and safe transportation of special commodities without delay.

Xi'an Airport has also made a number of breakthroughs, including the first case of international bonded maintenance in Shaanxi, the first contract of bonded financial leasing of large equipment, the first contract of bonded stocking of cross-border e-commerce, and the first pilot qualification of VAT general taxpayer. At present, the average clearance time for imports is 25 hours, and that for exports is 2.7 hours at Xixian Airport Comprehensive Bonded Zone, both less than the national average clearance period.

2. Improving the Rule of Law to Ensure Unimpeded Economic Cooperation

In recent years, Shaanxi has actively promoted the building of the Belt and Road Demonstration Zone for International Commercial Legal Services, as well as the creation of a versatile legal service support system for the entire ecological chain, so that the rule of law can safeguard the BRI cooperation.

Located in Xi'an International Trade and Logistics Park, the Belt and Road Demonstration Zone for International Commercial Legal Services is the only Belt and Road demonstration zone for legal services in China, focusing on international commercial litigation, mediation, arbitration, legal services, judicial personnel cooperation and international law research. Since its approval in December 2018, the demonstration zone has introduced a large number of professional international legal platforms and service institutions, including the China-Shanghai Cooperation Organization Legal Service Committee Xi'an Center, the Belt and Road Lawyers Association Xi'an Center, the Belt and Road Center for International Commercial Dispute Resolution at Xi'an, the National Biosafety Evidence Foundation, the Second International Commercial Court of the Supreme People's Court, the Sixth Circuit Court of the Supreme People's Court, the Xi'an Intellectual Property Court, the Shaanxi Pilot Free Trade Zone Court of Arbitration, and well-known law firms, providing great support for performing the core functions of the demonstration zone.

Attaching great importance to intellectual property protection, the demonstration zone has established the Belt and Road Industrial Intellectual Property Alliance to explore the creation of the Belt and Road Intellectual Property Protection Demonstration Zone. Seventeen legal service agencies have established the Belt and Road Intellectual Property Legal Service Cooperation Platform in Shaanxi Province. In addition, the demonstration zone has played a leading role in the implementation of innovative policy for the lawyer system in China (Shaanxi) Free Trade Pilot Zone, explored and created a new one-stop resolution model for international commercial dispute litigation, arbitration, and mediation, and formulated the *Implementation Plan for Supporting Chinese Lawyers to Go Out to Serve the Overall Situation of China's All-Round Opening-Up*.

3. Ensuring Standards Alignment to Break Market Trading Barriers

Fragmentation of standards is a major constraint on the BRI cooperation across borders. Shaanxi has fully leveraged the technical strengths of scientific research institutions in related fields, carried out research into different standards to align Chinese standards with international standards and promote Chinese standards abroad, and contributed Shaanxi strength to the alignment and mutual recognition of Chinese and foreign standards.

In September 2017, Shaanxi was approved to set up the Belt and Road National Metrology Center (Shaanxi), aiming to build an international platform for metrological exchange and cooperation based on the technical capabilities of the Northwest National Center of Metrology and the Shaanxi

Institute of Metrology Science. The Center gives full play to the fundamental role of metrology in supporting technology and quality, thus making greater contribution to the BRI cooperation through metrological services. In May 2021, the Center was officially inaugurated as the only national metrological technology research institution serving the BRI.

Since the preparations for the Belt and Road National Metrology Center (Shaanxi) started, more than 200 metrology laws, regulations and management systems of the BRI countries and regions have been sorted out, and three volumes of background information on those countries and regions have been compiled and printed. In response to the metrological demands of enterprises "go global", equipment verification in such projects as Fiji road and hydropower station in Mali has been conducted to help the enterprises reduce project costs. Research programs on the metrological laws and regulations of the BRI countries and regions have been carried out together with the International Law School of Northwest University of Political Science and Law, to study the metrological laws and regulations of key countries, and promote the internationalization of the metrological system in China.

(iii) Promoting People–to–people Exchanges and Connectivity

Amity between the people holds the key to sound state-to-state relations. Over the past decade, Shaanxi has leveraged its profound culture and history and rich scientific and educational resources to continuously promote people-to-people exchanges and scientific and educational cooperation, injecting impetus to people-to-people connectivity among people in BRI countries and regions. Shaanxi has actively organized Silk Road archaeological excavations to promote exchanges and mutual learning among civilizations. The advancement of international education cooperation has made Shaanxi a popular destination for students from Central Asian countries. Greater efforts have been made to develop cross-border tourism and promote friendly exchanges between Chinese and foreign people. Shaanxi has taken an active part in building scientific and technological innovation platforms, establishing demonstration bases, and promoting scientific and technological achievements that benefit people's wellbeing. It has provided strong support for non-governmental organizations in establishing a people-to-people exchange alliance to enhance mutual understanding and traditional friendship. Over the past decade, Shaanxi has newly established international friendship with 48 cities. In total, it has established international friendship with 108 cities in 41 countries, including 54 cities in the BRI countries.

1. Silk Road Cultural Tourism Promotes Mutual Learning Among Civilizations

Shaanxi boasts abundant historical and cultural resources, where tourists can explore the origin of rituals of the Zhou and Qin system, and marvel at the grace and charm of the Tang and Han Dynasties. Thanks to its unique cultural tourism resources, Shaanxi strives to build an international cultural tourism center carrying forward Chinese civilization and inheriting the spirit of the Silk Road.

To explore the Silk Road civilization, Northwest University has established the Silk Road Archaeology Center and the Belt and Road Joint Laboratory on China-Central Asia Human and Environment with approval. It has also carried out exchanges and cooperation with prestigious universities and cultural & museum institutions in over 30 countries. Being the first to go abroad and carry out overseas archaeological excavations and research, the archaeological team of Northwest University has completed joint archaeological excavations and investigations in Rabat Site in Uzbekistan and Beshkent Valley in Tajikistan. Currently, the team is engaged in the excavation, protection of and research on the cultural relics at major sites in Uzbekistan, the investigation on an archaeological program in Turkmenistan, and the construction of the Belt and Road international joint laboratory. It will also resume or launch archaeological and cultural heritage protection programs in Kazakhstan, Nepal, Myanmar, Iran and other places.

Over the past decade, Shaanxi Province has successfully held eight Silk Road International Arts Festivals, three World Culture and Tourism Forums, and seven Xi'an Silk Road International Expositions. Shaanxi Culture Week titled "Regional Songs·Qin Rhythm" has been held in sister cities in more than 20 countries and regions such as Italy, Belarus. Cultural exchange programs such as "When Chang'an Meets Rome" series exhibitions and performances have been well received at home and abroad. The Silk Roads: The Routes Network of Chang'an-Tianshan Corridor became the first world cultural heritage project to be successfully inscribed through transnational cooperation.

To facilitate personnel exchanges, Shaanxi has cooperated with international organizations such as the United Nations World Tourism Organization and the Asia Pacific Tourism Association to establish the first inter-provincial cooperation mechanism for inbound tourism in China along with Beijing and Shanghai. Xi'an and Xiamen have entered into strategic cooperation on tourism to promote the collaboration between Maritime Silk Road and Land-based Silk Road. The first local action hub of the World Alliance of Cities and Local Governments - the Youth Education and Dialogue Hub Project, has been launched in Xi'an. The development of Xi'an consulate area has been accelerated, with the establishment of Consulate General of Thailand, South Korea, Cambodia and Malaysia, and Visa Centers of 32 countries including France, Britain and Germany.

2. Education-research Cooperation Enhances Mutual Acquaintance

The mission of joint building the BRI belongs to young people. Relying on its rich scientific and educational resources, Shaanxi has actively promoted Chinese-foreign cooperation in running school among institutions of higher learning and vocational schools to meet the needs of the future and the world. It has held the Silk Road Education Cooperation Expo for six consecutive years. At present, there are 50 Chinese-foreign cooperative education programs and institutions in Shaanxi, ranking first in Western China and eighth across China. Eighteen national and regional research centers have been established in Shaanxi, and eight foreign-aid programs have been approved by the Ministry of Education. Over the past decade, Shaanxi has attracted more than 100,000 foreign students, cultivating a large number of companions for the joint building of the BRI.

To strengthen inter-university exchanges, Xi'an Jiaotong University has initiated the "Silk Road Academic Belt" and the establishment of the University Alliance of the Silk Road. Since its inception eight years ago, the Alliance has made consistent efforts to advance cooperation among universities in the BRI countries and regions in such fields as personnel training, scientific research, cultural communication, policy research, and medical services. The Alliance has been expanding its membership, and more than 150 universities from 37 countries and regions have joined the Alliance. Shaanxi Normal University has led the establishment of the Silk Road Teacher Education Alliance, the Silk Road Humanities and Social Sciences Alliance and the Silk Road Books and Archives Publishing Alliance. Twenty-seven universities and research institutions from seven countries have joined the Alliances.

In terms of the research on jointly building the BRI, Xi'an Jiaotong University has led the establishment of the Collaborative Innovation Center for Silk Road Economic Belt Studies, Northwest University has led the establishment of the Belt and Road Think Tank Alliance among universities in Shaanxi, and Xi'an University of Finance and Economics has initiated the establishment of the Silk Road Think Tank Alliance of Finance and Economic Universities in Western China. Relevant think tanks have produced a number of legal, political, social and cultural research results, contributing wisdom and strength to the joint building of the Belt and Road.

3. Scientific and Technological Exchanges Enable Practical Cooperation

Innovation is an important driving force for development. Over the past decade, Shaanxi has deeply participated in the *Action Plan for the Belt and Road Science, Technology and Innovation Cooperation* to strengthen cooperation with participating countries in scientific and technological innovation, achievement transformation, industrial collaboration, and talent exchange. So far, 19 national and 64 provincial bases for international science and technology exchange and cooperation have been established in Shaanxi, and the International Science and Technology Cooperation Base Alliance in Shaanxi has been set up. Shaanxi has also established multi-layered cooperative relations with over 400 institutions in more than 40 countries and regions. Since 2015, various innovation entities in Shaanxi have signed 561 technology contracts with foreign countries, with a total contract value of more than 8 billion yuan.

In October 2020, the SCO Demonstration Base for Agricultural Technology Exchange and Training was officially inaugurated in Yangling. With a focus on the core functions of exchange, training and demonstration, the Base has carried out exchanges and cooperation in agricultural scientific research among SCO member states, training of personnel in modern agricultural science and technology, popularization and application of agricultural scientific and technological achievements, and development of international agricultural industrial parks, so as to achieve mutual benefit and win-win results for all stakeholders. The Base has carried out modern agricultural cooperation with more than 60 countries, established eight modern agricultural demonstration parks and one agricultural science and technology industrial park in Kazakhstan, Uzbekistan and other countries, and successfully held more than 30 exchange activities including a roundtable conference on the development of modern agriculture among SCO member states. More than 28,000 trainees from SCO member states have participated in technical training.

(iv) Strengthening Economy and Trade to Deepen Production Capacity Cooperation

On the basis of "hard connectivity" and "soft connectivity", Shaanxi has accelerated its integration into the global industrial chain and supply chain. As a result, foreign trade has been substantially advanced with the total import and export volume in Shaanxi nearly quadrupling since 2013. Foreign investment attraction goes hand-in-hand with outbound investment. High-quality "bringing in" helps to accelerate the formation of industry clusters of advanced manufacturing and modern service, as well as the upgrading and optimization of the industrial structure in Shaanxi. The high-level "go global" continues to deepen international production capacity cooperation, supporting the BRI countries and regions in improving the level of industrial development.

1. Foreign Trade Delivers Strong Growth

Shaanxi has actively developed various foreign trade clusters such as national bases for transformation and upgrading of foreign trade, and export bases with provincial characteristics, and sped up the establishment of national innovation demonstration zones for promoting import trade. Currently, there are 11 national bases for transformation and upgrading of foreign trade in Shaanxi, and 7 enterprises serving as provincial foreign trade comprehensive service platforms. These bases have helped to drive small and micro enterprises to achieve leapfrogging growth in foreign trade.

In 2022, total import and export volume in Shaanxi reached 483.5 billion yuan, 3.88 times that of 2013, with an average annual growth rate of 18.5%, far exceeding the national average of 6.3% over the same period. Among them, total exports reached 301.1 billion yuan, with an average annual growth of 21.5%, and total imports reached 182.4 billion yuan, with an average annual increase of 14.6%. The trade between Shaanxi and other BRI countries and regions has enjoyed rapid growth, with an average annual growth rate of 28.1% since the "13th Five-Year Plan", exceeding the average growth rate of Shaanxi's trade volume over the same period by 11.2 percentage points. In 2022, the imports and exports between Shaanxi and other BRI countries and regions exceeded 100 billion yuan, an increase of 41% year-on-year, with its proportion in Shaanxi's total trade volume increasing from 13.5% in 2015 to 23.3%.

With the explosive growth of cross-border e-commerce, Shaanxi has seized the opportunity of the "Online New Silk Road" to develop the comprehensive pilot zone for cross-border e-commerce in Xi'an and promote the prosperity of new formats and modes of foreign trade. By the end of 2022, Xi'an had been home to more than 1,800 enterprises related to cross-border e-commerce, with the annual transactions reaching 14.427 billion yuan, an increase of 46.4%.

The comprehensive pilot zone for cross-border e-commerce in Xi'an has taken advantage of pilot policies to smooth communication channels and remove data barriers among various links including "customs, taxation, foreign exchange, national inspection, industry and commerce and finance", and ensured the full coverage of cross-border e-commerce regulatory modes, including the 1210 bonded warehouse mode, the 9610 consolidation mode, the 9710B2B direct export mode, and the 9810 export overseas warehouse mode. The Chang'an China-Europe freight trains dedicated to cross-border e-commerce have been sent to Duisburg, Hamburg, Moscow and many other cities. Cross-border e-commerce packages are promptly inspected and released upon arrival and customs clearance and inspection are completed within 24 hours. In 2022, a total of 198 trips were made by the Chang'an China-Europe freight trains exclusively for cross-border e-commerce, an increase of over 60% year-on-year.

2. Industrial Structure Continues to Upgrade

"Hard connectivity" and "soft connectivity" continue to optimize business environment in Shaanxi and boost its attraction for investments. So far, the world's top 500 enterprises have set up 144 enterprises in Shaanxi. Foreign giants such as Samsung and Micron have been increasing investment and expanding production capacity. In 2021, the foreign capital actually utilized in Shaanxi exceeded 10 billion U.S. dollars for the first time (including profit reinvestment by foreign-invested enterprises), with an average annual growth rate of 18.3% since 2013. A number of leading domestic enterprises such as Huawei, ZTE, BYD, Geely, Skyworth and Konka have invested and built factories in Shaanxi. Over the past five years, the added value of high-tech manufacturing industry has registered an average annual growth rate of 13.1%, more than twice that of the industries above designated size. The high-quality "bringing in" has promoted the upgrading and optimization of Shaanxi's industrial structure, and significantly improved Shaanxi's capacity to participate in jointly building the BRI.

According to the data released by the Shaanxi Semiconductor Industry Association, boosted by leading enterprises such as Samsung, Micron and Infineon, Shaanxi's semiconductor industry sales has increased by more than 10 times from 10 billion yuan in 2011 to 122.8 billion yuan in 2022, with its national ranking rising from eighth to fourth, second only to Jiangsu, Shanghai and Guangdong. A large number of large-scale processing trade enterprises at home and abroad such as those engaged in silicon wafer manufacturing and display manufacturing have entered Shaanxi, expanding the emerging electronic industry clusters in Shaanxi.

New-energy vehicle (NEV) industry has developed rapidly in Shaanxi, adding another hundred billion-level industry in the province. In 2022, the output of NEVs in Xi'an exceeded 1 million for the first time in China, among which 995,000 vehicles were produced by BYD. As a result, Xi'an has surpassed Shanghai to become the top city in terms of NEV output in China. BYD has also set up a battery production base in Shangluo, and signed a strategic cooperation agreement with Baoji to invest in the construction of an NEV parts base. According to incomplete statistics, as of July 2023, BYD has invested more than 55 billion yuan in Shaanxi on projects covering new-energy passenger cars and parts, power batteries, intelligent terminals and Semiconductor R&D Center. Apart from Shenzhen where the BYD headquarters is located, Xi'an has become the best developed northern base with the most comprehensive industrial layout. In addition, the "BYD special line" has been launched in Xi'an to introduce the rail freight line into the freight yard on the west of the BYD Phase 4 factory. Once put into operation in 2025, it will be more convenient to export vehicles, spare parts manufactured in the industrial zone and finished products of related enterprises in the high-tech zone to Central Asian countries through the China-Europe freight trains.

Geely Auto has also actively increased its production capacity in Shaanxi. With the launch of the 300,000 NEV Project (with an investment of 7.8 billion yuan) in Xi'an, Geely had possessed its world's first smart black light factory with a full architecture and a full range of models. The first batch of vehicles rolled off the production line in 2022, and were first transported for export by the special Chang'an China-Europe freight trains for Geely Auto in April 2023.

3. Production Capacity Cooperation Continues to Deepen

Thanks to the BRI, Shaanxi has steadily expanded its outbound investment and deepened practical cooperation with the BRI countries and regions. During the "13th Five-Year Plan" period, Shaanxi's average annual ODI reached 796 million US dollars, 65.7% higher than that of the "12th Five-Year Plan" period. The average annual value of newly-signed contracts for foreign projects was 3.677 billion US dollars, double that of the "12th Five-Year Plan" period.

A number of leading enterprises in Shaanxi have accelerated their presences in overseas markets. Shaangu Group has provided system solutions and services for over 100 countries and regions around the world. Longi has established 32 production bases and more than 150 branches globally. Shaanxi Automobile Group has sold heavy trucks to more than 110 countries and regions. TOP International Engineering Corporation Limited, a wholly-owned subsidiary of Shaanxi Construction Engineering Group which is responsible for overseas business, has set up local operations in 32 countries (regions).

Fast Group is one of the first batch of national manufacturing individual champion demonstration enterprises, which has ranked first in the world for 17 consecutive years in terms of the output and sales of heavy-duty vehicle transmission. Fast's first overseas factory under sole proprietorship, Fast Auto Drive (Thailand) Co., Ltd. was fully put into operation in October 2014. It is now the only heavy-duty transmission manufacturer in ASEAN.

Targeting the Thailand, Vietnamese and Indian markets, Fast has established a sales and service network covering major commercial vehicle markets in ASEAN and radiating into the global market. In consequence, it has successfully joined the global supply chain system of many world-famous automobile and parts companies such as Daimler, Caterpillar and Eaton. In 2023, Fast introduced a new generation of NEV powertrains to the Thailand market and has received orders for 500 NEV powertrains.

In 2016, PV giant Longi Green Energy Technology invested 311 million US dollars in Malaysia to build the first overseas production base Longi (Kuching) SDN.BHD. In 2020, it spent 1.78 billion yuan acquiring a PV project in Vietnam. Longi has now built a whole industrial chain base with four factories for crystal pulling, slicing, battery and components in Malaysia. It has completed the upgrading of the battery and component factories in Vietnam, and is planning to set up a battery and component production base in India. All these efforts have provided strong support for the expansion of green energy product exports and the development of PV power generation in the host countries. In the last three years, overseas revenue has accounted for 40% of Longi's total revenue.

As a national leading enterprise for agricultural industrialization, Xi'an Aiju Grain and Oil Industry Group, based on the function of Xi'an International Trade and Logistics Park as a port and the channels of the Chang'an China-Europe freight trains, has carried out production capacity cooperation with Kazakhstan, and built a trilateral logistics and processing system between Northern Kazakhstan, the Alashankou Port in Xinjiang, and the Xi'an International Trade and Logistics Park. Aiju has also signed a contract farming agreement covering an area of 1.5 million mu (100,000 hectares) with North Kazakhstan to purchase locally produced oil and wheat. Once completed, the project will be capable of processing 300,000 tons of oil and flour and can create more than 1,000 local jobs. As of 2022, Aiju Group has cumulatively imported nearly 300,000 tons of agricultural products from Kazakhstan, earning more than 100 million US dollars in foreign exchange to Kazakhstan.

Thanks to the BRI cooperation, the signed contract value for overseas engineering projects undertaken by Top International Engineering Co., Ltd. has grown at an average annual rate of over 20% in recent years, of which the value of newly signed contracts in 2022 was 12.085 billion yuan, an increase of 20.7% year-on-year. In recent years, Top International has won 8 Luban Prize for overseas projects and 4 National Quality Engineering Awards for overseas projects, and a number of high-quality projects have become heart-winning projects for the benefit of local people. For example, Osh Hospital, which was completed in 2018, is the largest and most modern hospital in southern Kyrgyzstan. The hospital has improved the local backward medical infrastructure and made it easier for the locals to see a doctor. Uzbekistan's Bustan Channel Restoration Project was successfully completed in March 2023, addressing the water shortage for more than 100,000 hectares of local farmland, increasing the irrigation efficiency by 60%, and saving nearly 300 million cubic meters of water every year.

Theme Chapter

The *Implementation Plan of Shaanxi Province for Promoting the Building of the Silk Road Economic Belt and the 21st Century Maritime Silk Road* (2015-2020), issued in 2016, proposes for the first time the main goals of building Center for Transportation, Trade and Logistics, Center for International Industrial Capacity Cooperation, Center for Science and Technology Education, Center for International Cultural Tourism, and Center for Regional Finance-five major centers of the Belt and Road-as Shaanxi's practice of implementing the national requirements of "Five-Pronged Approach".

Over the past decade, based on its advantages in traffic location, industry, science and education, history and culture, and focusing on the construction of the five major centers, Shaanxi has introduced policies, implemented measures, invested funds, and made solid efforts to deeply integrate into the overall pattern of the BRI, striving to develop an open pattern by building connections with other countries over land and sea while creating synergy between its eastern and western regions.

Nowadays, important breakthroughs have been made first in the construction of the center for logistics, trade, and transportation. Shaanxi plays a prominent role as the Belt and Road commerce and trade logistics hub of the Belt and Road. It has kept promoting the construction of the center for international production capacity cooperation center, and achieved practical results in "go global" and "bringing in". Efforts have been made to build a center for the Belt and Road science and technology education, and promote the increase and expansion of international cooperation in science, education and humanities. Giving full play to its unique resources, Shaanxi has granted highlights to the construction of an international cultural tourism center, and witnessed enhancement in development vitality and international influence of its cultural tourism. In building the Silk Road financial center, greater efforts have been made to develop innovative products and services and carry out pilot projects to leverage the supporting role of finance in the construction of the Belt and Road.

I. The Function of the Center for Transportation, Trade and Logistics as a Hub Becomes Prominent

Over the past decade, based on its geographical advantages, Shaanxi has introduced policies and measures to ensure capital investment, and taken the construction of high-level channels as the first step. The development of the Asia-Europe land-sea trade corridor with high efficiency, low cost and quality service has been accelerated, and the international-oriented transportation and logistics network has gradually taken shape. With all these efforts, function of the center for transportation, trade and logistics as a hub has become increasingly prominent. The Chang'an China-Europe freight trains have lead the country in many aspects and made more than 20,000 trips, with 17 regular international routes reaching 45 countries and regions. The "Air Silk Road" has been expanded to fully cover "six cities in five countries" in Central Asia for the first time in China. Foreign trade has maintained steady growth, and the layout of overseas warehouses and centers for storage, processing and distribution of imports and exports has been constantly improved. From 2013 to 2022, the total trade volume between Shaanxi and the BRI countries and regions has increased by 18.4% annually.

(i) Speeding up the Formation of Asia-Europe Land-sea Trade Corridor

1. Chang'an China-Europe Freight Trains Take the Lead in China

The Chang'an China-Europe freight trains made its first trip from Xi'an on November 28, 2013, the year when the BRI was proposed. The number of trips annually made by Chang'an China-Europe freight trains has increased from more than 100 to more than 4,000 through three stages of development over the past decade, with indicators including number of trips, heavy container rate and freight volume all ranking first in China. 17 regular international routes have been opened reaching 45 countries and regions, and 21 "+ Western Europe" routes have been opened, with number of trips accounting for more than 20% of the national total. Today, the Chang'an China-Europe freight trains has become a freight service with the fastest running time, the highest degree of intelligence, the widest radiation range, the most complete service functions and the lowest comprehensive costs. At the same time, the construction of the China-Europe freight train assembly center in Xi'an has been accelerated to create a "golden channel" for international trade with high efficiency, low cost and quality service.

Initial exploration period (2013-2017). China Railway Xi'an Group Co., Ltd. was responsible for the organization and operation of the Chang'an China-Europe freight trains at the beginning of its service, which was mainly launched to the Central Asia. Xi'an International Inland Port Multimodal Transportation Co., Ltd., the operation platform of Chang'an freight trains established in 2016, has opened up five trunk routes between Xi'an and five Central Asian countries, Poland, Germany, Hungary and Russia, realizing the first Europe-bound freight train service. A total of 486 trips were made during this period.

Breakthrough and development period (2018-2019). The innovative service idea of China-Europe freight trains featuring government-led, multi-platform and market-oriented operation has been put forward, with the establishment of Xi'an Free Trade Port Construction and Operation Co., Ltd., and the building of a macro-controllable multi-platform operation model. The radiation range of Chang'an freight trains has been expanded continuously, with regular operation of 13 trunk lines from Xi'an to five Central Asian countries, Iran (Afghanistan), Germany, Poland, the Czech Republic, Finland, Hungary, Belgium, Belarus, Turkey and Russia and stable service of international rail-sea intermodal freight trains from Xi'an to Qingdao and Ningbo. During this period, the annual number of trips reached 2,000 with the total number reaching 3368, as Xi'an ranking top among the cities in China where China-Europe freight train was launched.

High-quality development period (2020 to present). Efforts have been made to comprehensively renovate and upgrade the port facilities of Xi'an International Trade and Logistics Park, and create new service modes of Chang'an China-Europe freight trains to improve operation. Domestic and foreign cooperation has been expanded to promote the port-industry-city integration, and accelerate the construction of China-Europe freight train assembly center in Xi'an. 17 international transport trunk lines of Chang'an freight trains have basically covered the entire Eurasian continent, including newly opened routes traversing the Black Sea and Caspian Sea, and China-Laos and China-Vietnam routes. The number of "+ Western Europe" assembly routes has increased to 21. To the east, the international sea-rail intermodal freight train running at fixed time, fixed routes, fixed train number, fixed schedule and fixed price from Xi'an to Qingdao has been launched to meet the cross-border transportation needs of Japan and South Korea, thus realizing the integration of North-South and East-West international logistics channels in Xi'an. From January to September 2023, the Chang'an China-Europe freight trains made 3,991 trips in an increase of 29.54% year-on-year, with a total cargo weight of 3.552 million tons in

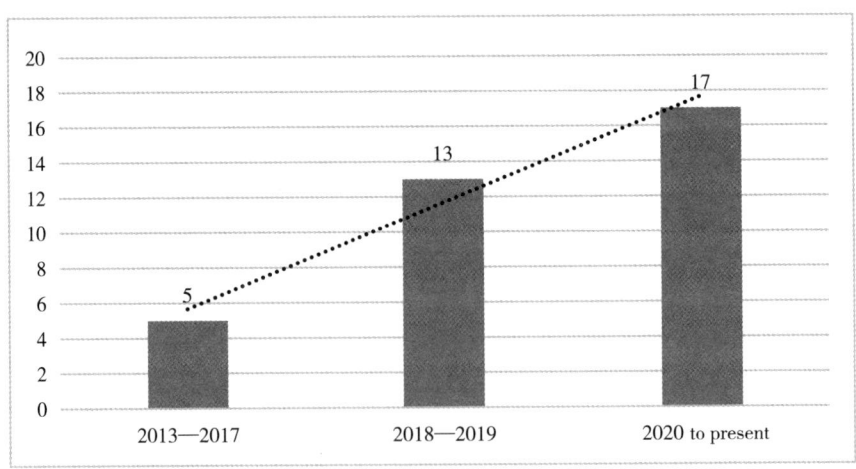

Figure 1: Number of Routes of Chang'an China-Europe Freight Train Service (2013-2023)

Data source: Shaanxi Belt and Road Portal

an increase of 35.2% year-on-year. Among them, 3,541 trips were made to Central Europe and 450 trips were made to Central Asia. Overall, the core indicators such as the number of trips, freight volume and heavy container rate of the Chang'an China-Europe freight trains rank first in China.

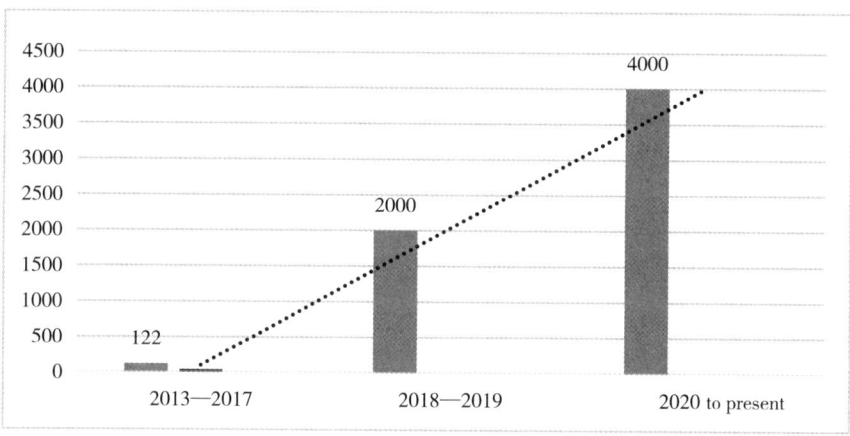

Figure 2: Average Annual Number of Trips Made by Chang'an China-Europe Freight Trains (2013-2023)

Data source: Shaanxi Belt and Road Portal

As a new international transportation organization mode featuring convenience, safety, stability and green economy, Chang'an China-Europe freight train service is a major practice for Shaanxi to participate in global opening-up and cooperation and an integrate into the BRI, promoting the exchanges and cooperation between Shaanxi and the BRI countries. During the COVID-19 pandemic, the Chang'an China-Europe freight train service maintained safe and stable operation and achieved growth against trend, reflecting Shaanxi's role in stabilizing the international industrial chain &

supply chain and supporting international cooperation against the pandemic. The strategic role of the China-Europe freight train service had also become increasingly prominent.

2. The "Air Silk Road" are Connected

Over the past decade, based on Xi'an Xianyang International Airport and Airport New City of Xixian New Area, Shaanxi has expanded "Air Silk Road" by opening international air routes between Xi'an and Tashkent, the capital of Uzbekistan, Bishkek, the capital of Kyrgyzstan, Astana, the capital of Kazakhstan, Ashgabat, the capital of Turkmenistan and Dushanbe, the capital of Tajikistan. Shaanxi is the first in China to achieve full coverage of routes in "six cities of five countries" in Central Asia.

Today, Xi'an Xianyang International Airport has opened a total of 386 passenger and cargo routes, including 83 international passenger routes, 45 all-cargo routes, and 4 fifth freedom flight routes, accelerating the construction of the "air route network running through Silk Road and connecting five continents with direct access to Europe and the United States". A 2-hour flight departing from Xi'an can cover 75% of China's territory and 85% of its economic resources, a 5-hour flight can cover all Asian cities, and a 12-hour flight can cover all European cities, providing a strong support for Shaanxi to build an inland opening-up highland.

As an important carrier of the Belt and Road, air logistics channel plays an important supporting role in serving the "dual circulation" and the new development pattern. As the only national airport logistics hub in Northwest China, Airport New City of Xixian New Area in Shaanxi Province accelerates the construction of an international aviation hub and trade logistics channel with wide radiation, high efficiency, low cost and quality service through the construction of air freight corridors, the creation of distribution centers for international trade, and the innovation of customs clearance supervision modes.

Nowadays, Airport New City of Xixian New Area has become the largest gathering area of aviation enterprises in Northwest China and the most versatile national airport-type logistics hub, home to nearly 200 modern logistics enterprises such as GLP, Mapletree, Hitachi, YTO Express, ZTO Express, STO Express and Yunda Express. 13 logistics parks have been built, regional headquarters of 14 airlines such as China Eastern Airlines and Hainan Airlines, and offices of 15 foreign airlines such as Finnair and Korean Air have been located here.

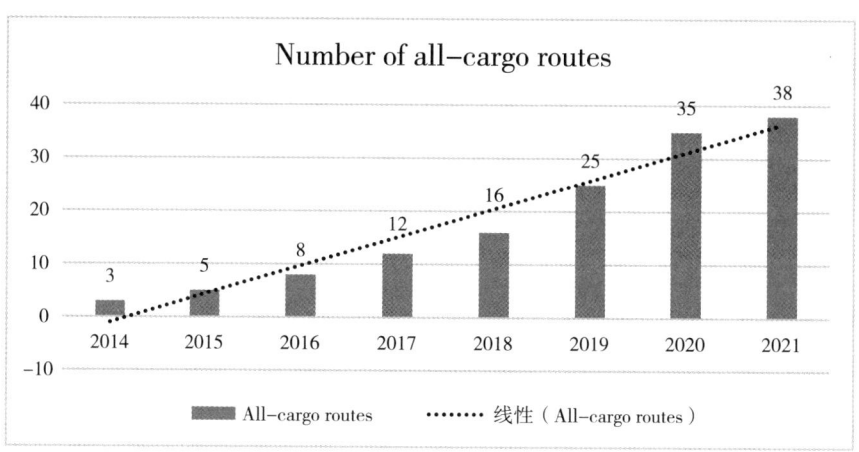

Figure 3: Number of All-cargo Routes in Xi'an (2014-2021)

Data source: Department of Commerce of Shaanxi Province and the Internet

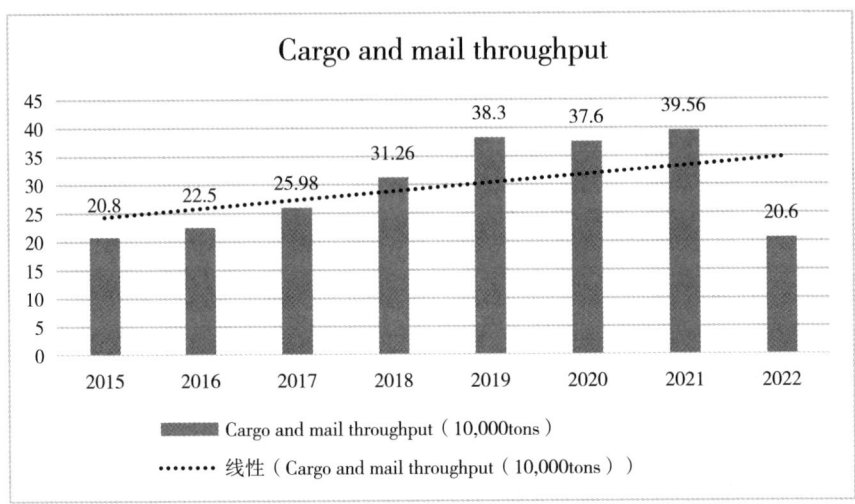

Figure 4: Cargo and Mail Throughput of Xi'an (2015-2022)

Data source: Department of Commerce of Shaanxi Province and the Internet

3. The Collaboration and Coordination of Land-sea-air Networks Gradually Constitutes a System

Shaanxi has actively carried out pilot demonstration of multimodal transportation including air-rail, road-rail and sea-rail transportation, and promoted the construction of two national demonstration projects-the Belt and Road inland transit hub in Xi'an Port and the intelligent backbone network of containers by CRIntermodal featuring "land-sea linkage and multi-point coordination", to accelerate the formation of the collection and distribution system for the coordinated development of airport and land port in the province.

The first TIR (International Road Transport System) international cross-border road freight line has been opened. In June 2023, four TIR trucks set off from the check point of Xixian Airport Comprehensive Bonded Zone in Shaanxi Province and headed for Kazakhstan, marking the opening of the first TIR international cross-border road freight line in Shaanxi Province (Xi'an - Kazakhstan). This move has further improved the open channels from Shaanxi to Central Asia and even the world, strengthened land-air multimodal transport in Xi'an, and effectively promoted the economic and trade cooperation between Shaanxi and the BRI countries, especially the Central Asian countries.

The layout of the road network has been further optimized. Efforts have been made to promote the construction of the land transportation network in the shape of Chinese character " 米 " centered on Xi'an, and develop a safe, convenient, green and intelligent land transportation system with smooth connection. The expressway network has been continuously improved. Since 2015, the expressways from Yan'an to Yanchuan, Taibai to Fengxian, Pingli to Zhenping have been built successively. At present, the total operation mileage of expressways in Shaanxi has reached 6,696 kilometers, forming a rapid radiation network of expressways such as Lianyungang-Khorgos Expressway, Beijing-Kunming High-Speed Railway, Baotou-Maoming Expressway, Fuzhou-Yinchuan Expressway and Shanghai-Xi'an Expressway The high-speed railway network has been continuously improved. The Zhengzhou-Xi'an High-speed Railway, Baoji-Lanzhou High-speed Railway, Xi'an-Chengdu High-Speed Railway and Yinchuan-Xi'an High-speed Railway have been put into operation successively. Positive progress has been made in the preliminary construction of the Xi'an-Yan'an High speed

Railway, Xi'an-Ankang High-speed Railway, Xi'an-Shiyan High-speed Railway and Ordos-Yulin-Yan'an High-Speed Railway. The operation mileage of the high-speed railways has reached 1,019 kilometers, with fast and direct routes between Xi'an and Beijing, Zhengzhou, Chengdu, Lanzhou and Yinchuan.

(ii) Building an Efficient and Convenient Logistics Collection and Distribution System

1. Improving the Collection and Distribution Functions of the Assembly Center as a Hub

According to the Plan for *the Construction of China-Europe Freight Train Assembly Center in Xi'an* issued in May 2022, Shaanxi has implemented the national "1+N+X" policy system, and sorted out and planned 45 key projects with a total investment of 224.157 billion yuan in three areas: infrastructure guarantee, informatization and intelligent construction, and port-industry-city integration. Nowadays, these projects have delivered substantial results by accelerating the construction of the assembly center and enhancing the distribution function of Xi'an as an international logistics hub.

The trade channel system has been completed with effective results, achieving the shift from "line" to "area" orientation. To the west and north, routes traversing the Caspian Sea and Black Sea have been opened, and the number of Chang'an trunk lines has increased to 17, basically covering the entire Eurasian continent. To the east, the international sea-rail intermodal freight train running at fixed time, fixed routes, fixed train number, fixed schedule and fixed price from Xi'an to Qingdao and Ningbo has been launched on a regular basis to meet the cross-border transport demands of Japan and South Korea and seamlessly connect with the global shipping system. To the south, the China-Laos and China-Vietnam international freight train service and road-rail routes from Xi'an to Nepal and Pakistan have been launched, realizing the integration of North-South and East-West international logistics channels in Xi'an. Through the "combination of trunks and branches", the "+ Western Europe" assembly system has been built with 21 assembly lines, continuously boosting the attraction of resource elements.

The comprehensive service function of the assembly center continues to improve. A container yard of 690,000 square meters and 59 railway lines have been built at Xi'an Guojigang Railway Station, with a daily handling capacity of 3,700 TEU. With the drive of the assembly center project, efforts have been made to constantly improve the port function, and speed up the improvement of the road-rail express line and customs inspection facilities. The consolidation center for Chang'an China-Europe freight trains has been approved for use. With 48 arrival and departure sidings, Xi'an Guojigang Railway Station has a designed annual throughput of 3.1 million TEU.

The agglomeration effect of the China-Europe freight trains serving Shaanxi has been unleashed at a faster speed with construction of assembly center as the key. In recent years, Xi'an International Trade and Logistics

Park has successively introduced leading enterprises such as China Forestry Group Corporation, Shandong Port Group Co., Ltd, China Minmetals Corporation, Shanxi Forestry Group Co., Ltd, and Shanxi Investment Group, to develop a port function zone of the China-Europe freight train assembly center in Xi'an integrating container transportation, cold chain logistics, futures delivery, bulk commodities, and truck-load transportation. So far, the zone has introduced 31 of the global top 500 enterprises, 8 of China's top 500 enterprises and 5 of China's top 500 private enterprises. At the same time, key logistics industries including express delivery, cold chain, commerce and e-commerce have gathered here, and a number of corporate headquarters or logistics transfer centers have settled such as "three headquarters" of JD and Alibaba Silk Road headquarter. Consequently, Shaanxi has become home to more than 230 A-level logistics enterprises.

2. Facilitating Customs Clearance to Boost Direct Freight Transportation

The construction of cross-border e-commerce comprehensive pilot zone has been promoted steadily, and freight train service exclusively for cross-border e-commerce has been launched. On January 1, 2022, carrying 50 containers full of electronic accessories and cross-border e-commerce products, the Chang'an China-Europe freight train service (Xi'an - Saint Petersburg - Mannheim) exclusively for cross-border e-commerce departed from Xi'an Guojigang Railway Station and headed for Mannheim, Germany. The launch of freight train service exclusively for cross-border e-commerce has improved the efficiency of international freight logistics and enriched the functions of the China-Europe freight train assembly center in Xi'an. Up to now, Shaanxi has sent a number of the Chang'an China-Europe freight service exclusively for cross-border e-commerce to Duisburg, Hamburg, Moscow and many other places, and opened the Chang'an China-Europe freight train special line for international mail, sending cross-border goods directly to more than 20 European cities. In 2022, a total of 198 trips cross-border e-commerce trains were launched, an increase of 60.9% year-on-year, remaining the first place in China.

The "railway express customs clearance for the inbound and outbound" and China's first departure land port tax refund pilot program have been launched. In April 2022, Xi'an International Trade and Logistics Park became the first inland port in China to carry out the departure land port tax refund pilot program, and the Chang'an China-Europe freight train became the first train to enjoy the tax refund policy of departure port. All customs clearance procedures for cross-border goods can be instantly completed at the Xi'an Station Customs, reducing the customs clearance time by half, and the tax refund time limit is cut down from an average of 30 days to a minimum of 2 days, effectively reducing the comprehensive logistics costs of enterprises conducting cross-border trade.

Informatization enables efficient customs clearance. A consolidation center for the Chang'an China-Europe freight trains for cross-border e-commerce, as well as an informationalized, visual and intelligent customs clearance service system has been built in Xi'an International Trade and

Logistics Park to realize informatization management and efficient customs clearance. With the new mode of "customs declaration before packing" for cross-border e-commerce bulk goods, the customs clearance time has been saved by 2 to 3 days. The full coverage of regulatory modes has been implemented, including 1210 bonded warehouse mode, 9610 consolidation mode, 9710B2B direct export mode, 9810 export overseas warehouse mode, the "green channel" for cross-border e-commerce has been opened, and "priority loading, bill filling and pull transport" has been conducted for cross-border e-commerce package transportation. Instant inspection and release of goods have been conducted upon arrival to ensure the completion of customs clearance and inspection within 24 hours.

3. Helping Enterprises Reduce Costs and Increase Efficiency with Service Platforms

Services including railway bill approval, market supervision, taxation, and administrative approval can be handled in an integrated way at the Office of Xi'anxi Railway Station in Shaanxi, and a full-chain comprehensive service system integrating policy consultation, registration, tax payment, cargo shipping and storage have been built. At the same time, Shaanxi has built a comprehensive service platform of digital finance for the Chang'an China-Europe freight trains, and developed digital application scenarios and functions such as space booking, container leasing, shipping, customs declaration, logistics and transportation, container dynamics, digital finance, and cross-border settlement, so as to realize the "Unified Online

Service" for space booking and financing services. Eight cross-border e-commerce overseas warehouses have been built in Germany, Kazakhstan, Belarus and other countries to connect the local truck flights network and distribution centers, and provide cross-border enterprises with "end-to-end, door-to-door" full-link logistics services, reducing the comprehensive cost of enterprises by about 10%. The average inspection cost of declared cross-border e-commerce goods per container has been cut down by 1,800 yuan through such measures as the purchase of self-provided boxes, the reduction of terminal handling charge and inspection fees of cross-border e-commerce goods on the declaration list, significantly reducing the operating costs of enterprises.

(iii) Fostering Foreign Trade to Achieve Leapfrogging Development

1. High-end Platforms Lead Foreign Economic and Trade Cooperation

Silk Road International Exposition helps build a new highland of inland opening-up. Since 2016, the Investment and Trade Forum for Cooperation between East and West China has been officially renamed the Silk Road International Exposition and the Investment and Trade Forum for Cooperation between East and West China. Up to now, the Silk Road International Exposition has been held for six consecutive years by countries including Russia, Britain and Serbia. The exhibition area, the number of exhibitors and exhibits have reached a new high, and the level of specialization, internationalization, branding and informatization has been greatly improved. As a result, the Exposition has become an important platform to promote the joint building of the Belt and Road, the development of the western region in China, and the coordinated development of the eastern, middle and western regions. In the first five sessions of the Silk Road International Exposition, the value of signed contracts for foreign-funded projects totaled 34.2 billion dollars, and the value of contracts for high-tech achievement transaction totaled 20.2 billion yuan. Overseas guests and merchants from more than 70 countries and regions such as South Korea, Thailand and Singapore, as well as domestic merchants from more than 20 provinces participated in the 6th Silk Road International Exposition both online and offline. An innovative exhibition area themed Regional Comprehensive Economic Partnership Agreement (RCEP) was set up. The Round-Table Meeting of RCEP Regional Economic and Trade Cooperation 2022, Shaanxi, China was held to further expand the cooperation among RCEP member states.

China Yangling Agricultural Hi-Tech Fair leads the high-quality Belt and Road agricultural cooperation. China Yangling Agricultural Hi-Tech Fair is a national 5A-level comprehensive agricultural exhibition certified by the Global Association of the Exhibition Industry (UFI) and recognized a well-known trademark in China, with a brand value of 87.119 billion yuan. Since its inception in 1994, China Yangling Agricultural Hi-Tech Fair has been held for 29 consecutive sessions, which is the largest comprehensive agricultural exhibition in China, displaying domestic and foreign agricultural high-tech achievements and advanced applicable technologies. Since the BRI was proposed, the scale of China Yangling Agricultural Hi-Tech Fair has been expanded year by year, and the level of internationalization, marketization and specialization has been continuously improved. The Fair has become an agricultural science event which is "well-known in the world and first-class in China, recognized by the market and loved by farmers." The 29th China Yangling Agricultural Hi-Tech Fair was successfully held in Shaanxi both online and offline, with a total of 2.948 million visitors and 338 signed projects with a total value of 98.8 billion yuan, of which 49 projects were signed on site with a contract value of 29.508 billion yuan.

The Eurasian Economic Forum has promoted frequent economic and trade interactions under the BRI. The Eurasian Economic Forum is a large-scale institutional foreign-related forum at the national level, with the Shanghai Cooperation Organization member countries as the main body facing the vast Eurasian region. It's held every two years. Xi'an is the permanent site of the Eurasian Economic Forum, which has been held for nine sessions since 2005, and has become an important platform for international exchanges and cooperation to promote the economic and cultural development of relevant countries and regions. Participating countries have signed a series of programmatic documents on regional exchanges and cooperation, including *Xi'an Accord, Xi'an Initiative, Xi'an Initiative on Promoting Trade Security and Facilitation*, and *Xi'an*

Declaration on Jointly Building the Silk Road Economic Belt through the Forum, expressing their common desire and firm confidence in the joint development of the BRI, and expanding the space for cooperation among Eurasian countries. More than 30 outcomes have been achieved in the previous forums, including the signing or issuing of *Annual Report on SCO, Report on the Investment of Chinese Enterprises in Eurasian Countries* and *Golden Silk Road Tourism Corridor*, contributing to more than 90 cooperation projects.

2. Trade-production Integration Enhances Logistics Business Momentum

The spillover effect of the China-Europe freight train has become increasingly significant, serving more than 16,500 enterprises and accelerating the port-industry-city integration. More than 40 manufacturing enterprises such as Konka and Huixin, and 886 enterprises conducting block trade have established themselves in Xi'an International Trade and Logistics Park.

Accelerate the port-industry integration. Xi'an International Trade and Logistics Park, relying on the National Processing Trade Industrial Park and Xi'an Comprehensive Bonded Zone, has accelerated the construction of the Belt and Road Lingang Industrial Park and carried out transfer of southeast coastal industries. Up to now, the construction of Lingang Industrial Park has been completed, with 11 enterprises entering the park, and 9 enterprises in operation, including Jinghong Display Technology, Shaanxi Shuoda

Vision Electronic Technology Co., SEEKBOOC, Warmasun, Deshimei and HuazhanSoft. The Konka Smart Home Appliance Headquarters Co was put into operation in October 2022, and the construction of the Konka Silk Road Technopole and the Industry Base for Future Information Technology Application and Innovation of Huixin has started. Taking the construction of Xi'an National Medical Center as an opportunity, Shaanxi has taken the initiative to make plans for the emerging medical science and technology industry, signed major projects of more than 1 billion yuan such as the Western Superconducting Medical Science and Technology Project, the Liando U Valley • Medical Science and Technology/Intelligent Manufacturing Innovation Port Project, and set up the first base for research, development and industrialization of superconducting heavy-ion accelerator in China. Efforts have been made to accelerate the concentration of science and technology innovation atmosphere, and introduce 11 high-quality R&D enterprises such as the Xi'an Branch of the Huixin National Innovation Center for Advanced Radio Frequency Devices and Shaanxi Konka Research Institute. Enterprise R&D centers of Stellar Hong Kong and Shenzhen Huasheng have been settled to build a regional center for science and technology research and development of small and medium-sized enterprises.

Accelerate port-trade integration. The construction of bulk commodity trading centers for metals, grain, timber, cold chain, and vehicles has been accelerated, with the volume of commodities trading revenue reaching 123 billion yuan in 2022, an increase of 17% year-on-year. Based on the rise of domestic goods, the "Silk Road E-commerce Center" has been built, and three global unicorn enterprises with an estimated value of more than 10 billion have been introduced, including Cainiao Global Express, J&T International Logistics and Dingdang Medicine Express. The national assembly center for cross-border e-commerce of the Chang'an China-Europe freight trains has been strengthened, with 198 high-quality trips dedicated to cross-border e-commerce, an increase of 61% year-on-year. Shaanxi has taken the lead in China to conduct rail assembly business for cross-border e-commerce bulk cargo, introduced Cainiao global non-empty transfer center project and global top 500 CEVA national railway intelligent consolidation center project, thus promoting the steady growth of imports and exports of the Park. The new field of foreign trade has been seized to develop the cross-border e-commerce live broadcast industry, build the Belt and Road e-commerce innovation center around the central business district, introduce 14 leading e-commerce live broadcast enterprises such as Hangzhou Peibo, Wuhan Shengliang, Shaanxi Weiju, thus creating an e-commerce live broadcast ecosystem integrating domestic live broadcast, cross-border live broadcast, short video production and anchor training.

Accelerate the port-city integration. On the basis of building headquarters of ten enterprises including China Merchants Group, China Resources, China Power Construction, COFCO, headquarters projects such as Sinopec, State Grid, and digitalization of Agricultural Bank of China have been introduced to build the central business district of China-Europe freight train assembly center in Xi'an. The Belt and Road Demonstration

Zone for International Commercial Legal Services (BRD-ICLS) with the Second China International Commercial Court at its core has been in effective operation, law firms such as Shaanxi Yunde and Heheng have been introduced, with the total revenue of law firms settled in the Zone in 2022 exceeding 130 million yuan. The construction of Xi'an International Arbitration Center has been accelerated, and the Xi'an Arbitration Commission has been successfully relocated to the Zone. The column for Belt and Road Demonstration Zone for China International Commercial Legal Services has been successfully opened on Shaanxi Legal Service Network, and the legal service module of the "Online Comprehensive Service Platform for China-Europe Freight Train" has been launched for test. Based on the Olympic Sports Center and the Silk Road International Sports Culture Exchange and Training Base, matters related to the grant of "National Comprehensive Sports Training Base" has been accelerated to build a national platform for people-to-people exchanges in culture, sports, education, science and technology, and law under the BRI, and build a Belt and Road-oriented urban meeting room.

The whole industrial chain of airport economy has been initially formed. Airport New City of Xixian New Area in Shaanxi has fully leveraged the advantages of six functional platforms of "airport, free trade, bonded system, cross-border service, port and air rights" to build a cargo route network embracing the Belt and Road and radiating the world. The crisscrossed air routes have contributed to the explosive growth of airport economy. Centering on the three leading industries-aviation hub guarantee industry, airport advanced manufacturing industry, and airport high-end service industry, and assembling industrial projects including aviation manufacturing, electronic information and biomedicine, the whole industrial chain of airport economy has initially taken shape, and is becoming a hot land for the development of high-end and sophisticated industries. By the end of 2022, a total of 30,626 new market entities have appeared in Airport New City, including 25 national high-tech enterprises, 104 other technology-based enterprises, and 134 SMEs applying for technology-based enterprises. Since the establishment of Xixian Airport Comprehensive Bonded Zone officially approved by the State Council in January 2020, the import and export volume has doubled to 8.22 billion yuan in 2022, with an average annual growth rate of 83.4%. With diversified businesses in the Zone, the airport economic output has exceeded 12 billion yuan.

II. Steady Progress in Building an International Production Capacity Cooperation Center

Over the past decade, as a major energy province and an important equipment manufacturing base, Shaanxi has given full play to its role as a node, actively integrating into the global industrial chain and supply chain, and building a center for international production capacity cooperation center Shaanxi has carried out high-quality "go global" with deep participation in the international industrial division of labor. A number of leading enterprises have accelerated distribution in overseas market, and a number of landmark projects have been fostered in a coordinated way. From 2013 to 2022, Shaanxi has invested 1.24 billion dollars in BRI countries, accounting for 23.8% of the province's total overseas investment over the same period. The turnover of Shaanxi's contracted projects in those countries reached 13.57 billion dollars, accounting for 52.6% of the province's total turnover of foreign contracted projects over the same period. Shaanxi has also carried out high-quality "bringing in" by giving full play to the pilot function of the free trade zone. It has constantly optimized the business environment to attract Samsung, BYD, Konka and other leading enterprises to establish production capacity bases facilitated by international industrial cooperation parks including the ones between China and Russia and China and Europe, so as to build a characteristic industrial cluster with international competitiveness.

(i) Solid Foundation for Expanding Cooperation

Since the proposal of the BRI, thanks to its industrial strength in energy and manufacturing, Shaanxi has promoted traditional industries and high-end equipment manufacturing to a new level, thus developing a number of highly competitive enterprise groups, enabling a number of enterprises such as Yanchang Petroleum, Shaanxi Coal and Chemical Industry, Shaangu Group, Fast, Longi, and Aiju to actively seek new development space overseas.

1. Strong Industrial Foundation of Energy and High-end Equipment Manufacturing

Competitive industry is the basis for promoting international industrial capacity cooperation as well as the prerequisite for institutional innovation.

In terms of energy industry, Shaanxi Province is an important energy base in China, with crude oil production and natural gas production ranking first and raw coal production ranking third in the country. Yanchang Petroleum and Shaanxi Coal and Chemical Industry Group have been on the list of the global top 500 enterprises, serving as key supporters of international industrial capacity cooperation.

In terms of manufacturing, Shaanxi has accelerated the building of a number of advanced industrial clusters, including traditional industries such as modern agricultural technology, energy and mineral resources, and project contracting, as well as sunrise industries such as clean energy, equipment manufacturing, and integrated circuits. By continuing to deepen practical cooperation with the BRI countries, leading enterprises in Shaanxi have accelerated distribution in overseas markets and developed a mutually beneficial international industrial capacity cooperation ecology with win-win results.

2. Joint Building the Park as a Carrier for Deepening Production Capacity Cooperation

Sino-Russian Silk Road High-tech Innovation Park has been built to create a platform for China-Russia production capacity cooperation. As one of the cooperation projects at the strategic level of the Chinese and Russian governments, the Sino -Russian Silk Road High-tech Innovation Park is built in two places. As one of the important carriers of energy cooperation between China and Russia, the Park is developed by two countries, who jointly set up the China-Russia Investment Cooperation Committee for unified management and coordination. Located in Fengdong New City, Xixian New Area, the Park in China focuses on high-tech industries. Located in the Greenwood International Trade Center in Moscow, the Park in Russia targets such fields as headquarters economy and information technology. At present, 53 enterprises and institutions have been introduced into the Park in China, and science and technology projects and research platforms such as the CIS Scientific and Technological Achievements Library, the China-Russia Joint Laboratory of Marine Technology and the workstation of foreign academicians and experts have been launched successively. A one-stop international enterprise service window and a National Test Center for Russia as a Foreign Language have been built. The Park in Russia has been committed to creating a base camp for Shaanxi enterprises to invest in Russia, and has introduced 22 enterprises.

The Sino-European Industrial Park supports high-end manufacturing. The Sino-European Industrial Park is aimed at building an industrial complex opening to the outside world which integrates scientific innovation research and development, business incubation and high-end business supporting, introducing European and domestic enterprises as intelligent manufacturing centers with cutting-edge technologies, and building high-standard intelligent factories such as intelligent manufacturing, robot research and development and manufacturing, and scientific and technological service. The Park is planned to be developed in two areas through two phases. With a planned area of about 800 mu, the first phase of the high-speed railway new town will be completed and put into operation in 2023. It has introduced 9 projects invested by European enterprises such as Bosch and BMW of Germany, Alstom of France, SNCF, Danone, Buhler and Oerlikon of Switzerland. The second phase of Jingwei new city, with a planned area of about 1200 mu, mainly introduces automobiles, high-end equipment, new materials, consumer goods manufacturing, military-civilian integration, general aviation, finance and modern service industries, launches and develops high-quality technology-based projects incubated in the high-speed railway new town, and forms a corresponding specialized industrial park for scientific and technological manufacturing.

3. Policies and Measures for Efficient Progress of Production Capacity Cooperation

Over the past decade, Shaanxi has introduced a number of policies and measures to promote the construction of international production capacity cooperation center.

In 2015, the People's Government of Shaanxi Province successively issued *the Implementation Opinions on Further Overseas Investment* and *Strategic Opinions on Accelerating the Implementation of "Go Global"* focusing on encouraging enterprises to participate in the construction of infrastructure in the BRI countries. In terms of agricultural cooperation, with a focus on Africa, Central Asia and Eastern Europe, Shaanxi has assisted qualified agriculture-related enterprises in overseas investment and project cooperation in crop planting, livestock farming and processing of agricultural products.

In 2016, Shaanxi Province issued *the Implementation Opinions on Promoting International Cooperation in Production Capacity and Equipment Manufacturing*, expressing support for the promotion of international cooperation in production capacity and equipment manufacturing in ten fields such as energy, chemical industry, non-ferrous metallurgy and building materials, so as to promote economic restructuring and industrial optimization and upgrading. In 2017, the State-owned Assets Supervision and Administration Commission of Shaanxi Province issued *the Opinions on Promoting Enterprises to Develop International Production Capacity Cooperation* to guide and standardize provincial enterprises' participation in the Belt and Road Initiative from four aspects.

The 14th Five-Year Plan for Shaanxi Province to Deeply Integrate into Belt and Road Cooperation and Develop into a Highland of Opening Up proposes that during the 14th Five-Year Plan period, the development of the international production capacity cooperation center should be improved by enhancing the international competitiveness of the industrial chain, promoting the construction of cooperation parks, and strengthening the cooperation in energy industry.

After the China-Central Asia Summit in 2023, Shaanxi proposed that it would support enterprises to set up overseas warehouses in five Central Asian countries, further promote the export of consumer goods of light industry and oil drilling machinery in Shaanxi Province, and expand the import of important energy resources, grain, vegetable oil and meat to promote the deepening and solid economic and trade cooperation with five Central Asian countries.

(ii) "Go Global" to Deeply Participate in the International Industrial Division of Labor

Over the past decade, Shaanxi has steadily advanced foreign investment cooperation, and Shaanxi enterprises have actively gone global to expand overseas markets and deeply participate in the international industrial division of labor. Longi has 32 production bases and more than 150 branches around the world, and Longi photovoltaic components production project in Malaysia has created nearly 4,000 jobs in the local area. Aiju Grain and Oil Industry Group has developed "contract agriculture" of 1.5 million mu in Kazakhstan, with an annual output of pressed oil and processed flour reaching 300,000 tons respectively. Xi'an Aiju Grain and Oil Economic and Trade Cooperation Zone in Kazakhstan has been one of the "55 projects on the China-Kazakhstan production capacity and investment cooperation list". Shanxi Automobile has exported its heavy trucks to more than 110 countries and regions around the world. The system solutions and services of Shaangu have covered more than 100 countries and regions globally. The Osh Hospital, a project undertaken by Shaanxi Construction Engineering Group, is the largest modern large-scale general hospital in southern Kyrgyzstan.

1. Traditional Competitive Industries "Go Global" for Mutual Benefits and Win-Win Results

Mutual benefit is the core of production capacity cooperation. Over the past decade, Shaanxi's traditional industries with advantages in oil and gas, agriculture, engineering contracting have actively gone global. The high consistency with the strategy of many developing countries to accelerate industrialization has served as the common ground for win-win cooperation between the two sides. In terms of oil and gas, Yanchang Petroleum has obtained the exploration and development rights of 11,300 square kilometers of oil and gas blocks in Kyrgyzstan, and carried out negotiation and cooperation with Kazakhstan in the development of several oil and gas resource blocks. In 2017, the 800,000 tons per year oil refining project of Zhongda China Petrol Company in Kyrgyzstan invested by Central Asia Energy Co., Ltd, a subsidiary of Shaanxi Coal and Chemistry Industry Group, was officially put into operation, playing an important role in ensuring the supply of various refined oil products and liquefied gas in Kyrgyzstan's market.

In terms of agriculture, Shaanxi has actively given play to its industrial advantages in agriculture, seeking for distribution in Central Asia and neighboring countries, and creating land routes for grain import and export under the BRI to build an overseas granary of China. Relying on SCO Demonstration Base for Agricultural Technology Exchange and Training in Yangling, Shaanxi Province, Shaanxi has continuously carried out exchanges and cooperation in agricultural scientific research, cultivation and training of personnel in modern agricultural science and technology, and construction of international agricultural industrial parks, so as to achieve mutual benefit and win-win results among regions.

Aiju Grain and Oil Industrial Group has cooperated with Kazakhstan in production capacity to build a trilateral China-foreign park among North Kazakhstan, Alashankou Port in Xinjiang, and Xi'an International Trade and Logistics Park. At present, Aiju Grain and Oil Industrial Group has completed the construction of a 300,000-ton oil processing plant in Kazakhstan, established a friendly cooperation mechanism with local farmers, signed a "contract agriculture" agreement of 1.5 million mu with a total purchase of nearly 400,000 tons of oil, wheat, etc., creating more than 1,000 local jobs both directly and indirectly and bringing more than 100 million dollars in foreign exchange for Kazakhstan.

In terms of engineering contracting, a number of enterprises such as Shaanxi Construction Engineering Group Huashan International Engineering Co., Ltd. have gone global to undertake various projects in the BRI countries, contributing strength of Shaanxi enterprises to promote infrastructure connectivity. Over the past decade, Top International Engineering Co., Ltd has accelerated go global by establishing branches in the United Arab Emirates, Pakistan and Malaysia responsible for overseas market development, conducting business with Sri Lanka, Bangladesh, Saudi Arabia, Uzbekistan, Tajikistan and other BRI countries.

Figure 5: Turnover of Foreign Contracted Projects of Shaanxi Province (2013-2022)

Data source: Department of Commerce of Shaanxi Province

2. Modern High-end Equipment Manufacturing Industry Opens a New Chapter in Overseas Market

Over the past decade, high-end manufacturing enterprises in Shaanxi have kept accelerating overseas market expansion by increasing investment in Malaysia, Thailand and other BRI countries, thus making constant breakthroughs in projects and markets, and achieving high-level overseas development.

Shaangu Group's energy-saving and environmental protection products, system solutions and services have been provided to dozens of countries and regions including Indonesia and Malaysia. In Vietnam, Shaangu Group has signed an EPC project of blast furnace with customers to become a global leader in blast furnace equipment in the field of metallurgy.

A Thailand plant was built and put into operation in 2014 by Shaanxi Fast Auto Drive Group, a leading enterprise in China's gear industry, with an annual production capacity of 30,000 transmissions. At present, Fast Thailand plant has provided dozens of auto factories in overseas regions with transmissions of over 20 varieties from more than 10 series including high-end, intelligent and automation types, and witnessed gradual increase in supporting range and sales, helping Fast move faster to the goal of strategic globalization, high-end orientation, market segmentation and brand internationalization.

3. Clean Energy Promotes Green Belt and Road

Currently, the global energy production and consumption pattern is facing profound adjustment with accelerated transformation of clean and low-carbon energy. Shaangu, Longi and other enterprises continue to innovate, participate in the development of national clean energy industry to promote green Belt and Road through technical support, capacity building and consulting services.

As a provider of distributed energy system solutions and energy-saving and environmental protection technologies, Shaangu has actively expanded the distributed energy market in the BRI countries, with contracts of such projects as the operation and maintenance of OSS coal-fired power generation in Indonesia. So far, Shaangu has undertaken overseas projects in nearly 100 countries, with continuous enhancement of its system solution capability.

In response to the BRI, Longi invested 311 million dollars in Kuching, Malaysia in 2016 to build its first overseas production base, Longi (Kuching) SDN.BHD. While developing the photovoltaic industry in Malaysia, Longi has actively performed its corporate social responsibility to improve local school conditions, reduce poor population, train technical personnel, increase employment opportunities and improve local people's livelihood to make photovoltaic better benefit the people in the backward areas of the BRI countries.

(iii) "Bring in" to Build Characteristic Industrial Clusters

Over the past decade, Shaanxi has taken advantage of its convenient land and air transportation, rich human resources and industrial strength to speed up the concentrated development of export-oriented industries, undertake the transfer of processing trade industries at home and abroad, and attract multinational companies such as Samsung, Micron and Schneider to launch projects. Display manufacturers such as BYD and Konka have established manufacturing bases in Shaanxi. A number of enterprises related to integrated circuit design, manufacturing, packaging and testing have enjoyed concentrated development, and industrial clusters such as chips, high-end manufacturing and new energy vehicles have taken shape.

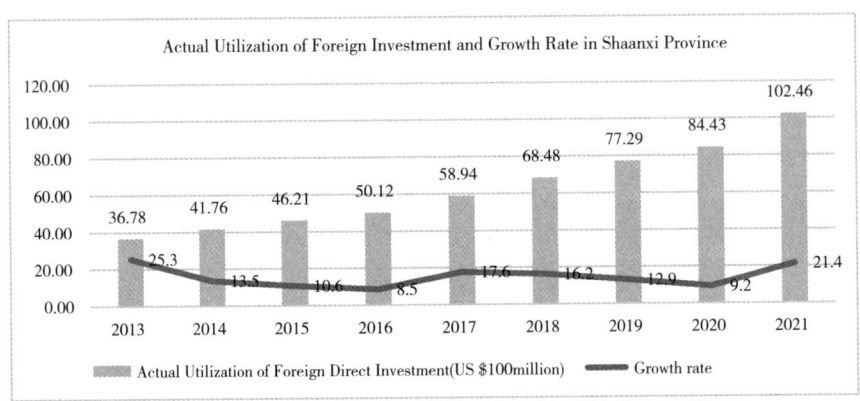

Figure 6: Actual Use of Foreign Capital of Shaanxi Province (2013-2021)

Data source: Statistical Communiqués on the Economic and Social Development released by Bureau of Statistics of Shaanxi Province over the years

According to the data, the global top 500 enterprises have invested to set up 144 foreign-funded enterprises in Shaanxi. By the end of 2022, 306 overseas enterprises in Shaanxi Province have made a total overseas investment of 6.88 billion dollars, of which 1.82 billion dollars were invested in the BRI countries, accounting for 26.5% of the total.

1. The Pilot Free Trade Zone Lays Solid Foundation for Enterprise Development

Since the official establishment of the Pilot Free Trade Zone in Shaanxi Province on April 1, 2017, a number of policies have been introduced to support its development. In December 2017, Shaanxi announced the implementation of the *Management Measures for China (Shaanxi) Pilot Free Trade Zone*. Shaanxi Provincial Development and Reform Commission issued *Opinions on Further Supporting the Development of China (Shaanxi) Pilot Free Trade Zone* in the same month. In September 2018, *Implementation Opinions on the Active and Effective Use of Foreign Investment to Promote High-quality Economic Development* was issued. In October, *Opinions of Shaanxi Provincial People's Government on Measures to Support the Deepening Reform and Innovation of the China (Shaanxi) Pilot Free Trade Zone*.

The Regulations for China (Shaanxi) Pilot Free Trade Zone, issued by Shaanxi Province in 2021, standardizes and refines the management system, investment promotion, trade facilitation, financial services, economic cooperation and people-to-people exchanges under the BRI, western development advancement, services and supervision, and legal protection. This marks the further standardization of the development of Shaanxi Pilot Free Trade Zone and ensures the law-based reform and innovation.

Shaanxi Pilot Free Trade Zone has expedited reform and innovation with institutional innovation at its core. A total of 792 innovation cases have been formed, and 36 reform and innovation achievements have been spread across the country. Efforts have been made to deepen the reform "separating operating permits from the business license", decentralize (delegate) 229 provincial administrative matters, carry out pilot programs to facilitate the entry and exit of foreign talents for innovation and entrepreneurship, set up a talent investment fund, and introduce policy measures including *36 Articles on the Development of Pilot Free Trade Zones in Financial Services*. Shaanxi has enhanced investment and trade liberalization and facilitation, fully implemented the pre-entry national treatment plus a negative list management for foreign investment, improved the "single window" function of international trade, set up an RCEP business service center, and built more than 20 functional platforms for trade finance and cross-border e-commerce, attracting a large number of foreign enterprises to settle in China. Shaanxi has also propelled the mutual empowerment between Qinchuangyuan Innovation-Driven Platform and the Pilot Free Trade Zone, set up 22 platforms such as offshore innovation centers around the world, upgraded the construction capacity of "free trade in science and innovation", and strengthened the demonstration role of "free trade in agriculture".

Through a series of institutional innovation and exploration, Shaanxi

Pilot Free Trade Zone has established distinctive industrial clusters in all function zones. The central area focuses on the development of strategic emerging industries and high-tech industries, including high-end manufacturing, aviation logistics, trade and finance and other industries, to create a high-end industrial highland for the Belt and Road. Xi'an International Trade and Logistics Park explores rules on the international multimodal transport logistics led by railway transport, and prioritizes the development of international trade, modern logistics, financial services, tourism and exhibition, e-commerce and other industries. With a focus on the agricultural science and technology innovation, demonstration and promotion, the Yangling Demonstration Zone accelerates the development in such fields as biotechnology and smart agriculture.

2. Integrated Circuit Industry Develops in Clusters

In recent years, based on its own industrial base, Shaanxi has introduced upstream and downstream industries including integrated circuit design industry, wafer manufacturing, packaging testing, and supporting industry, shaping a whole integrated circuit industry chain from wafer manufacturing to packaging testing.

In the upstream link of IC design, more than 120 semiconductor design enterprises such as ZTE Kris, Huawei, Unigroup Guoxin, and Toll Microelectronic have gathered in Xi'an, Shaanxi. In the midstream link of IC manufacturing, Xi'an, Shaanxi Province, is home to eight wafer manufacturing enterprises such as Samsung, Xiyue Electronics, Weiguang and Peri. In the downstream link of IC packaging, 13 enterprises including Samsung, Huatian, Micron, Powertech, Huayi have settled in Shaanxi. In terms of supporting industry, there are more than 70 enterprises in Shaanxi, such as ESWIN, Institute of Crystal Growing Technology, WaferChina, and Jili Electronic and Chemistry Engineering.

Taking the Samsung project as an example, in May 2014, the first phase of semiconductor investment project of Samsung, South Korea was completed and put into operation. From 2017 to 2020, Samsung Electronics has added an additional 15 billion dollars in the second phase of the memory chip project, with a total investment of 26 billion dollars. The launch of Samsung semiconductor project has attracted a large number of domestic and foreign enterprises such as Air Products and Chemicals of the United States, Sumitomo of Japan, Dongjin Semichem of South Korea, and Huaxunwei Electronics, creating more than 10,000 jobs directly or indirectly. The annual output value of Samsung semiconductor exceeded 100 billion yuan in 2022, and the total investment of the project has reached 27 billion dollars by 2022.

3. Modern Service Industry Innovation Booms

Thanks to the National Processing Trade Industrial Park and Xi'an Comprehensive Bonded Zone, Shaanxi has expedited the collaboration between "land port" and "airport," brought together hundreds of upstream and downstream enterprises in the industrial chain, which will generate an annual output value of 50 billion yuan and a total annual tax payment of 1 billion yuan, and provide 20,000 employment opportunities.

As for "land port", as of February 2023, the first phase of the Belt and Road Lingang Industrial Park has been fully put into service, with a rental rate of 81%. 12 enterprises have entered the Park with 9 enterprises in operation, including Jinghong Display Technology, Shaanxi Shuoda Vision Electronic Technology Co., SEEKBOOC, Warmasun, Deshimei and HuazhanSoft, whose products mainly focus on intelligent terminals and display panels, and have been exported to Europe, Central Asia, Russia, North America, Southeast Asia, Africa and other places.

As for "airport", the industrial pattern has been expanded from the single bonded logistics to the supporting development of diversified industries, such as processing and manufacturing, testing and maintenance, supply chain services, and cross-border e-commerce under the guarantee of bonded logistics. By the end of 2022, a total of 88 enterprises have been introduced with more than 540 practitioners, among which warehouse logistics accounts for about 80%, cross-border e-commerce about 10%, international trade about 5%, and other service industries about 5%.

(iv) Promoting the Construction of International Production Capacity Cooperation Center

At present, while Shaanxi Province's international industrial capacity cooperation has achieved pragmatic results, it still faces problems such as small scale of foreign investment stock, single source of foreign investment, and low quality and efficiency of processing trade.

To continue pushing forward the construction of international production capacity cooperation center, Shaanxi should give full play to the carrier function of cooperation parks. It should focus on promoting the construction of Sino-Russia Silk Road High-tech Innovation Park in Xixian New Area, Samsung City in Xi'an High-Tech Industries Development Zone, Sino-European Industrial Park in Xi'an Economic and Technological Development Zone, China-Korea Industrial Park in Xianyang, China-Japan International Cooperation Material Industrial Park in Shaanxi Coal and Chemistry Industry Group in Yulin, Modern Agricultural International Cooperation Center of the Belt and Road Initiative in Yangling, China-Japan Life Science and Technology Park in the Airport in Xixian New Area, China-Japan Modern TCM Industrial Park in Hanzhong and others, so as to form the advantageous carriers for opening-up and cooperation of Shaanxi to the world. In addition, Shaanxi should put more efforts on the promotion of international investment, and actively carry out online and offline thematic investment promotion, targeted investment promotion and investment banking thinking investment promotion to attract new momentum for industrial development.

Shaanxi should promote the construction of key international cooperation projects. Enhance the quality and efficiency of overseas investment, focusing on high-end equipment, power transmission equipment, automobile manufacturing and other advantageous industries, support Shaangu Group, China XD Group, Shaanxi Heavy Duty Automobile, FAST and other enterprises to lay out the industrial chain and supply chain for the Belt and Road Initiate. Promote the construction of the SCO Demonstration Base for Agricultural Technology Exchange and Training, encourage foreign design and consulting enterprises to jointly develop the market, drive the export of equipment, technology and services, and enhance the quality and efficiency of foreign contracted projects.

Shaanxi should deepen synergistic innovation continuously to promote the construction of the Pilot Free Trade Zone. It also needs to carry out pressure tests against high-standard economic and trade rules, and promote systematic and integrated institutional innovations in the areas of investment and trade, people-to-people exchanges, and financial services. Moreover, deepening the reform and innovation of the legal service industry in the Pilot Free Trade Zone, accelerating the gathering of innovative elements, the transformation of scientific and technological achievements, and the integration of the industrial chain and innovation chain are also important actions for Shaanxi to build the "Science and Innovation Pilot Free Trade Zone". Construct the second batch of Pilot Free Trade Zone Cooperative Innovation Zone, actively integrate into the Yellow River Basin Pilot Free Trade Zone Development Alliance, strengthen collaboration with other Pilot Free Trade Zones, and deepen economic, trade and investment cooperation with the BRI countries.

Shaanxi should further widen open platforms and trade corridors. Promote the integration and optimization of the resources of Xi'an High-tech Comprehensive Free Trade Zone and Xi'an Guanzhong Comprehensive

Free Trade Zone, and encourage the cities and development zones in southern Shaanxi to declare the establishment of Comprehensive Free Trade Zone. Promote the physical reorganization, functional integration and policy superposition of Comprehensive Free Trade Zone with Pilot Free Trade Zones, Economic Development Zones and other platforms to attract enterprises to gather. Give full play to the opening function of the Fifth Freedom of the Air, and support the official opening of Yan'an, Yulin, southern Shaanxi air ports and Xi'an railroad station ports.

Shaanxi should reinforce the support for the advantageous production capacity to go global. Accelerate the construction of key projects such as Longi Malaysia Photovoltaic Industry Cooperation Zone. Strengthen research on international trade norms and industry rules, focus on product services, engineering cooperation, investment cooperation, industry-financing integration, strategic cooperation and other areas, accelerate the construction of cooperation platforms, effectively dock Shaanxi's advantageous production capacity, developed countries' advanced technology and developing countries' development needs, and jointly promote the active expansion of cooperation in third-party markets, so as to realize win-win results for all parties.

III. Expanding Exchanges and Cooperation of Science and Technology Education Center

Over the past ten years, relying on various science and technology innovation subjects and university resources, Shaanxi Province has continuously strengthened scientific, technological and educational cooperation and exchanges with the BRI countries, and gradually formed a clear, well-planned, well-focused, and vigorously implemented system with Shaanxi characteristics. The University Alliance of the Silk Road has brought together 150 universities from 37 countries and regions; the construction of "Luban Workshop" has been further promoted, and the influence of the independent brand of "Qinling Workshop" has been continuously enhanced; a platform system for foreign science and technology innovation and cooperation has been formed, including 7 national and provincial "Belt and Road" joint laboratories and 147 International Science and Technology Cooperation Bases; and SCO Demonstration Base for Agricultural Technology Exchange and Training has carried out cooperation in modern agriculture with more than 60 countries and regions.

(i) Building Bridges for Technology and People-to-people Cultural Exchanges

In order to promote the construction of science and technology center, Shaanxi Province has focused on top-level design, and has formulated and issued the *Outline of the Implementation of the Strategy of Innovation-Driven Development* and the *"14th Five-Year Plan" for the Development of Science and Technology Innovation*. Led by the system, Shaanxi Province has made great efforts to build channels for scientific and people-to-people exchanges, coordinate international scientific and technological resources, build international innovation and cooperation platforms, expand international cooperation in science and technology parks, accelerate the transfer and transformation of scientific and technological achievements, and enhance the competitiveness of participation in global scientific and technological development.

1. Building a High-Quality International Innovation Cooperation Platform

Promote the construction of the Qinchuangyuan Innovation-Driven Platform. Qinchuangyuan is the general source and platform of innovation-driven development in the province. Shaanxi Province is committed to building it into a three-dimensional linkage "incubator", an achievement transformation "accelerator" and a two-chain integration "promoter", so as to actively integrate into the global innovation network, open up the "blocking points" of international scientific and technological exchanges and cooperation, and create a market-oriented, shared, open and comprehensive science and technology innovation platform.

Since the official launch of the Qinchuangyuan Innovation-Driven Platform in March 2021, with Xixian New Area and Western China Science and Technology Innovation Harbour as the general window, it has accelerated the integration of the two chains, deeply promoted the implementation of "Three Reforms" and the construction of the "incubator", "accelerator" and "promoter". These efforts have greatly accelerated the gathering of innovation resources, and created a good innovation ecology. Over the past two years, Qinchuangyuan's brand effect in China is obvious. The Qinchuangyuan phenomenon, Qinchuangyuan ecology, Qinchuangyuan model and Qinchuangyuan sector gradually emerged, the main body of the enterprise, the main force of the talent, the market-led, government-promoted innovation ecosystem is gradually perfected, the machine tool, photovoltaic, hydrogen, energy storage and other industrial chain planning and layout, advanced manufacturing, new energy, new materials, biomedicine and other areas of a large number of small and medium-sized enterprises to settle in the gatherings, a large number of traditional enterprises to innovate, and a large number of colleges and universities and research institutes of scientific and technological achievements transformed in the place.

Sino-Russia Silk Road High-tech Innovation Park is one of the parks in Qin Chuang Yuan Comprehensive Service Center, which has been opened and operated successively in East New Town, Xixian New Area, Shaanxi

Province and Greenwood, Moscow, Russia, and has brought in more than 50 organizations and enterprises. In addition, Shaanxi Province also focuses on promoting the construction of international cooperation parks in Western China Science and Technology Innovation Harbour, Samsung City in Xi'an High-Tech Industries Development Zone, Sino-European Industrial Park in Xi'an Economic and Technological Development Zone, China-Korea Industrial Park in Xianyang, China-Japan International Cooperation Material Industrial Park in Shaanxi Coal and Chemistry Industry Group in Yulin, The "Belt and Road" Modern Agricultural International Cooperation Center in Yangling, China-Japanese Life Science and Technology Park at Xixian New Area Airport, China-Japanese Modern Traditional Chinese Medicine Industrial Park in Hanzhong and other international cooperation parks.

Shaanxi Province encourages capable enterprises to go global to establish demonstration parks with innovative functions. In 2022, the China-Uzbekistan Overseas Demonstration Park for Water-Saving Agriculture of Northwest A&F University in Tashkent Oblast, Uzbekistan, was completed and put into operation. The intelligent water-fertilizer integration irrigation equipment in the demonstration park can effectively realize the informatization, precision and automation of irrigation and fertilization through information collection and transmission and remote control.

Build an International Science and Technology Cooperation Base. Shaanxi Province issued the *Measures for the Management of International Science and Technology Cooperation Bases in Shaanxi Province* in 2014, and the *Implementing Rules for the Assessment of International Science and*

Technology Cooperation Bases in Shaanxi Province in 2020. Up to now, Shaanxi Province has established international scientific and technological exchanges and cooperation relations with more than 40 countries and regions in an all-round, multi-level and wide range of fields. There are 23 state-level International Science and Technology Cooperation Bases and 124 provincial-level international scientific and technological cooperation bases.

Accelerate the transfer of international scientific and technological achievements. In recent years, the industry-university-research institutions in Shaanxi Province have undertaken to implement more than 50 state-level international scientific and technological cooperation projects and more than 350 provincial-level international scientific and technological cooperation projects, with nearly 300 million yuan of support funds. Since 2022, 15,900 science and technology-based enterprises have been registered in Shaanxi province, a year-on-year increase of 42%. The turnover of technology contracts has amounted to 305.3 billion yuan, a year-on-year increase of more than 30%. Shaanxi has carried out international cooperation in the fields of modern agriculture, new materials and earth sciences, and has applied for a total of 102 international patents.

2. Carrying out Multi-Level Foreign Scientific and Technological Cooperation and Exchanges

Actively applying for the establishment of the "Belt and Road" Joint Laboratory. In 2021, the "Belt and Road" China-Central Asia Joint Laboratory on Humanity and Environment of Northwest University was approved to build the third batch of national "Belt and Road" joint laboratories. The Joint Laboratory cooperates with universities and scientific research institutions in Uzbekistan, Kyrgyzstan and Tajikistan to focus on the cultural heritage and geological environment along the Silk Road, focusing on "geological tectonics-environmental change-human development-civilization inheritance", and revealing the mechanism of synergistic evolution of the geological tectonics and environment of the Silk Road. At present, around the aerospace, electronic information, precision medicine, photonics technology, ecological water conservancy technology and other fields, Shaanxi Province layout and recognized the first batch of six provincial-level "Belt and Road" joint laboratories, which vigorously support the main body of innovation to carry out joint research on key technologies, demonstration and promotion of advanced technologies to foreign countries, and play an important role in promoting Shaanxi's international scientific and technological cooperation to enhance the level of opening-up.

Organize various scientific and people-to-people exchanges activities. In recent years, Shaanxi has organized and participated in various science and technology exhibitions and forums at home and abroad for more than 40 times. Among that, the "Shaanxi International Science and Technology Innovation and Entrepreneurship Expo" has gradually become a regional science and technology innovation and entrepreneurship professional exhibition with great influence. Shaanxi has hosted the Global Key & Core Technology Conference for six consecutive years, the Global Programmer's Festival, the China Innovation Challenge (Xi'an) Key & Core Technology

Development Symposium, the Belt and Road Forum for Artificial Intelligence, and the International Forum on Advanced Materials for many years. The first Key & Core Technology Arbitration Court was formally established at the 2022 Global Key & Core Technology Conference.

Actively promote medical cooperation and exchange. Shaanxi Academy of Traditional Chinese Medicine and Xi'an TCM Hospital of Encephalopathy jointly built the "International Science and Technology Cooperation Base for Traditional Chinese Medicine Research," "International Science and Technology Cooperation Base for Diagnosis and Treatment of Traditional Chinese Medicine Diagnosis and Treatment" and "China-Kazakhstan Traditional Medicine Center" to promote the popularization of TCM diagnosis and treatment technology and TCM culture in Central Asian countries. The cooperation signed with the European Center for Traditional Chinese Medicine in the Czech Republic, the Faculty of Medicine of the University of Novi Sad in Serbia, the Embassy of Malawi in China, and the Belt and Road Joint Research Center of the University of Zambia aim to expand the influence of traditional Chinese medicine overseas, promoting traditional Chinese medicine to go global, and cultivating foreign traditional Chinese medicine practitioners. There are more than 16,000 overseas patients in total have received traditional Chinese medicine services.

3. Promoting the Gathering of Diversified Science and Technology Innovation Factors

Building a regional innovation base. Accelerate the construction of science and technology innovation cities such as Xi'an Science City, Western China Science and Technology Innovation Harbour, Agricultural Science City in Yangling, Science and Innovation City in Yulin, Science and Technology New City in Baoji, Aviation Intelligence New City in Hanzhong and so on. As a national agricultural high-tech industrial demonstration zone and the only Pilot Free Trade Zone featuring agricultural development in China, Yangling Demonstration Zone has taken the Belt and Road Overseas Agricultural International Cooperation Park as a carrier, endeavored to cultivate the service system of overseas agricultural parks, and successively established cooperative relations with more than 60 countries in the field of modern agriculture, and carried out more than 500 activities of international exchanges and cooperation.

Continuously enhance the role of China Israel Center (CIC) Northwest China International Science and Technology Innovation Center in gathering high-quality science and innovation resources. Promoting the construction of the Central Asia Scientific and Educational Cooperation Center, the China-German International Science and Innovation Center, and the Shanghai Cooperation Organization Agricultural Technology Training Base. Further play the role of the Belt and Road National Metrology Center (Shaanxi), accelerate the construction of Central Asia Standardization Research Center, and promote the standard "soft connectivity".

Accelerate the gathering of science and technology innovation talents. Through the mechanism of "Talent + Project" and "Unbundling + Empowerment", Shaanxi Province has attracted many domestic and foreign talents to stay in Xi'an for business and employment. By the end of 2022, Xi'an had 3.44 million talents of all kinds, including 1.04 million professional and technical talents, and more than 720,000 talents in modern industry.

Northwest A&F University initiated the establishment of the "Silk Road Agricultural Education and Science and Technology Innovation Alliance" in 2016. Now, there are 96 agriculture-related universities or research institutions in 18 countries to join the alliance, and eight modern agricultural demonstration parks have been built in Kazakhstan, Kyrgyzstan and other five countries. In addition, an overseas talent training base has been set up, initially forming a new model of "university-enterprise-government-farmer" cooperation. Taking this as a platform, Northwest A&F University has cooperated to set up a number of country-specific research centers, such as African Research Center, Kazakhstan Research Center, China-Russia Agricultural Science and Technology Development Policy Research Center, and South-South Agricultural Cooperation College, etc., and has cultivated professional technical and managerial talents in the field of agriculture for the BRI countries by holding agricultural workshops, organizing international conferences on agriculture and promoting the construction of overseas demonstration parks of agricultural science and technology. On October 22, 2020, SCO Demonstration Base for Agricultural Technology Exchange and Training was inaugurated in Yangling. Yangling has deepened the agricultural technology foreign aid training, trained more than 1,100 agricultural officials and technicians for SCO countries. More than 30 lectures on agricultural technology for SCO countries were held, and 31,000 people have participated in online learning.

Legal services escort science and technology innovation. Since the establishment of the Shaanxi Belt and Road International Commercial Legal Services (BRD-ICLS) in 2021, the Ministry of Justice's "three centers and one base", 17 legal service organizations and other foreign-related rule of law forces have continued to converge on the Demonstration Zone. The Belt and Road International Commercial Legal Services Platform is launched to provide a whole business and whole process service integrating consultation, inquiry, application, reservation and handling.

(ii) Deepening International Exchange and Cooperation in Education

Shaanxi is actively taking advantage of the abundant resources of universities, aiming to build a Belt and Road education community, and actively carrying out the construction of a Belt and Road education international cooperation and exchange center by focusing on the construction of systems and platforms, the cultivation of internationalized talents, the interoperability of languages, the study of countries and regions, and the running of schools by Chinese-foreign cooperation. Therefore, to make the level of internationalization of education achieve a qualitative leap.

1. Building a Platform for Quality Education Exchanges and Cooperation

Since 2014, Shaanxi Province has held eight consecutive sessions of the Silk Road Educational Cooperation Expo, with more than 10,000 domestic and foreign experts and scholars participating in the activities. More than 200 cooperation agreements were signed, more than 20 alliances and educational research institutions were set up, such as the University Alliance of the Silk Road. And nearly 50 events such as the Chinese traditional culture display and the outdoor performance of the Belt and Road International Students' Cultural and Artistic Season were organized. It constructed an all-around, multi-layered and wide-ranging platform for educational cooperation and exchanges, and created a new highland for educational cooperation and exchanges with the Belt and Road countries.

Since 2020, Shaanxi Province has hosted the Silk Road International Industry-University-Research and Application Cooperation Conference for three consecutive years, with a cumulative total of more than 3,000 Chinese and foreign experts from more than 60 countries discussing and exchanging views on major issues such as key core technology PR, efficiency improvement of science and technology transformation and application, and cultivation of internationalized scientific and technological talents. The conference builds a platform for cooperation between Chinese and foreign universities, research institutions and enterprises.

In 2015, Xi'an Jiaotong University initiated the establishment of

University Alliance of the Silk Road, adhering to the Silk Road spirit of "peace and cooperation, openness and inclusiveness, mutual learning and mutual benefit". At present, 150 universities from 37 countries and regions on five continents have participated, forming 13 discipline sub-alliances around energy, chemical engineering, global health, law and many other directions. In 2018, the "Project to Promote Regional Cooperation and Development of the University Alliance of the Silk Road" won the Fifth National Special Award for Education Reform and Innovation. The establishment of the alliance effectively promotes the cooperation between Chinese and foreign universities in the field of science and technology applications, innovates new modes of university-enterprise and university-local cooperation, and facilitates the communication and cooperation between universities and enterprises in the BRI countries.

In 2017, Shaanxi Institute of Vocational Technology initiated the establishment of the Belt and Road Vocational Education Alliance, which has been joined by 105 vocational colleges and universities, industries, and enterprises from 17 countries. It is to provide support for the Belt and Road in the areas of applied talent cultivation, professional training and exchanges, and educational assistance in remote areas.

In the same year, Shaanxi Normal University took the lead in establishing the "Silk Road Teacher Education Alliance", "Silk Road Humanities and Social Sciences Alliance" and "Silk Road Book and Archives Publishing Alliance". There are 27 universities and research institutes of seven countries have joined the alliances. By promoting cooperation in school running, student exchanges, teacher exchanges, mutual recognition of credits, construction of education and practice bases, cooperation in scientific research, joint publishing, resource sharing, and so on, it aims to promote people-to-people exchanges and cooperation among member institutions.

In addition, Northwestern Polytechnical University initiated the establishment of the Belt and Road Cultural Heritage International Cooperation Alliance. Chang'an University set up the "Five Central Asian Countries Transportation Infrastructure Talent Cultivation Alliance". Northwest University set up the "Silk Road Cultural Heritage Alliance Preservation and Inheritance Union". Xi'an International Studies University set up the "Belt and Road Language and Culture University Alliance". Northwest University of Political Science and Law set up the China-Central Asia Law Identification and Research Center, and continue to enhance the quality of cooperation and exchange of education with the five countries in Central Asia.

2. Optimizing the Training Model for International Students in Shaanxi

Since the proposal of the BRI, the proportion of international students with academic qualifications in Shaanxi Province in the total scale has been increasing steadily, from 46.6% in 2013 to 70% in 2022. Among them, the proportion of students from the BRI countries has been increasing year by year, from 51.2% in 2013 to 71% in 2022. Shaanxi universities are more and more attractive to students from the BRI countries, especially Central Asian countries.

Shaanxi has become one of the most popular destinations for students from Central Asian countries to study abroad. From 2013-2022, the province received about 109,200 international students. The number of international students in Shaanxi nearly doubled in 2019 compared to that in 2013, and there was only a small decrease in the number during 2020-2022 due to the pandemic.

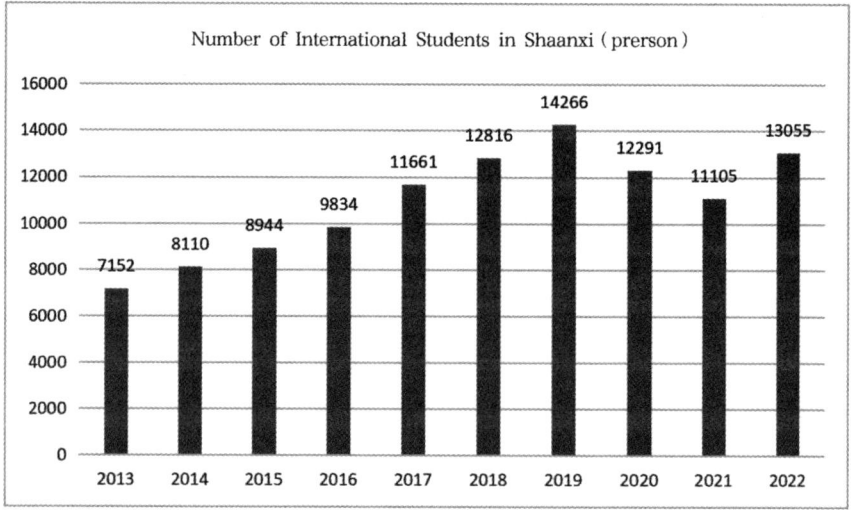

Figure 7: Number of International Students in Shaanxi (2013-2022)
Data source: Education Department of Shaanxi Provincial Government

In order to further improve quality and efficiency, Shaanxi has innovated the mode of international student cultivation, joined hands with the advantageous enterprises in the industry, strengthened the cooperation between schools and enterprises as well as the cooperation with overseas colleges and institutions, and set up joint cultivation bases for international students. By connecting universities and enterprises, it is to gradually form an order-type and academically-oriented cultivation mode of international students, and vigorously cultivate the localized, international and complex talents who have a good command of the language as well as their professions.

Chang'an University and China Civil Engineering Construction Corporation have cooperated to train a total of more than 300 Nigerian students, and signed an agreement in September 2020 to jointly establish the Nigerian University of Transportation. This will cultivate professional technical and managerial talents in the transportation and infrastructure construction industry for Nigeria as well as Africa, and create opportunities for local economic development. Northwest University and Xi'an Shiyou University took the cultivation of oil and gas talents as a pivot point, cooperated with enterprises, and adopt the mode of "order class" to cultivate nearly 700 professionals in petrochemical industry, oil and gas pipeline construction and operation for Kyrgyzstan, Tajikistan and other countries.

The quality international education resources are continuously expanded, and the scale of cooperative education is widened as well. As of August 2023, a total of 27 colleges and universities in Shaanxi have carried out cooperative education with 40 colleges and universities in 14 countries and regions. The number of cooperative education institutions and programs reached 46. Among them, there are ten cooperative education institutions and 30 programs at the undergraduate level and above. The number of institutions is the highest in the west part of China. More than 13,000 students were enrolled in the program, 430 students have been admitted to world-renowned colleges and universities, and more than 640 innovation prizes at the national level and provincial and ministerial levels were rewarded to the students.

3. Strengthening Language Services for Foreign Exchanges

With the continuous advancement of the Belt and Road, Shaanxi's foreign exchanges have become more active, and the demand for language services has been increased. Shaanxi vigorously cultivates international and complex talents who are proficient in both language and profession, and actively pushes forward the construction of new majors and compound language education in non-common languages of the BRI countries. Up to now, 20 non-common languages have been opened in five universities in Shaanxi Province. Xi'an High School has been guided to set up the international curriculum class of Russian language to cultivate all kinds linguistic talents of non-common language at early ages.

Xi'an International Studies University, together with the relevant departments of Shaanxi Province, has jointly developed and established the Shaanxi Province Belt and Road Language Service and Big Data Platform to meet the language needs of Shaanxi Province and even the western provinces of China for BRI, and to lay a solid foundation for promoting the enterprises of Shaanxi Province and even the western region of China to go global. Shaanxi Province has accelerated the construction of the Belt and

Road Intellectual Property Language Service Talent Cultivation Center, focusing on the cultivation of talents for the intellectual property in foreign scenarios, education and training, enterprise cooperation and high-end language services, so as to serve and promote foreign exchanges and cooperation.

Carry out country-specific and regional research in relevant universities. Twelve country and regional research centers at eight universities, including Northwest University, have been successfully approved. Research institutes such as the Collaborative Innovation Center for Silk Road Economic Belt Legal and Policy Studies, the Legal Research Institute for Regional Cooperation and Development on the Silk Road, and the Institute of Silk Road Studies have been set up. The research centers and institutes have undertaken a great deal of research on Central Asia and other Silk Road countries, promoting the construction of the Ministry of Education's country-specific and regional research centers and other think-tanks, and providing policy advice and opinions on the development of educational cooperation and exchanges with the countries on the Silk Road. In 2022, the 16 country-specific regional research centers in Shaanxi Province have presided over or participated in a total of 70 topics at the provincial and ministerial levels and above throughout the year. It has strongly enhanced the reputation and influence of the research strength of Shaanxi universities.

4. Promoting the Cultivation of International Vocational Education Personnel

Actively participating in the construction of the Luban Workshop initiated by the Ministry of Education. Shaanxi Railway Institute-Kenya Railway Training Center was approved as the first national project of Luban Workshop (25 in total), and Shaanxi Polytechnic Institute-China-Zambia Polytechnic Institute was approved as the national project with conditional operation (8 in total). By these great efforts, Shaanxi Province became one of the leading provinces of the construction of Luban Workshop. In 2019, Shaanxi Polytechnic Institute set up the Machinery Manufacturing and Automation Branch of China-Zambia Vocational and Technical College and Zambia Branch of Shaanxi Polytechnic Institute to promote vocational skills training and academic upgrading for foreign students.

Creating the independent brand of "Qinling Workshop" In 2022, Shaanxi Province innovatively set up the "Qinling Workshop", based on the principles of "complementary advantages, mutual benefit, pragmatism and efficiency, and common development", highlighting Shaanxi's regional characteristics and cultural connotations, and cultivating vocational skilled personnel adapted to the international market. At present, a total of four higher vocational institutes have set up "Qinling Workshop" for the first time in Greece and other three countries. At the same time, they have also researched and developed nine state-level vocational standards and supporting talent training programs for Tanzania, which have helped local enterprises to expand the international market.

(iii) Continuing to Enhance the Openness of Science and Education

Shaanxi Province has actively undertaken the action plan for the Belt and Road educational cooperation and science and technology innovation, and has continuously promoted the high-quality development of science education. Promoting the Belt and Road science and technology innovation as well as educational exchanges and cooperation is a brand new exploration and practice. To continue enhancing the opening-up of Shaanxi's science and technology education and to promote the construction of science and technology education centers to strengthen international cooperation in science and education, it is appropriate to focus on the following aspects.

1. Strengthening Policy Support for Scientific and Educational Cooperation

It is necessary to strengthen the coordination, organize experts to carry out top-level design and overall planning, and formulate a medium- and long-term development plan for Shaanxi as the Belt and Road science and technology education center. Moreover, the strengths and specialties of colleges and universities, enterprises and research institutes in the province should be clearly defined, and the positioning of the governmental departments as the organizers, coordinators and servicers of the docking process should be emphasized as well. It is also of great significance to arrange the governmental departments, colleges and universities, enterprises and research institutes to carry out scientific and technological and educational cooperation with the BRI countries in a hierarchical and planned manner to ensure mutual cooperation, high-quality and efficient synergy.

2. Integrating the Resources to Expand Opening-up to the World

To coordinate the science and technology, education, culture, tourism and other resources in the province, and strengthen the integration of resources, Shaanxi may take cultural and tourism exchanges as the first step. And the policy inclination enhances the exchanges and cooperation between Shaanxi and more countries, and expands the international influence of Shaanxi as the Belt and Road science and technology education center. It is also needed to strengthen the internationalization of innovative talents and cooperative research, closely exchange scientific and technological information, promote the enhancement of scientific and technological capabilities, invite foreign experts for in-depth exchanges and cooperation, as well as enhance mutual mobility and overseas research.

3. Expanding the Scope of Scientific and Educational Cooperation Programs

It is vital to vigorously expand project cooperation in science and technology education with the BRI countries and some developing countries. The province set up research programs to encourage cooperation in science and technology education and training programs for scientific and people-to-people exchanges, and guide scholars at home and abroad to participate in scientific research and human resources training in the BRI countries. Also, it set up a fund for the construction of Shaanxi as the Belt and Road science and technology education center, rewarding colleges and universities, enterprises, scientific research institutes, and research teams that have made outstanding achievements in their cooperation with the partner countries, and supporting the training of human resources and research programs in cooperative laboratories and research centers.

IV. The Vitality of Shaanxi as the International Cultural Tourism Center is Increasing Day by Day

Over the past ten years, Shaanxi Province has focused on the strategic goal of promoting the construction of Shaanxi as an international tourism hub, relying on the natural advantages of Shaanxi's rich history and culture, abundant landscape resources. With its superior geographic location and tourism flow, Shaanxi has explored international people-to-people exchanges channels, innovating the Belt and Road related cultural resources and tourism products, promoting the high-quality development of Shaanxi's tourism in different dimensions, as well as enhancing the influence of Shaanxi's cultural and tourism brands. During the past ten years, Shaanxi has organized nine Silk Road International Arts Festivals, eight Xi'an Silk Road International Tourism Expo, and three World Culture and Tourism Forums. A number of cultural exchange projects, such as the "Regional Songs · Qin Rhythm" Shaanxi Culture Week and the Exhibition of Intangible Cultural Heritage, have attracted a strong response overseas. There have been 108 cities from 41 countries have paired sister cities with Shaanxi, among which 54 are the cities of the BRI countries.

(i) Building a Cultural and Tourism Center by Taking Advantage of the Strengths

As the starting point of the ancient Silk Road and the gateway of the western development, Shaanxi has endeavored to explore the historical and cultural values of the city as the ancient capital and the origin of Huaxia, and carry forward the spirit of the Silk Road. Relying on the unique advantages of building Shaanxi as an international cultural tourism center, the province has been actively working on the construction of the brand of "the starting point of the Silk Road Tourism."

1. Strengthening Cultural and Tourism Policy Support

The *Implementation Plan of Shaanxi Province for Promoting the Building of the Silk Road Economic Belt and the 21st Century Maritime Silk Road* (2015-2020) puts forward the goal of creating Shaanxi as a Belt and Road international cultural tourism center. The *Shaanxi Silk Road Economic Belt Tourism Action Outline* provides the guidance on the practical and orderly promotion of international tourism cooperation and exchange, and establishes a program for the construction of a corridor of the starting point of the Silk Road Tourism. *Shaanxi Province the Belt and Road Construction Plan* specifies the development goal of "building the core area of Chinese civilization-Silk Road tourism to be the first choice of history and culture to highlight Huaxia civilization, making the added value of the province's cultural industry to account for more than 3.5% of GDP, the total income of tourism to exceed 1 trillion yuan, and the total number of tourist trips to reach 900 million". For nine consecutive years, Shaanxi Province has issued annual action plans or working instructions to promote the Belt and Road Initiative, clarifying the annual task requirements of the construction of Shaanxi as an international cultural tourism center.

2. Relying on the Advantages of Cultural and Tourism Resources

Culture is one of Shaanxi's greatest resources and the profound heritage of Shaanxi's image. The Mausoleum of Xuanyuan Huang Emperor, the Terracotta Warriors and Horses, the Pagoda of Yan'an, and the Qinling Mountains in Shaanxi are the spiritual and natural markers of Chinese civilization, revolution, and geography. Xi'an, the capital of Shaanxi Province, was called "Chang'an" in ancient times, and was known as one of the world's four great ancient capitals of civilization together with Ancient Rome, Cairo, and Athens. With 13 dynasties such as the Zhou, Qin, Han, and Tang establishing their capitals here successively over a period of 1,180 years, it has been an indispensable and important part of the human history and a valuable asset for all human beings.

Shaanxi has nine World Cultural Heritage sites in three categories: the first is the Mausoleum of the First Qin Emperor and the Terracotta Warriors and Horses. The second is the Silk Roads: the Routes Network of Chang'an-Tianshan Corridor, which includes the ruins of the Weiyang Palace in Chang'an City of the Western Han Dynasty, the ruins of Daming Palace in Chang'an City of the Tang Dynasty, the Big Wild Goose Pagoda, the Small

Wild Goose Pagoda, the Pagoda of Xingjiao Temple, the Grottoes of the Great Buddha Temple in Binxian County, and the Tomb of Zhang Qian. The third is the Great Wall (shared with other provinces).

Shaanxi's historical and cultural heritage concentrates the essence of Chinese civilization for quite a long period of time, embodies the advanced culture of the ancient East, and witnesses the history of the intermingling and collision of Eastern and Western civilizations. During the Western Han Dynasty, Zhang Qian traveled from Chang'an to the Western Regions and opened up the Silk Road. As the starting point of the ancient Silk Road, Shaanxi Province is rich in Silk Road tourism resources and has a large number of Silk Road heritages. In the face of new historical opportunities, Shaanxi Province has grasped the advantages of the Silk Road tourism resources and demonstrated the charm of Silk Road tourism.

3. Showcasing the Advantages of Transportation Location

Shaanxi Province is an important transportation hub of China and a gateway from China to Central Asia and Russia. At present, the Longhai and Baocheng Railways and the Xibao Passenger Line pass through the province, and Xi'an Xianyang Airport has opened 83 international airlines for passengers. Shaanxi Province has been identified by China as one of the important railway hubs and operation and dispatch centers, becoming one of the eight major aviation hubs and an important highway hub. The perfect land and air networks have laid a good foundation for the development of Silk Road tourism in Shaanxi Province.

(ii) Building on the New Chapter of Culture and Tourism

Civilization is wonderful because of exchanges, and culture is enriched by diversity. Adhering to the concept of "people-to-people communication, culture goes first", Shaanxi has continuously strengthened friendly exchanges and practical cooperation in the field of culture and tourism with the BRI countries, giving full play to the important role in the promotion of people-to-people communication, and increasing its vitality as an international cultural tourism center with each passing day.

1. Building and Refreshing the Silk Road Brand to Enhance the Exchange Platforms

Comprehensively build the Silk Road cultural tourism brand. Shaanxi Province has made efforts to build cultural tourism brands such as "Regional Songs · Qin Rhythm" and "Starting Point of the Silk Road - Home of the Terracotta Warriors and Horses", and has played the role of a bridge for the people to communicate and exchange with each other. The "Regional Songs · Qin Rhythm" project makes Shaanxi's outstanding traditional culture to go global through international tours and exchanges and domestic exhibitions and performances. Overseas publicity and promotion of the "Regional Songs · Qin Rhythm" has been strengthened. The activity "Regional Songs · Qin Rhythm-Shaanxi Traditional Culture Week" has been organized in more than 20 countries and regions, promoting Chinese folk music, Shaanxi shadow play, Shaanxi opera, Shaanxi paper-cutting, Xi'an wind and percussion ensemble, Ansai waist drums and other intangible heritage fine arts. It has achieved considerable results overseas. Shaanxi Province also continues to expand and strengthen the Shaanxi Literature, "Chang'an School of Painting", "Western Film and Television", "Shaanxi Opera" and other well-known brands. The province has also continued to work on the key brand projects, such as "Silk Road Chinese New Year Gala" and "Trips alongside the Silk Road", so as to build the brand of intangible cultural heritage projects.

Solidly promote the construction of international exchange and cooperation platforms. Over the past ten years, Shaanxi has successfully organized nine Silk Road International Arts Festivals, eight Xi'an Silk Road International Tourism Expos, and three World Culture and Tourism Forums. A series of cultural exchange activities, such as the "Regional Songs · Qin Rhythm" Shaanxi Culture Week, the exhibition of intangible heritage products, the "Starting Point of the Silk Road - Home of the Terracotta Warriors and Horses", the 10th anniversary of the Belt and Road Initiative and the opening ceremony of the China-Kazakhstan Commodities Exhibition, the Silk Road International Film Festival, and a series of cultural and creative activities in Xi'an, all of which have caused a strong reaction overseas, fully highlighting Shaanxi's status as an international tourism center.

Since the Silk Road International Exposition was held, 11 countries, including Thailand, Kyrgyzstan, Georgia and so on, have been participated as guests of honor, with more than 9,000 overseas merchants from more than 190 countries and regions around the world, exhibiting and selling more than 30,000 kinds of special commodities, and the number of visits exceeding 600,000. The Silk Road International Arts Festival is the first national comprehensive international arts festival on the theme of "Silk Road." The Eighth Silk Road International Arts Festival attracted the participation of 29 countries, including the United States, Japan, Argentina, etc. A total of 58 cultural and artistic activities were held, benefiting more than 3,990,000 audiences, which strongly promoted cultural exchanges on the Silk Road, people-to-people communication and mutual understanding of civilizations. Over the years, Shaanxi's diversified international exchange platforms have built ties for artistic exchanges, channels for business exchanges, and bridges for people-to-people communication, and have gathered humanistic strength for the high-quality construction of the Belt and Road.

2. Developing both Interconnections and Exchanges to Continuously Promote the Cultural and Tourism Projects

The interconnection mechanism of culture and tourism has been continuously improved. Shaanxi is having more and more international friends. As of May 2023, the international sister cities of Shaanxi have involved in 41 countries on five continents. The number of international sister cities amounted to 108, among which 54 are the BRI countries. The ten municipalities in Shaanxi Province and Yangling Demonstration Zone all have paired international sister cities. Shaanxi has established the first inter-provincial cooperation mechanism for inbound tourism in China in conjunction with Beijing and Shanghai, realizing the mutual exchange of tourism information, mutual delivery of passenger sources, market construction and product promotion. The construction of the Xi'an consular district has been accelerated. Thailand, South Korea, Cambodia, Malaysia and Kazakhstan set up their consulates-general in Xi'an, and 32 countries, including France, the United Kingdom and Germany, set up visa centers in Xi'an, making Shaanxi's foreign exchanges more convenient.

The 72-hour transit visa-free policy for Xi'an Xianyang International Airport port has also attracted many international travelers to Shaanxi. From

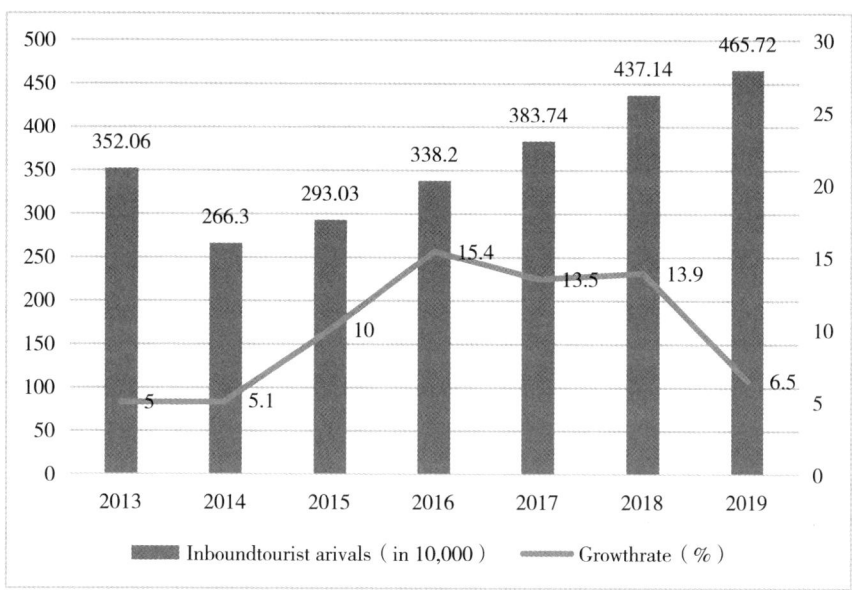

Figure 8: Inbound Tourist Arrivals and the Growth Rate of Shaanxi Province (2013-2019)

Data source: Shaanxi Provincial Department of Culture and Tourism, Shaanxi Belt and Road Portal

2013-2019, the province received a total of 3.357 billion domestic and foreign tourists, with an average growth rate of 16.34%, 25,361,900 inbound tourists, and a total tourism revenue of 29,49.501 billion yuan, with an average growth rate of 22.49% for the province, of which the international tourism revenue totaled 16.228 billion US dollars, with an average growth rate of 12.25%.

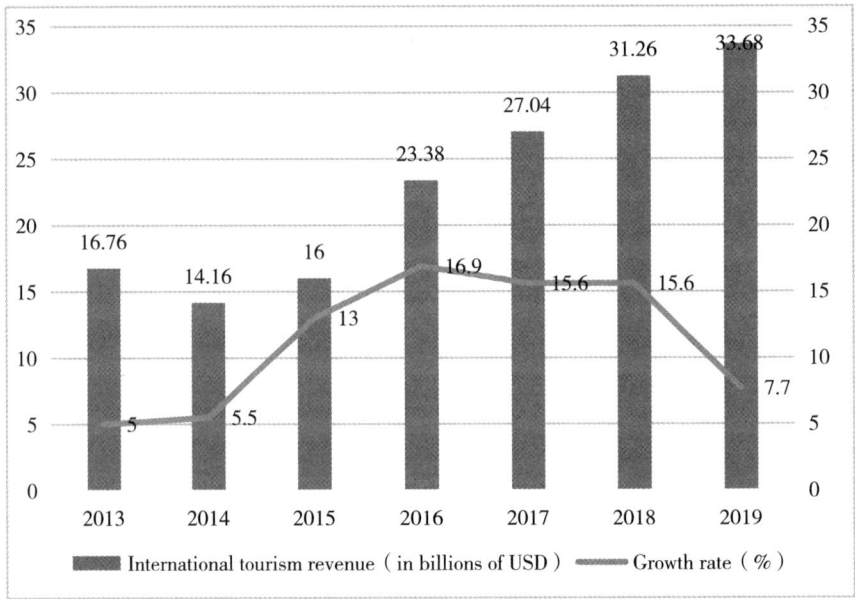

Figure 9: International Tourism Revenue and the Growth Rate of Shaanxi Province (2013-2019)

Data source: Shaanxi Provincial Department of Culture and Tourism, Shaanxi Belt and Road Portal

Foreign cultural exchanges have been continuously expanded. Shaanxi Province has hosted more than a dozen major cultural and tourism exchange activities, including the Tourism Ministerial Meeting of Countries Along the

Silk Economic Belt and the 7th United Nations World Tourism Organization (UNWTO) International Meeting on Silk Road Tourism, and the China-Arab Cultural Journey along the Silk Road - Chinese Cultural Week in Saudi Arabia.

In addition, it has also organized the training program for young sinologists. A total of 130 young sinologists from nearly 60 countries on six continents have participated in training activities in Shaanxi since 2016, becoming the ambassadors for spreading Chinese culture. It also hosted the 2022 Media Cooperation Forum on Belt and Road, in which more than 120 Chinese and foreign media representatives from more than 40 countries and international organizations had extensive exchanges and communication through online and offline means.

3. Putting Efforts on Cooperation and Collaboration to Actively Promote the Participation of all Parties

Shaanxi has been continuously endeavored on the deepening of international cooperation. Shaanxi Province has cooperated with international organizations such as the United Nations World Tourism Organization (UNWTO), the World Tourism Alliance (WTA), the Pacific Asia Travel Association (PATA), and the International Congress and Convention Association (ICCA) to deepen cooperation in the fields of culture and tourism by joining as a member and hosting large international conferences. By building a demonstration zone for the inheritance of outstanding Chinese culture along the Belt and Road, Xi'an was elected as the "Culture City of East Asia" in 2019, and has carried out more than 100 cultural exchange activities. In 2021, the UCLG ASPAC Tourism Committee organized Asia's first Local 4 Action Hubs, the Youth Education and Dialogue, to settle in Xi'an. Xi'an has also been selected as one of the first batch of members of the Lancang-Mekong Tourist Cities Cooperation Alliance to form the Silk Road International Tourism Cities Alliance, which continuously expands Xi'an's international influence in tourism, and enhances the right of discourse on international tourism. Shaanxi Library joined the Silk Road International Library Alliance and participated in the First Conference of the Silk Road International Library Alliance, which enhanced Shaanxi's cultural and tourism influence in the BRI countries.

Cooperation in the field of cultural heritage has been continuously strengthened. Shaanxi Province has set up the Belt and Road Cultural Heritage Global Alliance, linking cultural heritage protection and research forces to form a synergy and innovate research on the protection and utilization of cultural heritage. "The Silk Roads: The Routes Network of Chang'an-Tianshan Corridor" became the first world cultural heritage project to be successfully inscribed through transnational cooperation. The archaeological team of Northwest University is the first team that go out of China to Central Asian countries to carry out overseas archaeological excavations and research. The team brilliantly completed the joint archaeological excavations and investigations at the Rabat site in Uzbekistan and the Behikent Valley in Tajikistan. Moreover, they found the traces of the Yuezhi people after their westward migration, clarified their distribution in Central Asia, and moreover verified the records in Chinese historical documents, established China's discourse on the archaeology of the Silk Road, and used the artifacts and relics to restore the true history of the Silk Road. Following the establishment of Shaanxi Provincial Archaeology Center of the Silk Road, in April 2023, the Collaborative Research Center for Archaeology of the Silk Roads was established. It is to carry out joint archaeological work for Central, West and South Asia, and to study the history of the Silk Road and the history of interaction between the civilizations of the East and the West in ancient times. These efforts have made the international cooperation in the field of cultural heritage between China and the BRI countries entered a brand-new stage.

The cultural relics are like Shaanxi's "diplomats". In 2022, "Terracotta Warriors and Ancient China: Heritage from the Qin and Han Dynasty" was held in Japan. The renovation project of Thatbyinnyu Pagoda aided by China has been officially launched in Myanmar's Bagan. Shaanxi Institute for the Preservation of Cultural Heritage undertook this task, demonstrating Shaanxi's international responsibility for cultural preservation and playing an important role in enhancing people-to-people communication. The conservation of paintings in Gongshutang was shortlisted for the Innovation Award for Franco-Chinese Teams, the "Smithsonian Digital Education Project of Terracotta Warriors and Horses of Qin" was selected as the WHITRAP Global Awards for World Heritage Education Innovative Cases and *The Story of Xijing* was selected as the key project of the national cultural export in the year of 2021-2022.

4. Putting both Offline and Online Efforts to Expand Communication Channels

Therefore, to let the artworks go global. Shaanxi Province actively participated in international travel exhibitions such as the Macau International Travel (Industry) Expo and well-known overseas art festivals, and continued to organize "Happy Chinese New Year" and other activities in Sydney, Paris and other cities. "Ancient Procedures, New Realizations" Shaanxi Culture and Art Exhibition was successfully held in Paris, and the dance drama *The Gate* along with the acrobatic drama *Dreaming of Chang'an* were brilliantly unveiled at the Jeju Haevichi Arts Festival in South Korea. The exhibition of "Qin-the Past and Present of Terracotta Warriors" and the online broadcast of the dance drama *Bronze* were open to the public through the official website and WeChat account of the Centre Culturel de Chine à Paris, as well as overseas social media platforms such as Facebook, Twitter, etc. These events and programs have been highly acclaimed by the overseas netizens.

The mutual communications are having strong momentum. The "Silk Road Channel" of Xi'an Radio and Television Station is the only TV channel officially approved by the State Administration of Press, Publication, Radio, Film and Television of the People's Republic of China named in "Silk Road," which has been on the air for six years. Over the past six years, the "Silk Road Channel" has carried forward the spirit of the Silk Road, the dissemination of Silk Road culture of creating a platform for the display of the results of the Belt and Road Initiative. It has created a number of columns and programs, such as "Walking on the Silk Road", "From Chang'an to Rome" and other programs. Moreover, many heartwarming events are organized, such as the "Spring Festival Gala for the Silk Road Cities" and other cultural activities, to help build a Silk Road cultural highland with the power of the media.

Since 2014, Shaanxi Province has opened 14 official accounts in English, Japanese and Korean on 8 internationally recognized platforms such as Facebook, Twitter and Photo Wall, and has planned and implemented hundreds of online and offline promotional activities by adopting precise communication methods close to audiences in different regions, countries and groups, so as to build an integrated media matrix for overseas communication of Shaanxi Culture and Tourism, and to bring together the powerful force of spreading the voice of Shaanxi. As of May 2023, the total number of followers of Shaanxi's overseas social media accounts was nearly 1.1 million, with a total of more than 20,000 posts, more than 255 million views, and more than 12.8 million interactions. Its comprehensive communication power ranked in the top tier of international new media accounts of Shaanxi's administrative agencies at all levels and the provincial cultural and tourism agencies of China.

5. Paying Attention to both Creativity and Quality to Develop Culture and Tourism Industry

The cultural industry is flourishing. Xi'an High-Tech Industries

Development Zone, which was selected in the first batch of national cultural export bases in 2018, focuses on the development of high-value-added cultural industries such as digital publishing, animation and games, creative design, and internet services. There are more than 4,000 cultural enterprises set their offices up at here. In 2021, Xi'an High-Tech Industries Development Zone ranked the second in the performance evaluation of the first batch of national cultural export bases. Xi'an Qujiang New Area was approved as a national cultural export base in 2021, focusing on the development of cultural industries such as film and television production, performing arts and performances, cultural and creative design, and e-sports services, with 207 cultural enterprises above a designated scale. Xi'an Qujiang Culture and Tourism Co., Ltd. and other outstanding cultural enterprises continue to emerge, creating tourism landmarks and scenic spots such as the Datang Everbright City and the Datang Furong Garden, as well as a series of tourism brands such as "Marks of the Silk Road" and "Culture of the Tang Dynasty".

  Shaanxi has been actively implementing the cultural tourism project-driven strategies. Shaanxi Tourism Group and the Italian urban design and engineering company signed the cooperation agreement of *Marco Polo* water live-action performance, which is a strong promotion of cultural exchanges between China and Europe. Additionally, Huaxia Culture and Tourism City Project, Han Culture Project in Xinghan Ecotourism Demonstration Zone, Zhangqian Cultural Park, Silk Road City and other key projects are progressing smoothly.

(iii) Telling the Story of Shaanxi with Multiple Approaches

Over the past ten years, the construction of Shaanxi as an international cultural tourism center has achieved fruitful results. While at the same time, the province still has to deal with the difficulties, such as scattered resources, the improvement needs of brand core competitiveness, lack of in-depth foreign exchanges and cooperation, etc. In order to better play the fundamental role of strengthening the foundation, to build a bridge for the people-to-people exchanges between China and foreign countries, and to effectively transfer Shaanxi's unique cultural and tourism resources into a driving force for the Belt and Road cultural and tourism high-quality cooperation, Shaanxi shall strengthen the regional collaboration, make good use of the unique resources. Besides, it shall also enhance the level of exchanges and cooperation from a high level of service to the overall situation of the foreign affairs, and promote the construction of Shaanxi as an international cultural tourism center by developing the cultural and tourism investment and trade.

1. Strengthening Regional Collaboration to Make Good Use of the "Silk Road" Brand Values

Shaanxi should strengthen cooperation with the BRI countries, integrate cultural and tourism resources with distinctive Silk Road logos, jointly build cultural and tourism belts such as the Qinling Mountains and the Yellow

River, and tourism cooperation zones such as the five northwestern provinces and Sichuan, Shaanxi and Gansu, strengthen cooperation with Beijing, Tianjin and Hebei, the Yangtze River Delta, Guangdong, Hong Kong and Macao, the Greater Bay Area, and Chengdu-Chongqing, cultivate high-quality tourism routes, and strengthen integrated marketing and promotion, so as to jointly build an international cultural and tourism belt along the Silk Road.

Moreover, expanding the people-to-people exchanges and cooperation in the field of cultural heritage protection, cultural tourism, intangible cultural heritage and other areas, actively participating in the Asian cultural heritage protection action, continue to enhance the influence of Shaanxi Silk Road Archaeological Center and Silk Road Archaeological Cooperative Research Center, and promoting the intangible cultural heritage projects and excellent art plays to go global are all need to do.

2. Serving the Overall Situation of Diplomacy to Enhance the Level of International Exchanges and Cooperation

Shaanxi should continuously make good use of foreign exchange platforms and overseas organizations, and strengthen the mechanism of foreign exchange and cooperation in culture and tourism. Continuing to promote the conference and festival tourism economy by organizing a series of high-profile key festivals, conferences and exhibitions and other activities, Shaanxi will be built into a Belt and Road international conference and exhibition center and an international tourist distribution center. Shaanxi should also strengthen the communication and docking with the relevant ministries and commissions of China, actively bid for the high-level meeting under the framework of the Belt and Road Forum for International Cooperation, and strive to incorporate the Silk Road International Exposition into the scope of the national mechanism of foreign exhibitions, so as to further enhance the international influence of the province.

Promoting practical cooperation with sister cities of the BRI countries, as well as making the cooperation more sincere is necessary. Shaanxi should strengthen cultural and tourism exchanges and cooperation, and strengthen relevant cooperation with our institutions abroad and international organizations such as the United Nations and the World Tourism Alliance relying on various international exchange and cooperation mechanisms and platforms.

3. Promoting the Construction of Bases to Enlarge the Scale of Cultural Tourism Investment and Trade

Shaanxi should promote the construction of the fourth national foreign cultural trade base, help itself accelerate the formation of an important industrial and people-to-people exchanges base for Central Asia and South and West Asian countries, and construct a unique international trade channel in the inland area. By focusing on key areas such as film and television production, publishing and distribution, and cultural and artistic performances, as well as cultivating a number of competitive export-oriented cultural enterprises, a new pattern of foreign cultural trade and investment will be built, which is combining government guidance and market operation, with state-owned cultural enterprises taking the lead to link up with private cultural enterprises to go global.

Shaanxi should also pay attention to the development of inbound tourism, by improving the use of the Beijing-Shanghai-Shaanxi China Inbound Tourism Hub cooperation mechanism, and furthering explore the role of the visa-free transit policy to attract more international travelers. Furthermore, Shaanxi should be supported to implement a more convenient endorsement policy, expand people-to-people exchanges, and continue to create favorable conditions for building an international cultural tourism center.

V. Silk Road Financial Center Pilot Explores Innovations

Focusing on the construction of the Silk Road financial center, the *14th Five-Year Plan for Shaanxi Province to Deeply Integrate into Belt and Road Cooperation and Develop into a Highland of Opening Up* clearly proposes the goal of becoming a regional financial center with important influence and distinctive characteristics, radiating to the western and Eurasian countries, with the added value of the financial industry to account for about 8% of the regional GDP. In response to this goal, Shaanxi has put forward specific initiatives in terms of promoting the agglomeration of financial factors, innovating financial products and services, and promoting pilot financial reforms.

Over the past ten years, Shaanxi has continued to deepen financial reform, encourage innovation in the financial industry, focus on building a Silk Road financial center, and continue to accumulate financial products and innovative services that meet the needs of the BRI in innovation and exploration, making the service and support capacity of the financial industry continuously upgraded.

(i) Building a Regional Financial Center Through Factor Clustering

1. Financial Organization System Tends to be Perfect

On the basis of the overall planning and design of the *Implementation Plan of Shaanxi Province for Promoting the Building of the Silk Road Economic Belt and the 21st Century Maritime Silk Road* (2015-2020) and other overall planning and design, Shaanxi has successively issued the *Action Plan for Development of Xi'an Silk Road Financial Center* (2020-2022), the *Development Plan for Xi'an Silk Road Financial Center*, the *Opinions on the High-quality Development of Financial Support to the China-European Freight Train (Xi'an) Assembly Center and the Pilot Free Trade Zone of China (Shaanxi)* and other policies and measures on the construction of the Silk Road Financial Center. Over the past ten years, Shaanxi has improved its financial organization system by attracting investment and establishing new financial institutions, and by taking advantage of its location, science and technology, and talents.

It has put efforts on attracting domestic and foreign financial institutions of all kinds to settle in the country. Ping An Bank, China Guangfa Bank, Bohai Bank opened branches in Shaanxi, and all 12 joint-stock banks have completed their layout in Shaanxi. Singapore DBS Bank, South Korea's Asiana Bank, Samsung Property and Casualty Insurance, and Fubon Bank have settled in Shaanxi. Qinnong Bank, the China's sixth provincial-level agribusiness bank has been established. BYD Auto Finance, the first automobile finance company in Northwest China, Changyin Consumer Finance, the first consumer finance company, Ruihua Health Insurance, the first corporate health insurance company, and Rosefinch Fund Management Company Limited, the first public fund company opened one after another, filling the gap of financial licenses in the province. In addition, Shaanxi Investment Group Finance Company Limited also opened. The Silk Road Rural Commercial Bank Development Alliance was established, which is the agricultural and commercial banks alliance with the largest number of member institutions in China.

It has also put efforts on introducing functional headquarters-type organizations of national financial institutions. The Xi'an Data Center and Development and Testing Base of China Development Bank, the Financial Science and Technology Center of Agricultural Development Bank, the Xi'an Customer Service Center of Bank of China, the National Card-Making Center of Industrial and Commercial Bank of China and China Zheshang Bank, and other middle platforms and back offices of national financial institutions have settled in Shaanxi, which initially formed a cluster of financial industry in the province.

2. Status of Financial Pillar Industries Tends to be Stable

Over the past ten years, Shaanxi's financial industry has been developed steadily and rapidly, with the added value of the financial industry increasing from 79.11 billion yuan in 2013 to 210.97 billion yuan in 2022. There is a 2.7-fold increase in the ten years, with an average annual growth rate of 11.5%, which is 3.1% higher than the average annual growth rate of GDP in the same period. Among them, in 2014, the added value of the province's financial industry exceeded 100 billion yuan for the first time, and the added value of the financial industry accounted for more than 5% of GDP for the first time, making financial industry one of the pillar industries.

During the past ten years, the average proportion of the added value of Shaanxi's financial industry to the GDP has risen from 5.0% at the end of 2013 to 6.4%. The status of the financial industry as a pillar industry has been continuously consolidated, and financial industry has already become the second-ranking productive service industry in the tertiary industry.

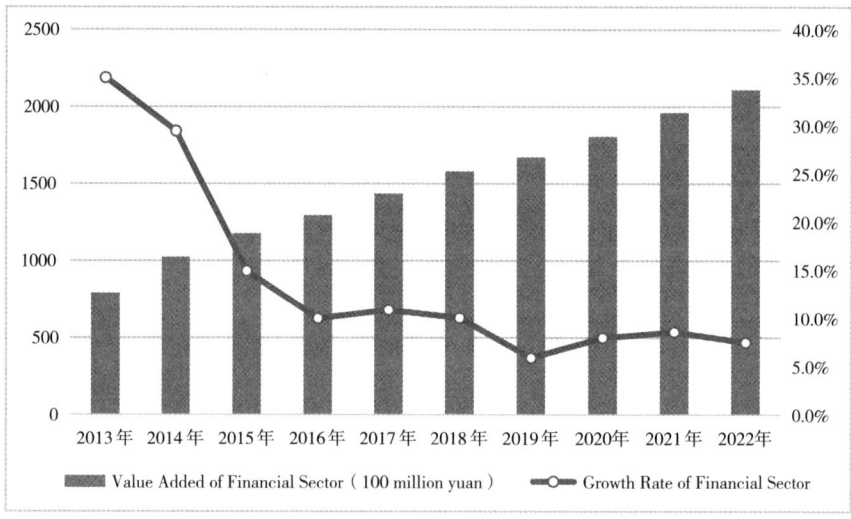

Figure 10: Value Added and Growth Rate of Financial Sector in Shaanxi (2013-2022)

Data source: People's Bank of China Xi'an Branch

As of 2022, Shaanxi has realized 453.699 billion yuan of cross-border payments and receipts, radiating to 148 countries and regions. Among that, there are 96 BRI countries, realizing 181.317 billion yuan of cross-border payments and receipts, which is about 20% higher than the average level of China.

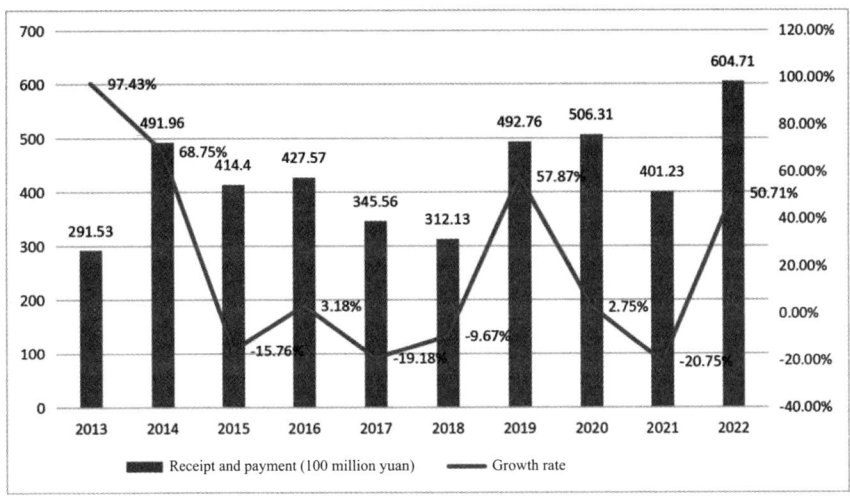

Figure 11: Cross-Border RMB Receipts and Payments in Shaanxi Province (2013-2022)

Data source: People's Bank of China Xi'an Branch

(ii) Strengthening Financial Support Functions Through Service Innovation

1. Taking the Initiative to Carry Out Financial Reform and Opening-up Pilot Projects

Through proactive planning and active actions, Shaanxi Province has been identified by the central financial management department as one of the 13 pilot financial science and technology, eight "science and technology innovation section" of the pilot regional equity market, six pilot cross-border business blockchain service platform, three pilot provinces for independent pricing of commercial automobile insurance. Xi'an has been approved as a pilot city for digital RMB, Tongchuan has been identified by the State Council as a national-level financial inclusion reform pilot area, and the Shaanxi Equity Exchange has been approved as the pilot for the construction of a blockchain in the regional equity market.

Focusing on the reform and innovation of the Pilot Free Trade Zone, the province has carried out pilot projects for the facilitation of capital project income payment and trade foreign exchange balance, promoted the pilot project for the unification of the local and foreign currency settlement account system, and actively carried out the pilot project for the management of capital remittance in and out of the Qualified Foreign Limited Partners (QFLP) and for the facilitation of the amount of foreign debt of enterprises.

The "Silk Road E-commerce" Shaanxi cross-border e-commerce RMB settlement service platform is a representative case of Shaanxi's exploration of financial services for the BRI. Through this platform, a convenient "Online Silk Road of RMB" has been set up for small and medium-sized enterprises and farmers to promote Shaanxi specialty products to the global market. The "Silk Road E-commerce" platform won the third batch of "Best Practice Cases" of the National Pilot Free Trade Zone in 2019 of China, and was also selected as the "Pilot of Digital RMB Cross-border Payment and Settlement in Xi'an in 2022".

In August 2021, the "Silk Road E-commerce" platform was successfully connected to the RMB cross-border Inter-bank Payment System (CIPS), becoming the first e-commerce platform in Northwest China to deploy the CIPS standard transceiver, which facilitates the platform to accurately support cross-border e-commerce enterprises in their overseas development, and further enhances the experience of cross-border RMB payment and collection and efficiency of the enterprises, and saves cross-border payment costs. At present, more than 300 foreign trade certified enterprises are stationed on the platform, involving more than 200 categories such as equipment manufacturing, industrial products, agricultural products, etc., covering 80% of the counties in Shaanxi, whose products are exporting to a number of the BRI countries and regions. As of May 2023, the cumulative transaction volume of the "Silk Road E-commerce" platform has exceeded 50 million yuan.

The landing of China-Indonesia bilateral local currency settlement (LCS) mechanism is another representative case of Shaanxi's exploration of financial innovation to achieve practical results. In order to solve the difficulties of an enterprise in Xi'an that the bilateral local currencies of China and Indonesia could not be directly exchanged and could not completely avoid the exchange rate risk, Xi'an Branch of the People's Bank of China promoted the Jakarta Branch of the Bank of China to realize the settlement of the enterprise through the bilateral LCS mechanism of China-Indonesia and completed the first settlement business at 12,305,100,000 yuan. This is the first attempt of LCS operations outside the pilot area.

LCS was first proposed by Bank Indonesia as a local currency settlement mechanism in the context of the inability of capital to move freely, and was mainly applied to cross-border settlements under current account and direct investment. The framework design of the China-Indonesia Bilateral Local Currency Settlement Mechanism has three major operational innovations: An asymmetric cooperation mode is adopted. The use of Rupiah is strictly limited to trade and investment exchanges between the two countries. Chinese enterprises are not allowed to use Rupiah for settlements with third-country entities, while Indonesian enterprises are free to use RMB for settlements with third-country entities. The introduction of a number of local Indonesian banks in the RMB/INR regional market better matches the supply and demand, smooths the clearing and leveling channels, and enhances trading activity. Participating banks in the regional market are allowed to close out passively held positions in RMB or INR in the market, and for the first time, derivative transactions such as forwards and swaps are supported in the regional market, realizing the full coverage of foreign exchange products and fully meeting the needs of liquidity and exchange rate risk management.

2. Exploring and Innovating to Enhance the Support Function of the Financial Industry

Over the past ten years, Shaanxi has created a digitized comprehensive financial service platform for the China-European freight train Chang'an by carrying out a pilot project for the facilitation of income payment for capital items and a pilot project for a cross-border financial service platform, and has launched innovative financial products such as the "Central Bank-Chang'an Ticket and Transportation Pass", "Export Pool" and the "China-European Freight Train Loan", in order to solve the problems of difficult and expensive financing for foreign-related enterprises. The "Silk Road E-commerce" innovative platform was selected as one of the third batch of best practice cases in the National Pilot Free Trade Zone, and was successfully connected to the standard transceiver of the RMB Cross-border Inter-Bank Payment System (CIPS).

"Central Bank-Chang'an Ticket and Transportation Pass" is the first cross-border trade financial product created by the People's Bank of China (PBOC) for China-European Freight Train. The specific operation of the product is as follows: Xi'an Free Trade Port Construction and Operation Company needs to obtain the bank credit first, and then inversely share the bank credit to the logistics and commerce enterprises related to China-European Freight Train Chang'an; the logistics and commerce enterprises will then issue commercial acceptance bills with interest to the platform company; after the platform company applies for discounting of the commercial acceptance bills received from the cooperative bank, the cooperative bank will pay the freight charges to the platform company, and the logistics and commerce enterprises will only need to pay the interest on the freight charges to the bank when they are discounted on the bills in the first instance, then pay the freight charges to the bank during the repayment period.

This innovative product has constructed a multi-party mechanism of "rediscounting directional guidance + financial policy funds for risk prevention and control + core enterprise high-quality credit transfer + commercial banks' active credit guarantee subsidy", which has effectively alleviated the pressure of freight advances from logistics or export enterprises. For example, in October 2019, Shaanxi Triangle Logistics Company, Xi'an Feisheng International Freight Forwarding Company and Shaanxi Yiwanjia Agricultural and Side Products Company Limited issued a commercial promissory note of 840,000 yuan to Xi'an Free Trade Zone Construction and Operation Company for the payment of freight charges for the China-European Freight Train Chang'an.

The China-European Freight Train Chang'an digital financial comprehensive service platform is an important practice of Shaanxi Province to explore financial service innovation. Through the mode of "freight train + digital finance", this platform provides enterprises with a series of financial services such as "railroad bill of lading financing," aiming to solve the problems of difficult financing process, low financing efficiency and long financing cycle. By the end of 2022, the Chang'an train scenario has attracted 484 enterprises to settle in, and 13 pilot banks have provided financial support of 5.724 billion yuan to 43 enterprises related to the China-European freight train industry chain through the scenario.

The State Administration of Foreign Exchange Shaanxi Branch also puts efforts on promote financial institutions relying on the advantages of the application of the China-European Freight Train, developing innovative financial products and services that are more in line with the enterprises of China-European Freight Train Chang'an industrial chain. Many of the China's "first order" were settled and implemented. People's Bank of China Shaanxi Branch landed China's first international railroad intermodal bill of lading loan of 1.1 million yuan, which was awarded as the "Best Practice Case" of Shaanxi Pilot Free Trade Zone in 2021. Pudong Development Bank Xi'an Branch landed China's first facilitated foreign debt of USD 1.05 million for enterprises in the industrial chain of the Chang'an China-European Freight Train; and China Construction Bank Shaanxi Branch landed the first online credit-only freight loan of 7.3 million yuan, which has effectively eased the difficulties of enterprise financing.

(iii) Breaking the Bottleneck of Future Development Through Openness and Cooperation

Finance is not only the core of the modern economy, but also the veins and blood of the real economy. Compared with the coastal areas, Shaanxi has problems such as low innovation, backward financial service model, and less financial interconnection with the BRI countries and regions. In the future, Shaanxi is desirable to deepen financial openness and cooperation, break the current development bottleneck, and continue to promote the construction of the Silk Road financial center to the set goal.

1. Promoting Financial Connectivity

Shaanxi should vigorously utilize the roles of the currency, capital and insurance markets of the BRI countries to improve the integration capacity and allocation efficiency of the financial resources of the countries. Accelerating the reaching of consensus among the BRI countries and regions on financial development concepts, laws and regulations, financial supervision and other aspects is essential. The goal is to endeavor to build an open, transparent, efficient and harmonious financing mechanism for the Belt and Road Initiative. Shaanxi should also encourage the participation of social capital, actively empower the enterprises and individuals, take the initiative to develop financing channels, and realize the symbiosis and co-prosperity between various industries and the financial industry with the help of the development and growth of the capital market.

It is also necessary to promote the development of multilateral financial institutions continuously, such as the Asian Infrastructure Investment Bank and the Silk Road Fund, as well as multilateral financing cooperation mechanisms, and accelerate the establishment of the Industrial Development Fund for the Economic Belt along the Silk Road in Shaanxi Province, in order to provide financial support for the construction of national infrastructures and the development of production collaboration. Moreover, strengthening cooperation in trade digitization, cross-border financing, insurance and other areas is a priority. And increasing policy support for investment promotion is imperative to the enhancement of Shaanxi's economic and social development by attracting foreign investment.

2. Innovating More Financial Service Modes

In order to accelerate Shaanxi's integration into the "Belt and Road" pattern, the financial industry needs to strengthen the sense of innovation, closely meet the financial service needs of the main body of the economy, and continue to reform and innovate to build a trade and investment facilitation of the financial service system.

Financial institutions should cooperate with each other to explore the new mode of centralized operation and management of cross-border RMB funds of multinational enterprise groups, explore and formulate reform and innovation measures in key areas such as cross-border use of RMB, convertibility of RMB capital account, interest rate marketization and foreign exchange management, etc., which are compatible with the Shaanxi Pilot Free Trade Zone, so as to dock with the enterprises that are go global, satisfy the cross-border financial needs of the enterprises, and provide financial support in the areas of trade financing and cross-border fund management, thus effectively facilitating the financing and communication of funds.

3. Building a Platform for International Cooperation in Finance

Shaanxi should guide financial institutions to transfer capital demand, combine the *Development Plan and the Action Plan for Xi'an Silk Road*

Financial Center, build a platform for international cooperation in finance, construct systems such as financial market rules and standards and cross-border settlement and clearing, advocate the concept of green finance, promote the construction of a cross-border financial risk prevention mechanism, and create a stable and sustainable financial environment, so that it can become a mutually beneficial, win-win, and professional and efficient financial platform.

The role of finance in promoting the Belt and Road economic cooperation and the full use of the capital market to finance in various ways help Shaanxi become a Belt and Road regional financial center, a core hub of trade in Eurasia, and an important gateway for east-west mutual assistance. It is also needed to analyze the opportunities and challenges brought about by the signing of strategic agreements between countries and regions related to the Belt and Road and Shaanxi by macro-prudential supervision and other methods from multiple perspectives and in an all-round manner, so as to further promote the development of related industries.

Special Topics

In November 2021, General Secretary Xi Jinping emphasized at the third symposium on the Belt and Road Initiative (BRI) that "cooperation in new areas such as health, green development, digital industry and innovation should be carried out properly to cultivate new growth points in cooperation."

The *14th Five-Year Plan for Shaanxi Province to Deeply Integrate into Belt and Road Cooperation and Develop into a Highland of Opening Up* proposes to "deepen innovation and cooperation in multiple fields, expand complementary development space, strengthen the joint building of digital, health, and green areas of the BRI, and deeply cultivate new areas, directions, and advantages of open cooperation".

Shangxi explores new areas, new directions, and new results. Based on its own characteristics, Shaanxi has carried out in-depth work and extensive cooperation in the fields of health, green development and digital industry. A number of Shaanxi practices, Shaanxi explorations and Shaanxi experiences are being formed, contributing Shaanxi's strength to the BRI in the new era and new journey.

I. Building a Health Community in New Areas

Shaanxi is a large province of science and technology, and also a large province of medicine. Relying on medical resources, culture, climate, transportation, scientific research talents, parks and leading enterprises and many other advantages, Shaanxi has developed the biomedical industry one of its new pillar industries in recent years. Among them, the development of traditional Chinese medicine industry is more prominent. As early as 2002, Xi'an TCM Hospital of Encephalopathy as the representative of the medical institutions began to use acupuncture to drive the Chinese medicine to go global, and has made initial progress.

Cooperation in the field of health is an important element in the building of the BRI. With the aim of promoting the health and well-being of people from all countries, the Health Silk Road has become an important link for friendly exchanges between the people of the BRI countries. In 2016, General Secretary Xi Jinping proposed to build the Health Silk Road. Relying on its own advantages in the pharmaceutical industry, Shaanxi has been sailing with the opportunity of the Belt and Road Initiative. The industry has been upgraded continuously, with the formation of an all-round cooperation pattern of traditional Chinese medicine at home and abroad, and the cross-border health cooperation has been steadily advancing.

(i) Shaanxi Ushers in the Upgrading of the Medical Industry

Based on the new situation and new requirements of the current development at home and abroad, Shaanxi has gathered the resources of doctors, researchers, government, enterprises and capitals to build an industrial innovation ecosystem and seek ways of high-quality development, and provided a platform for the pharmaceutical and healthcare industry to go global and introduce in by aligning resources at home and abroad, so as to make the international exchanges and cooperation more convenient.

1. Biomedicine Becomes a New Pillar Industry

The opening up based on institutions and rules has created a favorable business environment for bringing in foreign resources for the medical and health industry, and has significantly increased the impetus for the global advanced medical power to seek cooperation with Shaanxi and achieve integrated development.

In October 1985, Xi'an Janssen Pharmaceutical Ltd. was established; in 2014, the Johnson & Johnson Global Supply Chain Production Base Project started its construction in Shaanxi, which has now become the largest supply chain production base of Johnson & Johnson in terms of global production capacity, and a typical representative of the 4.0 unmanned factory of the global pharmaceutical enterprises. Driven by the leading enterprises, talents, enterprises, technology have accelerated their gathering, and the industrial cluster effect has emerged.

Nowadays, the biomedical industry has become one of the six new major pillar industries in Shaanxi and one of the 14 key industries that Shaanxi strives to cultivate in the *Opinions on the Implementation of 'Made in China 2025'*. A complete industrial chain integrated product research and development, manufacturing and clinical application has been formed: there are leading enterprises engaged in traditional Chinese medicines, such as Tsing Hua Deren, Ginwa Enterprise, Beilin Pharmaceuticals and Shiji Shengkang; leading chemical and biological pharmaceutical enterprises, such as Janssen, Libang, Genor Biopharma and Giant Biogene; leading medical device manufacturers, such as Tianlong Technology, Kangtuo Medical, Our United Corp.; industrial application platforms, such as Xintong Pharma, Pharmaron; as well as biological diagnosis and biochip research and development enterprises, such as Lifegen, BGI and etc.

2. The Landing of Major Foreign Projects is Accelerating

The biomedical industry has a relatively strong requirement on airport, requiring high-end talents and global connectivity in cold chain air logistics. With the efficient and fast air transportation system of Xi'an Xianyang International Airport, the Airport New City gives full play to the superimposed advantages of the six functions of "airport + free trade +

bonded warehouse + cross-border + ports + traffic rights", promoting the accelerated landing of major projects.

In July 2021, Guorui Yinuo Drug Safety Evaluation and Research Co., Ltd. in Xixian New Area was awarded the national drug GLP certification by the National Medical Products Administration, filling the gap of GLP laboratories in Shaanxi. On this basis, the construction of Meili Omni-Honety animal vaccine project speeded up. This project will have an annual output of 140 million copies of foot-and-mouth disease vaccine. In addition, the Health Medicine City project in the Eurasian (Shaanxi) Pilot Free Trade Zone was also landed. This project focus on biomedicine, international diagnosis and treatment, medical equipment, etc. With the goal of "internationalized national healthcare and medicine industry base", this project adheres to the concept of "medical treatment, medicine, health insurance, healthcare and hospital", relies on the policy advantages of the National Airport Economic Demonstration Zone of the Airport New City, introduces domestic and foreign high-quality resources, and creates four innovative platforms featuring biomedicine in the Shaanxi Pilot Free Trade Zone, global consultation on the Silk Road, innovation of medical devices, and cross-border electricity business of healthcare products. It is expected that by 2030, the project will form an economy with an annual output value of more than 50 billion yuan in technology, industry and trade, and an annual profit tax of more than 1 billion yuan.

3. The Transformation and Upgrading of Pharmaceutical Foreign Trade is Accelerating

Shaanxi has established a pharmaceutical distribution enterprise organization and strengthened the safe sharing of healthcare big data to facilitate the open development of the health industry.

Shaanxi optimizes the business environment and enhances the convenience of ports. In May 2022, the People's Government of Shaanxi Province issued the measures for *Promoting the Pilot Project of Cross-border E-commerce Retail and Import of Certain Pharmaceuticals and Medical Devices* to support the development of cross-border e-commerce retail and import of certain pharmaceuticals and medical devices in eligible Pilot Free Trade Zones, and encourage eligible Pilot Free Trade Zones to apply for the establishment of ports for the first import of medicines and biological products. This is an attempt and innovation of Shaanxi with the help of the construction of five major centers, and another initiative of Shaanxi to continuously optimize the business environment and enhance the convenience of export, with accelerated burst of market vitality. Shaanxi enhances "Internet + Healthcare" and builds a platform for cross-border cooperation. Relying on Shaanxi's leading pharmaceutical companies, industrial development parks, etc., Shaanxi has set up a cross-border e-commerce sub-brand of big health (bonded) cross-border purchase, Eurasia International (Shaanxi) Health Industry Group Corporation, Free Traded Blue Bay No. 1 Industrial Park, Qinchuangyuan Shaanxi International

Biomedical Innovation Center, Shaanxi Provincial Clinical Medicine Demonstration International Science and Technology Cooperation Base and other international cooperation platforms.

(ii) The Pattern of International Cooperation in Chinese Medicine has Basically Taken Shape

The theory of traditional Chinese medicine is a comprehensive knowledge of life and health under the systematic view. The concepts of "prevention but not treatment" and "make people healthy" in the *Inner Canon of Yellow Emperor* are of great significance in guiding the lifestyle and health in modern times. In recent years, the exchanges and cooperation of traditional Chinese medicine have become a new highlight of the high-quality development of the BRI, and have played a major strategic role in serving human health and promoting people-to-people and cultural exchanges. The *Development Plan for Promoting High-Quality Integration of Chinese Medicine into the Belt and Road Initiative (2021-2025)* proposes that, during the 14th Five-Year Plan period, China will cooperate with the BRI countries to build 30 high-quality overseas centers of traditional Chinese medicine (TCM), promulgate 30 international TCM standards, create 10 brand-name projects for the dissemination of TCM culture overseas, build 50 bases for international cooperation in TCM, and construct a number of national bases for exporting TCM services. TCM culture is striding towards the world along the Belt and Road, providing a strong impetus for the promotion of exchanges and mutual understanding among world civilizations and helping to build a community of common health for mankind.

In recent years, Shaanxi Province, in response to the call of the country to "promote TCM to the world" and to promote TCM in the BRI countries, has established the idea of "culture goes first, medicine follows, and cooperation in trade". By organizing and declaring the international cooperation projects of traditional Chinese medicine with the National Administration of Traditional Chinese Medicine, Shaanxi gives full play to the roles of Shaanxi University of Chinese Medicine, Shaanxi Academy of Traditional Chinese Medicine, Xi'an TCM Hospital of Encephalopathy and other Chinese medical institutions, has implemented the strategy of letting TCM go global, and actively promoting cooperation and exchanges in the field of medical and health care with the BRI countries, and has achieved good results. The new pattern of the Belt and Road all-round cooperation in TCM in Shaanxi has basically been formed, and nine TCM overseas centers, one Silk Road TCM international cooperation base and one national TCM service export base have been built in cooperation with the BRI countries. Moreover, an international standard for TCM has been formulated.

1. Shaanxi's Traditional Chinese Medicine Becomes more Influential

Shaanxi is an important birthplace of traditional Chinese medicine. Since ancient times, there have been many famous physicians, including

Shennong, Bian Que, Sun Simiao, Wang Tao, etc.. They left behind the medical humanistic ideology of "a great doctor lies in excellent skill and sincerity" to the following generations, which has a pivotal position in the history of China's medicine.

Shaanxi is also a natural storehouse of traditional Chinese medicine. According to the data of the third national census of traditional Chinese medicine resources, Shaanxi Province has a total of 3,291 kinds of TCM in the catalog, 12 of which have been certified as National Product of Geographical Indication. Of the 364 species in the national key census of Chinese herbal medicine resources, Shaanxi Province has 283 species, accounting for 77.7%. Up to now, there are nearly 200 enterprises in Shaanxi for the processing of TCM decoction pieces, the extraction of TCM and the manufacturing of proprietary Chinese medicines, more than 3,000 approval certificates for the production of TCM, the annual output value of the TCM industry is about 43.3 billion yuan, and there are more than 80 varieties of proprietary Chinese medicines with an annual output value of more than 100 million yuan. Shaanxi is transforming the advantages of TCM resources into industrial and development advantages, continuously improving the brand influence of "Qin Medicine", promoting the high-quality development of Shaanxi's TCM industry, and providing strong momentum for TCM to go global.

Shaanxi has actively implemented the strategy of "bringing in" and "go global" in the foreign exchange of TCM. In recent years, Shaanxi has enthusiastically invited and received experts and scholars from more than 40 countries and regions to TCM organizations in Shaanxi for TCM diagnosis and treatment and cultural exchanges. Shaanxi Province also organized TCM delegations to visit Russia, Hungary, Kazakhstan, Uzbekistan and other countries to explore ways of exchanges and cooperation and to promote the dissemination and popularization of TCM in the BRI countries.

Shaanxi has continuously organized the Sun Simiao Traditional Chinese Medicine Cultural Festival and carried out the construction of a platform for the exchange and cooperation of new technologies and ideas for the development of TCM. At the 2023 festival, a total of 520 guests from 15 countries, including the United Kingdom, Turkmenistan and Uzbekistan, as well as the consuls general of the Republic of Korea, Malaysia and Thailand in Xi'an, gathered in Tongchuan to explore the cultural resources and contemporary value of Sun Simiao TCM culture, to promote international exchanges and cooperation in TCM, and promote TCM to go to the world.

2. Platforms for External Cooperation Mechanisms Increase Continuously

Shaanxi makes use of the existing intergovernmental cooperation mechanism to build a platform for eligible traditional Chinese medicine institutions to go global and provide policy support for foreign cooperation of traditional Chinese medicine by strengthening exchanges and experience sharing in traditional medicine policies and regulations, personnel qualifications, product registration, market access, quality supervision, etc..

Shaanxi has held several international TCM exchange and cooperation forums at the Eurasian Economic Forum, and hosted the Fifth Summer Summit of the World Congress of Chinese Medicine, "Shaanxi Province Silk Road Forum of Young Scholars", "China-Central Asia Five Countries Folks Forum-Traditional Medicine and Health Sub-Forum", etc., to conduct exchanges and seminars on the policies for the development of the TCM industry, the standardization and internationalization of TCM, and the culture of TCM, which have further expanded the international influence of TCM in Shaanxi.

Expanding the cooperation with medical institutions and medical personnel training are also important aspects. At present, Shaanxi University of Chinese Medicine, and some provincial and municipal TCM medical institutions have established cooperative relations with traditional medical schools, research institutes, medical universities and other medical, scientific research and educational institutions in Russia, Kazakhstan, Hungary, the Czech Republic and other countries, and have signed 19 strategic cooperation agreements on bilateral cooperation in TCM and cooperation agreements and memorandums on the cultivation of TCM talents. As one of the earliest institutions of higher education in China to have the eligibility to carry out TCM education for foreign students and students from Chinese Hong Kong, Macao and Taiwan, Shaanxi University of Chinese Medicine now has international students from 16 countries, of which students from Pakistan, Kazakhstan, Kyrgyzstan, Uzbekistan, Belarus, Myanmar, Bangladesh and other BRI countries account for more than 90% of the international students in the university. The university has established inter-university cooperation and exchange relationships with universities in the United States, Canada, the Republic of Korea, etc., and has trained more than 3,000 Chinese medicine talents for more than 30 countries and regions around the world.

3. The Trade in Traditional Chinese Medicine Products and Services is Gradually Expanding

Shaanxi has carried out a number of collaborations in the development of healthcare and health industries, including traditional medicine, hospital construction assistance, and the promotion and application of medical equipment made in China.

Shaanxi extends the Chinese medicine industry chain. Shaanxi has taken advantage of the fact that 183 countries and regions around the world have recognized the legal qualifications of traditional Chinese medicine and acupuncture to build a "Chinese medicine service chain which promotes the medical care with acupuncture, promotes the medicine with medical care, promotes medical training with medical care, promotes the sales with medical care, and promote the tourism with medical care". The mode has been widely recognized and successfully selected as one of the "Best Practices" in national service trade in China. Through the acupuncture, Shaanxi Province drives the traditional Chinese medicine and medical services to go global, and then through the Chinese medicine diagnosis and treatment services, drives the export of traditional Chinese medicine tablets, proprietary Chinese medicines and other medicines, and successively promotes the TCM diagnosis and treatment technology training, TCM diagnostic and treatment equipment and medical equipment sales, TCM health tourism and other links of the industrial chain to deepen the medical and health care cooperation, and enhance the popularization and application of medical equipment made in China. Some TCM medical institutions in Shaanxi Province have successively opened TCM hospitals, chain clinics and other international branches in foreign countries (territories) to provide TCM medical treatment, health care and rehabilitation services. Nine international TCM diagnostic and treatment (rehabilitation and traditional medicine) centers have been established in Geneva, Switzerland, Russia, Kazakhstan and other BRI countries. As one of the first national TCM service export bases in China, since 2002, Xi'an TCM Hospital of Encephalopathy has received about 12,000 times of patients from more than 20 countries and regions, including Kazakhstan, Tajikistan, Russia, Turkey and Pakistan. Shaanxi actively builds an "Internet + traditional Chinese medicine" platform. Utilizing the three major platforms of international smart hospitals, TCM product research and development, and technology research and development services, Shaanxi provides online consultation and group consultation services for users in Russia Kazakhstan and other countries, realizing tele-consultation and tele-education for medical institutions of both sides. In addition, Shaanxi also facilitates the export of TCM products through the Northwest Modern Pharmaceutical Logistic Center and the China-European Freight Train Logistic Shuttle Line, promoting the development of the trade of TCM products and services.

(iii) Cross-border Medical and Health Cooperation Progresses Steadily

1. The Development of International Health and Medical Assistance is Consolidated

In recent years, Shaanxi has given full play to its strengths by dispatching a joint working group to Tajikistan to assist in anti-pandemic cooperation, helping Tajikistan set up pandemic prevention and control mechanism, and donating anti-pandemic medical supplies valued 5 million yuan to the government of Tajikistan and other institutions. In cooperation with the Extraordinary China-Africa Summit on Solidarity against COVID-19, Shaanxi donated anti-pandemic medical supplies valued 8.3 million yuan to Guinea, and various anti-pandemic medical supplies valued 6.86 million yuan to 22 international sister cities, 26 Shaanxi overseas Chinese associations and organizations, and the organizations of Shaanxi overseas students, embassies and consulates of 15 countries, as well as four friendly organizations. Medical institutions in Shaanxi have carried out online video academic exchanges with more than 40 countries, sharing their experience in fighting the pandemic with the international community.

In terms of cooperation to promote the new system of integration of production, learning, research and utilization, Xi'an Tianlong Science and Technology Co., Ltd. cooperates with Xi'an Jiaotong University, Tsinghua University and other domestic and foreign universities and research institutes to establish a new system of integration of production, learning, research and utilization. The innovative integration mode of production, learning, research and utilization has attracted more than 20 medical and healthcare delegations from Belarus, Sri Lanka, Oman and other countries to visit and exchange ideas. The company's products, such as nucleic acid extractor, have obtained more than 150 overseas registrations and certificates. The products have entered into the global market, and have been exported to medical institutions, CDCs, scientific research institutes, and food enterprises in more than 100 countries and regions in North America, Europe, Asia-Pacific and the Middle East.

2. Information Sharing Bridges People-to-People Exchanges

Shaanxi has been continuously promoting the construction of the Health Silk Road, comprehensively launched the action plan for building a Silk Road Community of Common Health, and accelerated the cultivation of international talents.

In order to enhance international academic exchanges in the field of health care, Shaanxi has organized four sessions of the Belt & Road Initiative Global Health International Congress, three sessions of International Forum on Exchange and Cooperation of Traditional Chinese Medicine, as well as Northeast Asia Seminar on Traditional Medicine Cooperation, promotional seminars of the large-scale health industry in the Yangling Demonstration Zone, international conference on medical sciences, the first Belt and Road Forum for Traditional Chinese Medicine Development, and the China-Czech

Republic-Nepal Multilateral Academic Conference on Medical Sciences, deepening the interaction and exchange of ideas in the field of medical sciences and health care among various countries.

Shaanxi has cooperated with foreign countries to develop a medical and health curriculum system, relying on the First Affiliated Hospital of Xi'an Jiaotong University to carry out exchanges and cooperation with universities in Singapore, Japan, Belgium and the United Kingdom, Shaanxi has undertaken three Sino-African counterpart cooperation hospital mechanism projects, and launched a series of Lourses such as "Lectures on the Silk Road Community of Common Health", so as to bridge people-to-people exchanges.

(iv) Improving the Quality of Go Global Requires Concerted Efforts

Under the increasingly severe international situation, based on the needs of the domestic economic cycle and the comparative advantages of the BRI countries, it is an important measure to further promote the construction of the Health Silk Road by continuing to deepen the bilateral and multilateral medical cooperation between Shaanxi and the BRI countries and encouraging Shaanxi enterprises to take advantage of the situation. "Making use of each other's strengths and complementing each other's weaknesses" is a significant strategy to promote the regional division of labor and the cooperation in the health industry with a larger scope, a wider range of fields, and at a deeper level. In order to realize the transformation of Shaanxi from a large province of medicine to a strong province of medicine, it is still necessary to further optimize the top-level design, integrate the policy, and provide sustained incentives and support for Shaanxi's medical and health care industry to go global.

1. Building a High-Quality Health Silk Road Brand

The Health Silk Road is a complex and systematic practical project that requires the efforts of multiple parties, each with its own role and cooperation, from the government, enterprises and the public. Looking ahead, Shaanxi should realize a greater health working pattern with the synergistic efforts of many parties, make overall planning at the institutional level, and formulate a comprehensive and systematic cooperation program at a strategic level. At the same time, it should implement policies according to the country and the place, and take into full consideration of the differences of the BRI countries, so as to effectively promote the construction of practical health cooperation projects, and build a high-quality Health Silk Road brand in Shaanxi.

2. Playing a Pioneering and Demonstrative Role in Institutional Mechanism Innovation

At the regional level, Shaanxi should actively build Belt and Road overseas medical centers and international scientific and technological cooperation bases, so as to contribute to the sustainable development of medical care in the BRI countries. It should also participate more actively and deeply in global public health governance, accelerate the cultivation of medical and scientific talents by supporting the joint construction of major public health facilities, encouraging transnational academic exchanges and the transformation of scientific and technological achievements, and play a demonstration role in the innovation of institutions and mechanisms, so as to enhance Shaanxi's influence and global rescue and treatment capacity in the Health Silk Road.

3. Accelerate the Go Global of Shaanxi's Traditional Chinese Medicine

Shaanxi should give full play to the unique advantages and role of the TCM industry in the construction of the Health Silk Road. It is necessary to strengthen exchanges and cooperation in the field of traditional Chinese medicine with the BRI countries, broaden the field of cooperation and expand the scope of the project. It is also needed to create a high-level medical service platform, promote the construction of Chinese medicine service export base, Chinese medicine overseas (diagnosis and treatment) center project and other international cooperation windows. Besides, Shaanxi shall also support capable educational institutions to run schools jointly with foreign universities, guide relevant TCM institutions to provide academic education and short-term training for practitioners in the BRI countries in the form of online and onsite training, attracting more people to come to China to learn TCM, and strengthening the cultivation of overseas practitioners of Chinese medicine. Shaanxi should promote cooperation in the traditional Chinese medicine industry and strengthen the brand of "Qin Medicine". Shaanxi should encourage TCM enterprises to move into Chinese and foreign industrial parks, provide high-quality TCM products, and increase the number of overseas registrations of TCM products. It also should encourage cooperation in the establishment of overseas bases for Chinese herbal medicines, and promote joint efforts with the BRI countries to carry out the protection, development and utilization of medicinal plants, and strengthen the exchanges and cooperation of experts and technicians.

4. Building a Strong Digital Foundation for the Health Silk Road

Strengthening the use of digitalization in global healthcare and life health is an important focus for advancing the rapid development of Shaanxi's Health Silk Road. Shaanxi will carry out the construction of infrastructure such as the 5G smart medical system, build a 5G smart medical demonstration service platform, accelerate the promotion of Internet medical applications such as pandemic early warning, pre-hospital emergency care, remote diagnosis and treatment, and intelligent image-assisted diagnosis, and accelerate the transformation of scientific and technological achievements in biomedical and other fields. By building a strong foundation of digitalization and informatization, the Health Silk Road will continue to benefit the people of Shaanxi and the BRI countries.

II. Exploration of Ecological Environment Governance Samples in Green New Fields

With complex geology and diverse ecological environment, Shaanxi has accumulated rich experience in the building of ecological civilization. The *Implementation Opinions of Shaanxi Province on Promoting the Green Belt and Road Initiative* issued in 2018 clearly stated that with the overall goal of "improving green development and building Shaanxi into an important ecological and environmental barrier in the west", Shaanxi should implement four major tasks, namely, improving green development and ensuring ecological and environmental safety; strengthening the building of publicity and communication platforms and promoting communication on ecological and environmental protection policies; improving policies and measures to promote green development; and carrying out cooperation in the field of ecological and environmental protection to accelerate the pace of "go global".

In recent years, Shaanxi has continuously built a strong ecological security barrier. At the same time, it has accelerated the green and low-carbon transformation of the industrial structure and improved the level of green development. Shaanxi also continues to expand international cooperation in the field of ecological and environmental protection, actively participates in global green governance and the building of ecological civilization, providing an example for global ecological and environmental governance.

(i) Gradually Build a New Barrier for Ecological Security

Shaanxi is an important part of the national ecological security pattern characterized by "two barriers and three belts". It is the first batch of low-carbon pilot provinces in China, one of the major provinces in national comprehensive desertification prevention and control and the construction of key ecological projects such as "three norths" shelterbelts project. It is also one of the important areas gathering rich biological species resources and rare and endangered wild animals and plants. The special geographical environment has made Shaanxi "an important ecological and environmental barrier in the west" in the green development of the Belt and Road Initiative. To this end, Shaanxi continues to tap the potential of green development and gradually build a new barrier for national ecological security.

1. Overall Planning to Ecological Highlights

In terms of ecological and environmental protection, Shaanxi adheres to the idea of "focusing on protection and governance", coordinates and promotes various tasks such as problem rectification, water conservation and control, protection and restoration, and puts forward systematic plans and task goals for ecological protection, focusing on building a number of ecological environment models and ecological highlights.

As a natural boundary between China's north and south, Qinling Mountains are home to a huge variety of plants and rare wildlife, and play an important role in conserving water sources, maintaining soil and water and regulating climate. The Yellow River Basin is the birthplace of Chinese civilization and an important ecological security barrier in China. Shaanxi takes the ecological environment protection of the Qinling Mountains and the ecological protection of the Yellow River Basin as the baseline for high-quality development to build ecological security barriers.

Shaanxi systematically promotes ecological environment protection and restoration, comprehensively implements the "forest chief" scheme, and carries out vertical comprehensive compensation for ecological environment protection. At the same time, Shaanxi continues to improve information supervision, build a "grid" and "information" platform to initially build a "space-air-ground" integrated monitoring network for ecological environmental protection and explore a smart management and protection model.

2. Taking Precise Measures to Protect Blue Skies and Lucid Waters

In terms of protecting the blue sky, lucid water and clean land, Shaanxi has taken many precise measures. Shaanxi advances the "one city, one policy" to precisely control haze in the Guanzhong region, strengthens the coordinated control of multiple pollutants, strengthens early warning responses to heavy pollution weather, and actively promotes hierarchical management and control of corporate performance. It establishes a management and control system consisting of "two major river basins - three sections - 25 key river control units - 111 state-controlled sections". It strictly enforces environmental access to key construction lands and strengthens the management of priority land parcels. Data show that from 2015 to 2022, Shaanxi witnessed the increase of excellence rate of ambient air quality on the whole. From 2013 to 2022, Shaanxi witnessed the steady growth of the proportion of river sections with Class I-III water quality.

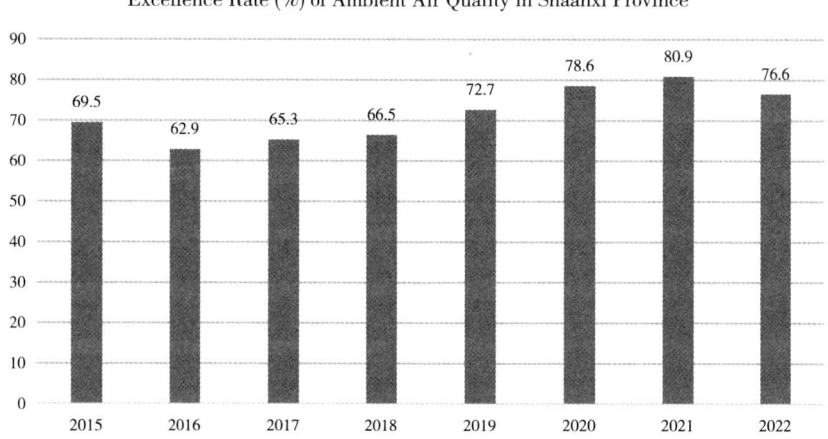

Figure 12: Excellence Rate (%) of Ambient Air Quality in Shaanxi Province (2015-2022)

Note: The statistical caliber has changed after 2015.

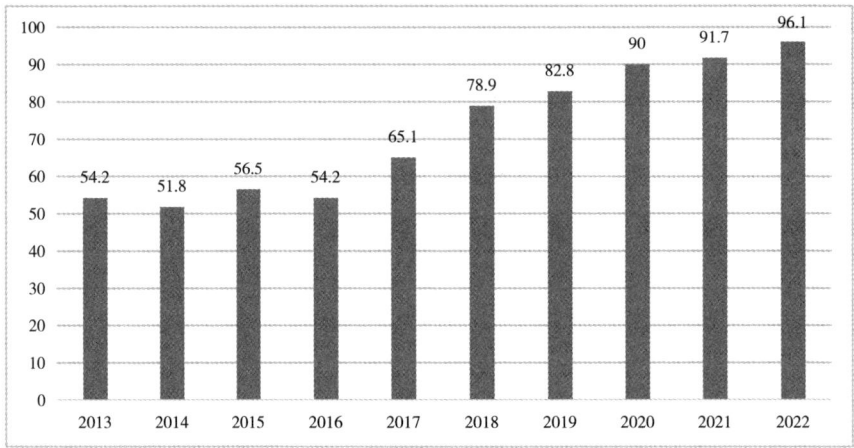

Figure 13: Proportion (%) of River Sections with Class I to III Water Quality in Shaanxi Province (2013-2022)

Data source: Ecological Environment Status Bulletin of Shaanxi Province over the Years

(ii) Continuously Expanding International Cooperation in the Green Field

While Shaanxi builds a strong ecological security barrier, it also gives full play to the concept of opening up in the BRI to continuously strengthen system governance and promote comprehensive green transformation of economic development. It has achieved remarkable results in developing clean energy and fulfilling international obligations. It has spread its ecological governance experience and achievements of industrial green transformation overseas through many ways like international exchanges and production capacity cooperation, showing China's image and responsibility as a major country to the world.

1. Acceleration of International Cooperation on Clean Energy

Clean energy cooperation is one of the key areas of high-quality development of the BRI. As a province with rich energy resources, Shaanxi vigorously develops new energy industries and actively carries out international cooperation under the guidance of the new energy security strategy of "four revolutions and one cooperation" and the carbon peaking and carbon neutrality goals.

In 2021, the Shaanxi Energy Administration issued the *Notice on Further Improving the Construction and Management of Renewable Energy Projects* to encourage and guide local governments and enterprises to prioritize the development of new energy sources such as photovoltaics and wind power. In July 2022, Shaanxi issued a hydrogen energy industry development plan, proposing to build the hydrogen energy industry as a new engine to promote Shaanxi's green and low-carbon energy transformation. With the support of multiple favorable policies, as of the end of 2022, Shaanxi witnessed the cumulative installed renewable energy capacity of 31.11 million kilowatts, accounting for 8.5% of all installed electricity capacity. At the same time, Shaanxi reasonably controlled fossil energy consumption and implement the "three integrated reform" of energy-saving and carbon-reducing transformation, flexibility transformation and heating transformation of 7.7 million kilowatt coal power units.

With the rapid development of clean energy, Shaanxi enterprises are also accelerating the pace of "go global". In recent years, Shaanxi has vigorously promoted the development of clean energy such as wind power, photovoltaic, hydropower and smart grids and completed the Maldives Malé Ring Network (Phase I) project, which has met local residents' electricity needs and improved local power supply capacity and reliability, promoting local economic and social development. It has actively promoted the construction of wind power, photovoltaic and energy storage projects such as Pakistan Dawood Wind Power Project, Adama Wind Power Projects in Ethiopia, and OYA Hybrid Energy Facility in South Africa. It has steadily and prudently promoted major hydropower projects such as the Baleh Hydroelectronic Power Project in Malaysia, the Kafue Gorge Lower Hydropower Station in Zambia and the Jatigede Hydropower Station Project in Indonesia to promote green and low-carbon energy development in the host countries. Through consultation, design, EPC general contracting and other methods, Shaanxi has participated in projects construction such as the 2.6GW PV Project in Alshubah, Saudi Arabia, laying a strong foundation for green development.

Longi is one of the representatives of Shaanxi's new energy enterprises "go global". In Kazakhstan, Longi provides high-efficiency and high-power monocrystalline modules with P-type PERC for the phase I of the Balkhash Thermal Power Plant, bringing environmental benefits to users by reducing carbon dioxide emissions by 70,000 tons per year. In Uzbekistan, Longi has participated in a number of government-led industrial and commercial projects, including the 2.3 MW industrial and commercial distributed photovoltaic project of the Taxation Bureau Building, the 750 kW project of the Almalyk Mining and Metallurgical Complex, the 120 kW project of the Uzbekistan State University of World Languages, 550-kilowatt industrial and commercial distributed photovoltaic project in the State Grid Building, the 300-kilowatt project of Shigan Administrative Building and the 260-kilowatt project of Regional Power Grid.

2. Sharing Green Development Experience with the World

Shaanxi takes the opportunity of the BRI to hold international forums and participate in international conferences, sharing Shaanxi's practical experience in green development with the international community and jointly exploring the future path of green development.

In the past ten years, Shaanxi has participated in the 15th meeting of the Conference of the Parties (COP) to the *UN Convention on Biological Diversity*, held the International Forum on Carbon Neutrality (Xi'an) during the Fifth Silk Road International Exposition, and participated in the informal discussion with the U.S. Embassy in China and Mongolian State Great Hural Democratic Party when they visited Shaanxi and the Third Chinese Arab Cities Forum to carry out international dialogue and exchanges in key areas such as climate change and biodiversity.

The International Forum on Carbon Neutrality (Xi'an) during the Fifth Silk Road International Exposition, with the theme of "Integration of the Two Chains towards Carbon Neutrality", brought together experts and scholars from all walks of life in government, industry, academia, research, finance and service to discuss strategies and ways of China to actively respond to climate change and achieve carbon peak and carbon neutrality under the current situation, contributing Shaanxi's strength to China's green and low-carbon development, seizing new strategic heights and effectively moving towards ecological civilization.

Shaanxi takes advantage of the provincial cooperation bases on the "International, Intelligent, Integrated Platform for Environmental Technology" and the Shaanxi-South Korea Joint Committee on Environmental Cooperation to carry out industry and technology exchanges. It held the 2021 China (Shaanxi)-Korea Environmental Protection Industry Cooperation Forum and Enterprise Online Negotiation Meeting, and participated in the Northeast Asia Autonomous Group Alliance Conference and the First China (Qinghai) International Ecological Exposition to promote industrial technology exchanges and cooperation.

Shaanxi actively undertook the mutual learning and exchange tasks of the "2019 Training Course for Solid Waste Management and Environmental Protection Officials from Developing Countries" organized by the Ministry of Commerce and the Ministry of Ecology and Environment, and met with 24 environmental officials from 11 countries including Tonga, Seychelles, South Africa, and Democratic People's Republic of Korea to communicate the overall situation, measures and results of ecological civilization construction, important ecological environment protection and solid waste treatment and disposal in Shaanxi Province. They also conducted on-site inspections.

3. Actively Fulfilling International Ecological and Environmental Protection Obligations

In the process of integrating into the overall pattern of the BRI, Shaanxi fulfilled its obligations stated in international conventions related to ecological and environmental protection. Shaanxi implemented the capacity-building project of the *Minamata Convention on Mercury*, promoted the implementation of the *Stockholm Convention on Persistent Organic Pollutants*, banned the production and use of hexabromocyclododecane, and conducted investigations on persistent organic pollutants (POPs) in Shaanxi. It has been developing the strategic emerging industries featured by green and environmental protection, and includes large-scale environmental protection and comprehensive utilization of resources and equipment into the key support areas of Shaanxi's first set of major technical equipment product projects, making Shaanxi's contribution to showing China's image to the world that it keeps its promises and actively participates in global governance.

(iii) Coordinated Layout for Green and Open Cooperation

In recent years, although Shaanxi has continued to improve the ecological and environmental quality, its foundation for promoting the green Belt and Road cooperation is still not solid. Next step, Shaanxi will put ecological and environmental protection into the overall plan of national ecological and environmental protection and promoting the Belt and Road cooperation.

1. Deepening and Optimizing the Policy System in the Field of Ecological Environment

Shaanxi, as a major province of energy, undertakes heavy ecological and environmental protection tasks. It needs to strictly adhere to the bottom line of ecological and environmental protection, continue to make up for shortcomings, and build a strong ecological security barrier for jointly building a green Silk Road. In the policy system of green development, it is necessary to effectively play the leading, optimizing and forcing role of ecological and environmental protection in economic development. In the production process, Shaanxi accelerates the structural adjustment of industrial energy, transportation and land use, strengthens the clean and efficient use of coal, and vigorously develops new and clean energy. In the consumption aspect, Shaanxi vigorously advocates green consumption, promotes resource conservation and intensive utilization to gradually form a green, energy-saving and carbon-reducing lifestyle, thus promoting the comprehensive green transformation of the economy and society, while laying a solid socio-economic foundation for jointly building a green Silk Road.

2. Comprehensively Improving Ecological and Environmental Governance Capabilities and Levels

Guided by climate change and biodiversity protection, Shaanxi makes great efforts to promote ecological and environmental scientific and technological innovation, achievement transformation and engineering technology upgrading, continues to expand the environmental protection industry, and creates more highlight demonstration projects, laying a solid foundation for jointly building the green Silk Road. Shaanxi also improves the green development supporting system, promotes pragmatic cooperation in green infrastructure, green energy, green transportation, green finance, green trade, green technology and other fields, and effectively serves the modernization of the ecological environment governance system and governance capabilities

3. Creating a Highland for the Building of Shaanxi Green Silk Road with Green Concepts

Shaanxi reflects the concept of building a green Silk Road in the planning and practice of its ecological environment work. Shaanxi gives full play to the leading role of the major diplomatic event of the China-Central Asia Summit and the equal cooperation role of the Eurasian Economic Forum, adheres to the principle of "bringing in" and "go global", and shares governance results and experience, to mobilize new momentum for Shaanxi's green development, form a new pattern of jointly building the Green Silk Road, and create a highland for the building of the Shaanxi Green Silk Road.

III. Promoting International Cooperation in New Digital Fields for the Future

Digital Silk Road is a combination of digital infrastructure and digital technology with the joint building of the BRI. It is an important measure proposed by China in the digital economy era to promote global common development and is becoming a digital bridge that promotes a new type of globalization.

In recent years, Shaanxi has taken the initiative to expand digital economic cooperation and promote cooperation with BRI countries and regions in the fields of digital technologies such as the Internet of Things, big data, artificial intelligence, 5G, industrial Internet and blockchain, making digital economy one of the important themes of Shaanxi's joint building of the BRI.

(i) Building a Solid Institutional Foundation for the Development of the Digital Economy

1. Improving the Top-Level Design for the Development of the Digital Economy

The *14th Five-Year Plan for Shaanxi Province to Deeply Integrate into*

Belt and Road Cooperation and Develop into a Highland of Opening Up and the *14th Five-Year Plan for Shaanxi's Digital Economy Development* have provided a framework for Shaanxi to build a Digital Silk Road from the top-level design to the implementation routes.

The *14th Five-Year Plan for Shaanxi Province to Deeply Integrate into Belt and Road Cooperation and Develop into a Highland of Opening Up* proposes to increase the application of digital technology and infrastructure construction, vigorously promote scientific and technological innovation, build an international digital cooperation platform, and continuously promote cooperation in the digital field and jointly build a high-quality Digital Silk Road. It provides a series of specific measures from three aspects: improving the digital level, innovating digital cooperation mechanisms, and deepening digital economic cooperation. The *14th Five-Year Plan for Shaanxi's Digital Economy Development* and the *Digital Economy Development Plan* propose to build a Digital Silk Road demonstration zone and make specific arrangements for expanding digital economic exchanges and cooperation with BRI countries and regions.

Shaanxi proposes in its 2023 government work report to pay equal attention to both digital industrialization and industrial digitization. It highlights the key points of network, information services, technological innovation, and informatization applications, strengthens research on key digital technologies, and promotes the integrated application of digital technologies such as the Internet of Things and big data to build a new national artificial intelligence innovation and development pilot zone. It also proposes to accelerate the construction of 100-billion-level industrial clusters such as big data and software information services, and strives to make added value of the core industries of the digital economy accounts for more than 8%.

2. Seizing the Opportunity of Digital Development to Establish a Demonstration Area for Project Library

Since 2020, Shaanxi has made it clear for two consecutive years that it will continue to promote the building of the Digital Silk Road, and clarify specific tasks and division of labor in the Action Plan for Jointly Building the Belt and Road. In 2022, the Shaanxi Provincial Development and Reform Commission issued a notice to solicit key digital economy construction projects and began to establish a key project library on digital economy in Shaanxi Province, including digital infrastructure construction projects, key digital industrialization projects, industry digital basic public service platform projects, and industry digital demonstration application projects, etc.

The People's Government of Shaanxi Province and local municipal governments are seizing digital development opportunities and vigorously promoting the development of digital technology and digital economy. In 2021, the Cyberspace Administration of Shaanxi Provincial Committee, together with the Shaanxi Provincial Development and Reform Commission and the Shaanxi Provincial Department of Industry and Information Technology, issued the *Notice on the Announcement of the First Batch of Provincial Digital Economy Pilot Demonstration List*, recognized the first batch of 5 provincial digital economy demonstration zones, including Baoji City Provincial Digital Economy Demonstration Zone (Weibin District), Tongchuan City Provincial Digital Economy Demonstration Zone (Yaozhou District including New Area), Yan'an City Provincial Digital Economy Demonstration Zone (Baota District), Yulin City Provincial Digital Economy Demonstration Zone (Shenmu City), and Xi'an Provincial Digital Economy Demonstration Zone which includes Xi'an Hi-tech Industries Development Zone, Xi'an Economic & Technological Development Zone, National Civil Aerospace Industrial Base, Yanliang National Aviation High-tech Industry Base, Chanba Ecological Area, etc.

(ii) Digital Economy Helps Build the Belt and Road

In recent years, Shaanxi has been promoting the construction of Information Silk Road and digital economy pilot demonstration zones in an orderly manner. A number of leading digital economy companies such as Huawei and JD.com have successively settled in Shaanxi, and a number of innovative local digital economy industries have been growing fast. The digital economy is becoming a powerful engine to promote high-quality economic development in Shaanxi and promote the joint building of the BRI.

1. Shaanxi's Digital Economy Growth Rate Ranks Among the Top in China

In recent years, Shaanxi has coordinated and promoted the building of a strong network province, digital Shaanxi, smart society, and Digital Silk Road, providing strong information support for high-quality development. As of May 2023, Shaanxi has built a total of more than 196,000 4G base stations and 63,000 5G base stations. The big data industry is accelerating its cluster development. A number of key projects, such as BYD Intelligent Terminal and Chang'an Kunpeng Industrial Base, have been completed and put into operation. Digital economy clusters have been created in various regions according to local conditions, and a large number of digital economy demonstration parks and digital economy demonstration platforms have been built. According to estimates, the total digital economy in Shaanxi accounts for more than 30% of its GDP.

In 2022, Shaanxi's digital economy exceeded 1 trillion yuan for the first time, with a growth rate of 13.9%, ranking fifth in China. The core industries of the digital economy such as big data, semiconductors, and network security are growing rapidly, and the industrial added value accounts for 7% of GDP. Among them, the scale of the semiconductor industry exceeds 170 billion yuan, ranking fourth in China. The digital economy industry has become an important engine for promoting high-quality economic and social development in Shaanxi.

At the same time, the core industries of Shaanxi's digital economy are developing rapidly and their capabilities are constantly improving. Merit Data Co. Ltd. ranks first among the National Industrial Big Data Companies. China Coal Aerial Survey Remote Sensing Group Co., Ltd., Shaanxi Tianrun Information Technology Co., Ltd. and others rank among the Top

100 Geographical Information Big Data Companies in China. Shaanxi Coal and Chemical Industry Group Co., Ltd. and others rank among the Top 100 Industrial Internet Companies, and Xi'an Jiaotong University Jump Network Technology Co., Ltd. and others are among the Top 100 Cybersecurity Companies.

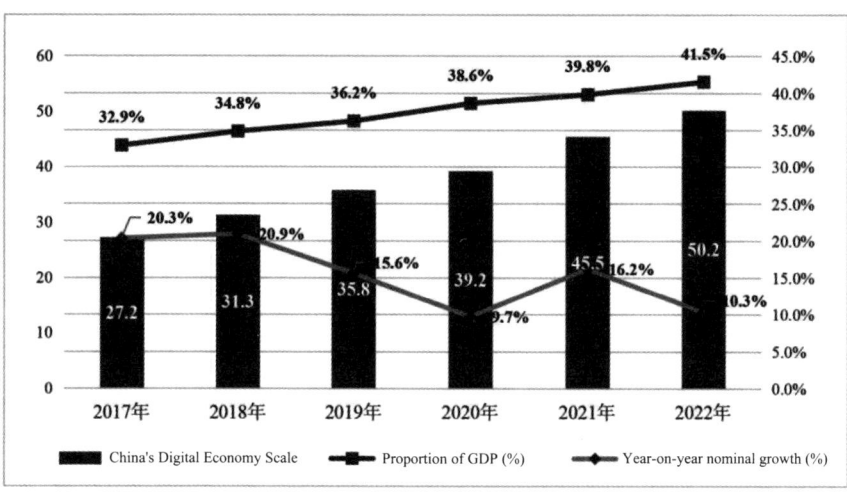

Figure 14: China's Digital Economy Scale and Growth Rate (2017-2022)
Data source: Xinhua Finance, Belt and Road Portal

2. Promoting the Coupling Development of Data Chain and Industrial Chain

Shaanxi takes the development of the digital economy as an "accelerator" to promote transformations in the quality, efficiency and motivation of economic development. It fully grasps the trend of integrated development of the digital economy and the real economy, vigorously promotes industrial digitization and digital industrialization, and forms a new synergy between digital and real economies to promote high-quality development.

Take Shaanxi Big Data Group Co., Ltd. as an example. The Group, headquartered in Shaanxi, with the direction of "operating government data, revitalizing social data, and driving industrial development", has built intelligent government platforms in many cities across China. It launched Shaanxi epidemic prevention and control code platform, digital platform of Online Silk and Road Expo, 2021 National Games of China APP, and unified platform for National Games big data, etc., contributing the wisdom and power to promote the development of Shaanxi big data industry and digital economy.

With a complete industrial system and abundant innovation resources, Shaanxi has significant advantages in innovation and R&D and rich application scenarios in the development of digital economy. Through the development of chain-circle combination, Shaanxi focuses on developing the digital technology application industry. Taking the assessment model of data management maturity as the standard, Shaanxi expands the development, gradually constructing the "ecosphere" of the big data industry. In 2022, Shaanxi became a pilot area for enterprises to carry out national standards for data management, and the first batch of 60 pilot enterprises were identified, including 17 leading enterprises in the key industrial chain of the manufacturing industry, such as passenger vehicles, heavy trucks, power transmission and transformation equipment, and coal to olefin conversion, initially realizing the coupling of the data chain with the industrial chain.

3. Digital Economy Integrating into the Pattern of BRI

Shaanxi grasps the opportunity of digital economy development, with digital industrialization as the focus and industrial digitization as the foundation, creates the BRI digital hub, builds the digital economy industrial clusters, strengthens the foundation for the development of the digital economy, and promotes the accelerated flow of digital resources and elements to advance to the first tier of the global digital economy.

Xi'an High-Tech Industries Development Zone is a leading innovation-driven development zone in Shaanxi and even the whole China. Digital economy has become the core of Xi'an High-Tech Industries Development Zone to cultivate new impetus and achieve new leaps. It focuses on breakthroughs in ground-breaking technologies such as artificial intelligence, big data and cloud computing, network information security and edge computing. It attaches importance to the development of integrated circuits, smart terminals and digital creativity. It is entering the first tier of digital economic development in China and becomes an innovation highland in the digital industry of the BRI and a national digital economy pilot demonstration zone.

Digital economy has also become an important theme of the Shaanxi Belt and Road International Conference. Since 2017, Xi'an High-Tech Industries Development Zone has held Global Key & Core Technology Conferences and Global Programmers' Festival in four consecutive years, providing important support for Xi'an to build a "capital of global key &

core technology" and a "pearl of digital silk road". In June 2023, the first Digital Silk Road Advanced Science and Technology Development Forum with the theme of "Sharing Digital Achievements and Creating a Digital Future" was held in Xi'an, aiming to promote pragmatic cooperation in the field of industrial Internet between China's scientific and technological enterprises in the field of Internet and advanced manufacturing and the member countries of Shanghai Cooperation Organization and expand opening up.

(iii) The Cross-Border E-Commerce Industry Chain and Ecosystem are Initially Formed

1. Cross-Border E-Commerce Comprehensive Pilot Zone Accelerates the Formation of Cross-Border E-Commerce Industry

At present, a cross-border e-commerce industry chain and ecosystem have initially taken shape in Shaanxi Province. Since the State Council officially approved the establishment of China (Xi'an) Cross-border E-Commerce Comprehensive Pilot Zone on July 24, 2018, Xi'an has successively established 9 pilot demonstration zones in three batches, including Airport New City, International Trade and Logistics Park, Qujiang New District, High-Tech Industries Development Zone, Economic & Technological Development Zone, and Beilin District, basically forming the development pattern of the cross-border e-commerce industry. Shaanxi has introduced well-known domestic cross-border e-commerce companies such as Kaola Online Shopping and Cainiao, and accommodates more than 1,300 companies engaged in cross-border e-commerce and related business, involving more than 30,000 employees. As of the end of 2022, Xi'an is home to more than 1,800 companies engaged in cross-border e-commerce and related business, with a cross-border e-commerce transaction volume of 14.427 billion yuan, a year-on-year increase of 46.4%. The cross-border e-commerce is growing rapidly and has become a new driving force for the development of the export-oriented economy.

2. Multiple Channels Jointly Promote the Agglomeration and Growth of Cross-Border E-Commerce

Xi'an relies on channels such as air and rail ports and comprehensive bonded zones to jointly promote the agglomeration and growth of its cross-border e-commerce industry. Since 2021, Xi'an has focused on building a national gathering center for cross-border e-commerce by the Chang'an China-Europe freight train, and implemented a new model of "packing after customs declaration" for cross-border e-commerce bulk cargo, shortening the customs clearance time by 2 to 3 days. In 2022, Xi'an launched a total of 198 cross-border e-commerce freight trains, achieving a cross-border e-commerce transaction volume of 3.51 billion yuan, a year-on-year increase of 40%.

Developing digital economy is important for accelerating industrial transformation and upgrading and enhancing independent innovation. The building of the Ddigital Silk Road is conducive to improving international competitiveness and influence of the BRI countries at a faster pace. Shaanxi will continue to promote opening up while building the Digital Silk Road, form a "community of interests" with the BRI countries, and finally form a "community with a shared future".

(iv) High-quality Development of the BRI Requires Digital Momentum

On the new journey, Shaanxi, taking the connectivity of digital infrastructure as the starting point, the deep integration of the digital economy and the real economy as the core, and core technologies as the key, promotes the healthy development of cross-border e-commerce and digital trade, to provide digital momentum for the high-quality development of the BRI.

1. Collaboratively Promoting Shaanxi Digital Industrialization and Industrial Digitization

Shaanxi vigorously promotes the integrated development of the digital economy and the real economy, and promotes investment in new infrastructure such as 5G, Internet of Things, artificial intelligence, and industrial Internet. It guides and drives digital development with the construction of digital government. Based on the building of Qinchuangyuan innovation-driven platform, it gives full play to the scientific, educational and industrial advantages, promotes the industrialization of digital elements and the high-level development of electronic information manufacturing, software and information service industries, and promotes industrial development such as the Internet of Things, big data, cloud computing and artificial intelligence, to create a new generation of information technology industry clusters with international competitiveness, guide the high-level concentrated development of the digital economy, and form a distinctive digital industry ecology.

2. Enhancing Shaanxi's Influence in Digital economy through International Exchanges and Interactions

Shaanxi actively builds an international digital cooperation platform, gives full play to the role of international digital economy events such as the Global Programmers' Festival, the Global Key & Core Technology Conferences, and the "Digital Silk Road" Advanced Technology Development Forum, and expand Shaanxi's influence in the development of the digital economy of the BRI. It encourages relevant enterprises to "go global", promotes international exchanges and cooperation in infrastructure construction, digital economic development, network security and other aspects, and continues to explore and carry out pilot projects such as cross-border circulation of data elements and digital trade.

3. Establishing Standards and Rule Systems for Digital Silk Road

Shaanxi gives full play to the role of the Silk Road Arbitration Center of the China International Economic and Trade Arbitration Commission and the China (Xi'an) Intellectual Property Protection Center, establishes the Belt and Road Industrial Intellectual Property Alliance, and explores the building of the Belt and Road Intellectual Property Protection Demonstration Zone, to provide intellectual property support for high-quality development of the digital economy. Standards and rule systems are also gradually established to assist the building of the Digital Silk Road.

Prospect

Prospect

In May 2023, the first China-Central Asia Summit was held in Xi'an, Shaanxi. On the occasion of the 10th anniversary of the Belt and Road Initiative (BRI), the world's attention once again focused on the starting point of the ancient Silk Road, Xi'an, and Shaanxi is facing new opportunities to promote the joint building of the BRI.

General Secretary Xi Jinping listened to the reports on the work of the CPC Shaanxi Provincial Committee and the provincial government before the China-Central Asia Summit. He pointed out that Shaanxi should open up wider and develop the inland province into a highland for reform and opening up, integrate and serve the new development pattern more proactively, and be more deeply integrated into the overall pattern of jointly building the BRI, so as to strengthen Shaanxi's momentum and vitality in expanding opening up and open a new development landscape.

The blueprint is drawn and the trumpet is blown. Faced with higher requirements of promoting high-quality development of the BRI under the new situation, Shaanxi will focus on the overall situation of China, give full play to its own advantages, clarify the main direction to integrate more deeply into the overall pattern of the BRI and develop the inland province into a highland for opening up. Shaanxi will strive to promote the implementation of the outcomes of the China-Central Asia Summit related to Shaanxi, continue to amplify the effect of the summit, actively expand areas of cooperation, strive to cultivate more new growth points, and establish a firm concept of openness, enhance openness awareness, to proactively integrate into and serve the building of new development pattern, promote high-level opening up, continuously enhance development momentum and vitality, and strive to open a new development landscape.

I. Clarifying the Main Direction and Making up for the Biggest Shortcomings of Openness

Insufficient opening up is the biggest shortcoming restricting the development of Shaanxi. With relatively low starting point for opening up and weak economic development foundation, Shaanxi still lags far behind the frontier areas of reform and opening up even after ten years of catching up. In 2022, Shaanxi's import and export volume only accounted for 1.1% of China's total volume. Its foreign capital utilization and outward direct investment accounted for 0.8% and 0.4%, respectively, and its per capita GDP is only half of the national average.

On the new journey of high-quality development of the BRI, Shaanxi will continue to strengthen top-level design, further improve the planning system, responsibility system, security system, and assessment system, strengthen coordination to gather joint efforts and clarify the main direction of the development. Shaanxi will play its role as a hub for transportation, clarify the key direction towards Central Asia, South Asia and West Asia, and continuously make up for the biggest shortcoming of opening up, making it more effective to develop the inland province into a highland for reform and opening up and promote the high-quality development of the BR further.

(i) The Role as Transportation and Logistics Hub is More Prominent

"Hard connectivity" of infrastructure is spotlighted. Shaanxi, located in an important area of the Asia-Europe land-sea trade corridor, is connected to the Western Land-Sea Corridor, which will continue to improve Shaanxi's international transportation hub level. In the future, Shaanxi will actively participate in the construction of the New Land-Sea Corridor in the West, give full play to the role of Xi'an as a gathering center for China-Europe freight trains, continue to enhance its radiating and driving role, further promoting the integration of ports, industries, trade, and cities. It will accelerate the formation of important opening channels for countries in Central Asia, South Asia and West Asia, and play a greater role in promoting domestic and international dual circulation.

(ii) The Key Directions towards Central Asia, South Asia and West Asia are Clearer

According to the location characteristics, Shaanxi will become the frontier of China's opening up to the west. Shaanxi is located on the main channel of the Eurasian Continental Bridge. Its original disadvantage of far away from the sea or border will gradually be transformed into the advantage of connecting the east and west and also connecting the north and the south. Opening up to and cooperation with Central Asia, South Asia, and West Asia will become Shaanxi's mission in the new stage, and it is also a necessary condition for Shaanxi to build a new development pattern that takes the domestic market as the mainstay while letting internal and external markets boost each other.

Under the new situation, Shaanxi has become one of the important regions opening up to Central Asia. The *Xi'an Declaration of the China-Central Asia Summit* and a series of important consensuses and institutional arrangements at the first China-Central Asia Summit have laid a solid foundation for Shaanxi to promote closer ties in the Central Asian region in economy, trade, culture and other aspects. Targeting the Central Asia and achieving common prosperity and development has become one of the main directions for Shaanxi to integrate into the overall pattern of the BRI.

Regional economic assistance will also become an important way for Shaanxi's opening up and development. In June 2023, the *Regional Comprehensive Economic Partnership* (RCEP) officially came into effect for the Philippines, marking that the free trade area with the world's largest population, largest economic and trade scale, and most development potential has entered a new stage of comprehensive implementation. Shaanxi actively participates in the implementation of the agreement, with its import, export and utilization of investment from trading partners growing steadily. With the RCEP taking full effect, Shaanxi will continue to improve the level of cooperation with Southeast Asian countries.

(iii) Developing the Inland Province into a Highland for Reform and Opening up is more Proactive

The joint building of the BRI is oriented by openness, adheres to the principle of mutual benefit and win-win cooperation, and builds an open cooperation platform to promote an open economy. For Shaanxi, which is located in the inland area, participating in the joint building of the BRI is an important way to promote the opening up to the outside and reform inside. It will help Shaanxi break the biggest shortcomings of insufficient openness that restricts its development and offer assistance in developing the inland province into a highland for reform and opening up.

High-quality development of the BRI and high-quality regional development are mutually prerequisites. By implementing the rules-based, open, transparent, and inclusive BRI multilateral trading system, promoting trade and investment liberalization and facilitation, and jointly building high-standard free trade zones, Shaanxi will continue to strengthen high-quality project support, create sound business environment, and improve modernization level of governance system and governance capabilities.

II. Giving Full Play to its Own Characteristics to Achieve New Breakthroughs in Key Areas

Achieving new breakthroughs in key areas based on its own characteristics is not only Shaanxi's responsibility to promote the joint building of the BRI in the future, but also a smooth way for Shaanxi to better play its role. Shaanxi will leverage its long history, cultural diversity and rich unique advantages in agriculture, health, green and other fields to create a "regional window" for mutual learning among civilizations, so as to further leverage its own characteristics to achieve new breakthroughs in multiple fields and levels.

(i) Cooperation in the Agricultural Field of the BRI is More Pragmatic

Shaanxi is an important agricultural province in China and plays an important role in demonstrating and leading agricultural cooperation under the BRI. With the establishment of the SCO Demonstration Base for Agricultural Technology Exchange and Training in the Yangling Demonstration Zone and the successive successful holding of the China

Yangling Agricultural High-tech Fair, Shaanxi has become an important representative of in-depth cooperation and exchanges between China and other countries in the agricultural field.

Looking forward to the future, Shaanxi, as a major agricultural province, will continue to give full play to its own advantages, take the initiative to carry out more pragmatic cooperation with the BRI countries in agriculture that benefits the most basic welfare of people, and promote cooperation to become more international, market-oriented and professional. Shaanxi will drive the BRI countries to jointly develop agriculture, promote agricultural planting technologies, varieties, and models, so that high-quality agriculture can benefit people in the BRI countries and even the whole world.

(ii) Cooperation in Health, Green Development and Other New Fields is closer

Shaanxi has rich traditional Chinese medicine (TCM) culture and is also an important province for TCM and biopharmaceuticals. Based on the previous international cooperation in TCM and other fields, Shaanxi will further promote the TCM to "go global", attract more international students and medical staff to study in Shaanxi, promote the inheritance and innovation of TCM, and carry forward the traditional culture of TCM. It will also promote people-to-people ties with the BRI countries, better advance the globalization of the TCM, and contribute the strength of Shaanxi TCM to the jointly building of a community of common health for mankind.

Creating a "Shaanxi model" of beautiful China and participating in global green governance are becoming one of the important features of Shaanxi. With the establishment of a long-term mechanism for normalizing the ecological environment protection in the Qinling Mountains and the ecological protection in the Yellow River Basin, the industrial structure is transformed and upgraded to the green and low-carbon, the quality and efficiency of leading green new energy enterprises is improved, and the level of green development continues improving. Shaanxi will gradually become an important participant, contributor and leader in the construction of global ecological civilization, injecting more distinctive green power into the ecological and environmental governance of the BRI countries.

(iii) The "Regional Window" for Realizing Mutual Learning Among Civilizations is Clearer

The joint building of the BRI provides a platform for cultural exchanges and mutual learning among civilizations of different countries. As the starting point of the ancient Silk Road, Xi'an is one of the main areas for the inheritance and demonstration of China's excellent traditional culture. Looking forward to the future, Shaanxi will take the opportunity of exploring the building of Xi'an's Belt and Road comprehensive experimental zone to implement the Chinese civilization logo protection project, build a city with the roots of Chinese civilization and a "natural history museum", protect the style of the ancient capital with thousands of years of history, and highlight the unique charm of the world's historical and cultural city. Xi'an will continue to deepen exchanges and cooperation with the BRI countries in the fields of cultural tourism, cultural relics and archaeology, and historical research, and continue to enhance Xi'an's international influence.

A single flower does not make a spring. Shaanxi's historical and cultural resources cover southern Shaanxi, northern Shaanxi and Guanzhong. The red culture and grassland culture in northern Shaanxi, the cultures of Zhou, Qin, Han and Tang dynasties in Guanzhong, and the Han and Ba cultures in southern Shaanxi are all important carriers of China's excellent traditional culture and have important influence that transcends geographical location. Those cultures are an important channel for cultural exchanges and mutual learning among civilizations between China and other countries in the world. In the future, Shaanxi will give full play to its local advantages, strengthen dialogue and exchanges with the BRI countries, and become a distinctive, pragmatic and in-depth "regional window" for external exchanges.

Cultural exchanges and mutual learning among civilizations have always been mutual, and overseas learning and exchanges are equally important. Shaanxi will give full play to its advantages as a province with cultural and tourism resources, strengthen its cultural confidence, actively build platforms, expand channels, innovate mechanisms and strengthen cooperation with the BRI countries. It will also explore new cultural exchange models and carriers such as the cultural train of China-Europe Railway Express (Xi'an) to achieve multi-level exchanges and communications with the BRI countries to enhance mutual understanding.

III. Deepen Innovation and Release Endogenous Power for High-Quality Development

The BRI has become a new platform for innovative development of the BRI countries, a driving force for achieving leapfrog development, and a new momentum for world economic development. Shaanxi will coordinate the three major driving forces of reform, opening up and innovation, further deepen reform, and deeply integrate into the overall pattern of the BRI to promote innovation-driven development, resolutely remove difficulties and blockages that restrict high-quality development, and continue releasing its inherent potential.

(i) The Radiation Effect of Xi'an as "Double Centers" is More Obvious

In 2023, Xi'an was approved to build a comprehensive science center and a science and technology innovation center (hereinafter referred to as the "dual centers"), becoming the fourth city to be approved to build a "dual centers" after Beijing, Shanghai and the Guangdong-Hong Kong-Macao Greater Bay Area. It marks that Xi'an's scientific and technological innovation has entered a new stage of high-quality development. Promoting the construction of "dual centers" will achieve the goal of creating a source of hard science and technology innovation with global influence, a cutting-edge and leading emerging industry hub and the first choice for top talents involved in the BRI.

Xi'an Comprehensive Science Center consists of "one core and two wings". The "one core" is located in the Silk Road Science City (Xi'an Science Park), and the "two wings" are located in the Western China Innovation Port and Chang'an University City. Xi'an Science and Technology Innovation Center will build a spatial layout of "one core, one circle, and one belt". "One core" refers to the core area of Xi'an Comprehensive Science Center, "one circle" refers to the collaborative innovation ecosystem centered on the Xi'an metropolitan area, and "one belt" refers to the Silk Road Science and Technology Innovation Cooperation Belt oriented to the BRI. The "dual centers" will create a source of hard science and technology innovation with global influence, a hub of cutting-edge emerging industries, and a gathering place for top talents involved in the BRI, which becomes a major advantage for Shaanxi to continue promoting the development of the BRI.

(ii) "Qinchuangyuan" Scientific and Technological Achievements are Transformed More Efficiently

The joint building of the BRI requires the establishment and utilization of a comprehensive open platform to achieve innovation-driven development. Qinchuangyuan is an innovation-driven platform established by Shaanxi in 2021. The platform is committed to creating a three-dimensional "incubator", a scientific and technological achievement transformation "accelerator" and a two-chain integration "promoter" to promote high-quality development of regional economy.

Shaanxi has established a science and technology innovation service system consisting of "one center, one platform, one company", created a number of demonstration models of "three-dimensional incubators, achievement transformation accelerators, and two-chain integration accelerators". It has implemented reforms such as the construction of a "scientist plus engineer" team, introduced various financial institutions and service agencies, and effectively promoted the integration of science and technology, economy and finance.

As various elements and resources are shared, flowed and recombined among the BRI countries, Qinchuangyuan innovation-driven platform will take its own advantages to cooperate and share with the BRI countries in terms of transformation of scientific and technological achievements, deepen innovation-driven development, and consolidate Shaanxi's status as a leading area for science and education innovation.

(iii) Digitalization Provides a Stronger Guiding Effect

The digital economy is in line with the priority directions of economic and social modernization of the BRI countries, and will become a new driving force supporting the economic development of various countries. China's digital economy is developing rapidly. There are many companies engaged in big data, artificial intelligence, various software and information service in Shaanxi Province, which are gradually becoming a strong engine for economic and social development.

The booming digital economy is one of the important ways to drive the economy. The joint building of the BRI must persist in promoting the development of big data, cloud computing and smart cities. Shaanxi will continue to strengthen international exchanges and cooperation in new technologies, new business formats and new models to facilitate the digital transformation of the BRI countries and achieve new growth momentum and development paths.

IV. Anchor Goals to Promote High-Quality Development of the BRI

In the future, Shaanxi will anchor the development goals of high standards, sustainability and benefiting people's livelihood, achieve multi-party connectivity among the government, enterprises and society, hold high-quality international activities to actively expand cooperation and promote the joint development of the BRI with high quality.

(i) The Goal of High Standards, Sustainability and Benefiting People's Livelihood is More Promising

Shaanxi will actively create a market-oriented, law-based and internationalized business environment and improve the quality and level of investment promotion. With its solid industrial foundation, strong scientific and educational strength and other advantages, Shaanxi attracts companies and entrepreneurs from all over the world to invest in Shaanxi, exchange and cooperate, and attracts talents at home and abroad to come to Shaanxi to find jobs, start businesses and realize their dreams. At the same time, Shaanxi will seize the new opportunity of international production capacity cooperation and combine the sustainable development of local advantageous industries and enterprises with the needs of economic development and growth in the BRI countries to achieve win-win or all-win results.

Shaanxi will continue to deepen mutually beneficial cooperation with partner countries and help more and more countries and regions to accelerate economic development. By promoting the construction of the free trade pilot zone, promoting the collaborative upgrading of the regional innovation chain, industrial chain, and value chain, and accelerating the agglomeration and transformation of domestic and foreign material flows, capital flows, talent flows, technology flows, and information flows, Shaanxi will actively develop modern industries, accelerate system integration innovation and strive to create a higher-level open platform. At the same time, Shaanxi will gradually implement all-round coordinated opening up.

(ii) Export–oriented Economy that can Make Profits and Promote Win–Win Results is More Diversified

"Bringing in" and "go global" not only help enterprises open up international markets, but more importantly, accelerate the transformation and upgrading of Shaanxi's economy, promote the high-quality development and enhance competitiveness of Shaanxi's economy in a more vigorous and open manner.

Shaanxi will continue high-level "bringing in". The investment and production capacity of foreign giants such as Samsung and Micron are expected to continue to expand. Foreign-funded enterprises in the starting area of the Sino-European Industrial Park and the Sino-Russian Silk Road High-tech Innovation Park are also expected to increase investment and expand production capacity.

Shaanxi will continue to accelerate high-level of "go global". Relying on its advantageous products of 23 key industrial chains, and targeting the BRI countries, RCEP countries and traditional European and American markets, Shaanxi will expand emerging markets such as Africa, promote enterprises in Shaanxi to team up and go global, and enhance Shaanxi product's share in the international market. A number of leading local companies such as Shaanxi Automobile, Longi and Aiju have established production bases, logistics parks and distribution networks in the BRI countries, and will continue to improve their market capabilities and profitability. Some traditional and new industrial enterprises will also gradually enter the BRI countries, go global with more diversified enterprise matrix and service systems, and foreign-funded joint ventures will enter Shaanxi more conveniently.

(iii) High-level and High-quality Forum Activities Increase

The international high-end platform is an important carrier for the realization of openness. High-level, high-standard and high-quality forum activities are important carrier and important symbol of regional external exchanges. The Silk Road International Exposition and the Investment and Trade Forum for Cooperation between East and West China, attended by 180 foreign politicians and 8,000 overseas merchants from more than 120 countries and regions around the world, have become an important platform to promote the joint building of the BRI and promote the coordinated development of the eastern, central and western regions.

With the success of the China-Central Asia Summit, the high-level, high-profile and high-quality forums represented by the Silk Road International Exposition and the Eurasian Economic Forum are expected to continue to raise the specifications and level, and become an important platform for international cooperation and exchanges among the BRI countries.

In the future, Shaanxi will promote the collaborative efforts of various open platforms such as free trade pilot zones, comprehensive bonded zones, airport economic demonstration zones, cross-border e-commerce comprehensive pilot zones, and the Yangling SCO Demonstration Base for Agricultural Technology Exchange and Training at a high level. It is necessary to promote high-quality development of the BRI through high-level external exchanges.

Conclusion

The development of history is magnificent and the road ahead is extremely broad. It is an inevitable result of historical development and a development opportunity for Shaanxi to deeply integrate into the overall pattern of the BRI. This is a peaceful, prosperous, open, green, innovative, civilized and honest road, in which the people of the BRI countries and the people of Shaanxi will share development opportunities and create a better life that "cherish one's own beauty, respect other's beauty and make the world a harmonious whole". It is the way to implement the concept of China's excellent traditional culture of "all people under the heaven are of one family and all nations should live in harmony" and build a community with a shared future for mankind.

Time and space intersect in the land of Shaanxi in the new era. From Xi'an, the starting point of the ancient Silk Road, to Hanzhong, the hometown of Zhang Qian who was envoy to the Western Regions, from Baoji where "Zhaizi China" was unearthed to Ankang where the symbol of the Silk Road "gilded copper silkworms" was discovered, from Yan'an, the holy revolutionary land, to Yulin, the camel city of the Silk Road, from Tongchuan, the hometown of Sun Simiao, the master of traditional Chinese medicine, to Weinan, the hometown of Sima Qian, who was the first to write about the "Western Regions" in China, from Xianyang, a famous capital on Silk Road, to Shangluo where has abundant walnuts from Eurasia, all cities in Shaanxi are involved in the BRI and carry out new cooperation with the BRI countries in new ways and new looks in the new era.

On the new journey of the joint development of the BRI, Shaanxi will focus on the primary task of high-quality development, show the ambition and courage to be a trend-setter of the times, expand high-level opening up to the outside world, and bravely set the trend, strive to catch up and surpass itself in implementing Chinese path to modernization, thus playing an exemplary role in the western region, and striving to write a Shaanxi chapter in Chinese path to modernization.

Major Events in Shaanxi's Advance of the Belt and Road Initiative (2013—2023)

In 2013

On September 7, President Xi Jinping proposed to jointly build the "Silk Road Economic Belt" during his visit to Kazakhstan.

On September 27, at the 5th Eurasian Economic Forum, representatives of Chinese and foreign cities on the Silk Road Economic Belt jointly initiated the release of the *Xi'an Declaration on Jointly Building the Silk Road Economic Belt*.

On October 3, President Xi Jinping proposed in his speech at the Indonesian Parliament to jointly build the 21st Century Maritime Silk Road.

On November 28, Shaanxi Province's first international freight train, Chang'an China-European freight train, set out.

In 2014

On March 19, the General Administration of Customs officially approved Xi'an as a national pilot city for cross-border trade e-commerce services.

From May 23 to 26, the 18th Silk Road International Exposition and the Investment and Trade Forum for Cooperation between East and West

China was held in Xi'an. 16 BRI countries set up exhibition halls.

On May 24, Shaanxi and Chuhe Prefecture of Kyrgyzstan formally established friendships and the signing ceremony was held in Xi'an.

On June 18, the launch ceremony of the first Silk Road Tourism Special Train was held at Xi'an Railway Station.

On June 22, "Silk Roads: The Routes Network of Chang'an-Tianshan Corridor" was successfully declared a World Cultural Heritage.

From September 12 to 27, the first "Silk Road International Arts Festival" was held in Xi'an.

From September 19 to 21, the first "China Xi'an Silk Road International Tourism Expo" was held in Xi'an, becoming an international marketing platform for Silk Road tourism.

In October, the Shaanxi Provincial Leading Group for Building the New Starting Point of the Silk Road Economic Belt was established.

From October 12 to 16, under the witness of the Prime Ministers of China and Russia, the Shaanxi Provincial Government and representatives of the Russian Direct Investment Fund, the China-Russia Investment Fund, and the Russian Skolkovo Innovation Center signed the *Memorandum of Cooperation on Joint Development and Construction of the China-Russia Silk Road High-tech Industrial Park*.

From October 20 to 26, the first Silk Road International Film Festival was held in Xi'an.

On October 27, four national ministries and commissions jointly issued a document approving the establishment of Shaanxi Xixian Bonded

Logistics Center.

On December 19, the international code (CNXAG) and domestic code (61900100) of "Xi'an Port" were officially put into use.

In 2015

From February 13 to 16, General Secretary Xi Jinping pointed out that Shaanxi is "the forefront of opening up to the west" and "Shaanxi must find its correct positioning and actively integrate into the overall pattern of the Belt and Road Initiative" when visiting and inspecting Shaanxi.

On March 28, the *Vision and Actions on Jointly Building the Silk Road Economic Belt and the 21st Century Maritime Silk Road* was released, which clearly stated that Xi'an would be built into a new highland for inland reform and opening up.

On April 1, the General Office of the People's Government of Shaanxi Province issued a notice on the establishment of a leading group for promoting the financial cooperation under the Belt and Road Initiative.

On May 6, the Summit for Enterprises of the BRI Countries was held in Xi'an.

On June 17, the *Action Plan for Jointly Building the Belt and Road in Shaanxi Province 2015* was released. Since then, Shaanxi began to release an annual action plan successively to deploy key tasks for the year.

On June 18 and 19, the Tourism Ministerial Meeting of Countries Along the Silk Road Economic Belt and the 7th UNWTO International Meeting on Silk Road Tourism were held in Xi'an.

On October 22, Shaanxi Province and the Bank of China signed a memorandum of cooperation on fully supporting Shaanxi's building of the Belt and Road.

On December 15, the Shaanxi Electronic Port comprehensive service platform was launched, marking the official launch of the "single window" operation of the Shaanxi Electronic Port.

On December 25, Xixian Bonded Logistics Center passed the formal acceptance.

On December 29, the Xi'an Railway Temporary Port in the Xi'an International Trade and Logistics Park passed the assessment and acceptance and became the only designated port for imported grain in Shaanxi.

In 2016

In March, the *Implementation Plan of Shaanxi Province for Promoting the Building of the Silk Road Economic Belt and the 21st Century Maritime Silk Road (2015-2020)* was issued.

On March 1, Longi invested 311 million US dollars to build its first overseas production base in Kuching, Malaysia, an important node on the Maritime Silk Road. Longi (Kuching) SDN.BHD.

On May 13, the 2016 Silk Road International Exposition and the 20th Investment and Trade Forum for Cooperation between East and West China were held in Xi'an, with the largest scale ever.

On August 31, Shaanxi was approved to establish the third batch of national free trade pilot zones.

On September 6, the Xi'an Silk Road Business Summit and the Silk Road Chamber of International Commerce Cooperation and Development Conference were held in Xi'an.

On October 18, Shaanxi Province and China Construction Bank signed a Strategic Cooperation Agreement on a series of the Silk Road funds.

On December 12, the international cargo flight from Xi'an to Amsterdam (Chang'an) was opened.

In 2017

On April 1, the China (Shaanxi) Pilot Free Trade Zone was unveiled in Xi'an, and the Shaanxi Pilot Free Trade Zone was officially established.

On May 18, Elegant Logistics Group Ltd. held its founding meeting in Xi'an. Two intercontinental freight routes, "Xi'an-Amsterdam" and "Xi'an-Shanghai-Anchorage-Chicago" were opened.

On May 22, JD.com Group signed a cooperation agreement with Xi'an Aerospace Base for JD Global Logistics Headquarters, JD Unmanned System Industry Center, and JD Cloud Operation Center, and plans to invest 20.5 billion yuan within five years.

On June 30, China (Shaanxi) International Trade Single Window was officially launched online.

On July 6, the Shaanxi Provincial Leading Group for Building the New Starting Point of the Silk Road Economic Belt was restructured into the Shaanxi Provincial Leading Group for Promoting the Belt and Road Initiative.

On August 19 and 20, the first World Xi'an Entrepreneurs Convention was held in Xi'an from.

On September 22, the first Belt and Road Forum for Traditional Chinese Medicine Development was held.

On September 25, the Belt & Road Initiative Global Health International Congress kicked off

On September 27, the National Belt and Road Leading Group Office went to Shaanxi to supervise and investigate the building of the Belt and Road.

On September 30, the *Implementation Opinions of the People's Government of Shaanxi Province on the Active and Effective Use of Foreign Investment to Promote High-quality Economic Development* was issued.

In October, the State-owned Assets Supervision and Administration Commission of Shaanxi Province issued the *Opinions on Promoting Enterprises to Develop International Production Capacity Cooperation* to guide and standardize provincial enterprises' participation in the Belt and Road Initiative from four aspects.

On October 13, the Belt and Road National Metrology Center (Shaanxi) was approved.

On November 27, Shaanxi Provincial Leading Group for Promoting the Belt and Road Initiative held a plenary meeting, at which the Shaanxi Belt and Road Portal was launched.

On December 12, the 12th Confucius Institute Conference was held in Xi'an.

On December 29, the *Opinions on Further Supporting the Development of China (Shaanxi) Pilot Free Trade Zone* was issued.

On December 14, the People's Government of Shaanxi Province issued the *Management Measures for China (Shaanxi) Free Trade Pilot Zone*.

In 2018

On January 2, the Shaanxi Branch of the State Administration of Foreign Exchange issued the *Implementation Rules for Further Promoting the Pilot Program of Foreign Exchange Administration Reform in the China (Shaanxi) Pilot Free Trade Zone*.

On January 29, the Shaanxi Provincial Environmental Protection Office, the Shaanxi Provincial Foreign Affairs Office, the Shaanxi Provincial Development and Reform Commission and the Shaanxi Provincial Department of Commerce jointly issued the *Implementation Opinions of Shaanxi Province on Promoting the Green Belt and Road Initiative*.

On April 9, Shaanxi Province and the Rheinland-Palatinate of Germany signed a letter of intent to develop friendships.

On April 9, the first Shanghai Cooperation Organization People's Forum opened in Xi'an.

On April 10, Shaanxi Province and Samarkand Oblast of Uzbekistan signed a Memorandum of Friendly Cooperation.

On April 16, the launch ceremony of the "Silk Road E-commerce" Shaanxi cross-border e-commerce RMB settlement service platform was held.

On May 12 to 13, scholars from China, Russia, Kazakhstan and other countries published the *Xi'an Consensus on the Protection of Archeology and Cultural Heritage on the International Silk Road*.

On May 25, Shaanxi Province formulated the *Implementation Plan for Promoting Integrated Development of Transportation and Logistics*, proposing that by 2020, Shaanxi's status as a comprehensive hub along the Belt and Road will be strengthened, and Xi'an's function as an "international aviation hub" will be significantly improved.

On May 31, the first Belt and Road International Forum on Automobile Industry Development was held in Xi'an.

On June 29, the Second International Commercial Court of the Supreme People's Court was unveiled in Xi'an.

On July 19, Beijing, Shanghai, and Shaanxi established an inter-provincial cooperation mechanism for inbound tourism.

On July 24, the State Council approved the establishment of cross-border e-commerce comprehensive pilot zones in 22 cities including Xi'an.

On August 14, the *Action Plan for Jointly Building the Belt and Road based on Shaanxi Provincial Standards and Connectivity (2018-2020)* was released.

On August 15, China (Shaanxi)-Russia Economic and Trade Cooperation Promotion Conference was held in Moscow.

On September 17, the 3rd Sino-French Cultural Forum opened in Xi'an

On September 17, the Second Sino-German Historical and Cultural Cities Dialogue opened in Xi'an.

On September 21, the first press conference on the theme of "Shaanxi's Five-Year Achievements in the Belt and Road Initiative" was held.

On October 9, the 2018 World Culture and Tourism Forum opened in Xi'an Chanba Ecological Zone.

On October 30, the activity to celebrate the operating of over 1,000 Chang'an China-Europe freight trains in 2018 was held at the Xi'an International Trade and Logistics Park.

On November 2, the 25th Yangling Agricultural Hi-tech Fair kicked off.

From November 5 to 10, the first China International Import Expo was held in Shanghai. A Shaanxi trading delegation composed of more than 3,000 business personnel presented at the expo.

On December 4, the 2018 "Belt and Road" Fair of Shaanxi Specialties co-sponsored by the Shaanxi Provincial Government and the Thai Ministry of Agriculture and Cooperatives was held in Bangkok.

On December 5, the Shaanxi Provincial Leading Group for Promoting the Belt and Road Initiative held a meeting.

On December 5, the *Implementation Plan for China (Xi'an) Cross-border E-Commerce Comprehensive Pilot Zone* was issued

In 2019

On January 11, the National Development and Reform Commission approved the project proposal for the third phase expansion project of Xi'an Xianyang International Airport.

On January 14, the Shaanxi Provincial Leading Group for Promoting the Belt and Road Initiative issued the *Overall Plan for Building the Belt and Road Comprehensive Reform and Opening-up Pilot Zone in Xi'an*.

On January 15, the Qinhan New Town Management Committee of Xixian New Area and the Alashankou Municipal Government of Bozhou, Xinjiang signed a strategic cooperation agreement.

On February 22, Xi'an International Grain and Oil Summit was held.

On March 11, the EXCO & OBOR Exhibition 2019, Italy Xi'an Station Conference was held.

On March 25, the China-Europe Railway Express (Xi'an) Collection Center Cooperation Forum and the Launch Ceremony of the Initiative to Jointly Build a Land-Sea Intermodal Transport Corridor were held, and the "Belt and Road Initiative (Xi'an) Land-Sea Intermodal Transport Corridor Initiative" was released.

On March 27, China (Shaanxi)-Belarus Economic and Trade Cooperation and China-Belarus Industrial Park Promotion Conference were held in Xi'an.

On April 2, Xi'an issued the *Implementation Opinions on the Active and Effective Use of Foreign Investment to Promote High-quality Economic Development*.

On April 8, Shaanxi's first cross-border e-commerce online shopping bonded imported goods were officially cleared at the Xixian Bonded Logistics Center (Type B).

On April 9, the 9th Western China International Logistics Industry Expo opened in Xi'an.

On April 9, Shaanxi Belt and Road Lawyers College was established in Northwest University of Political Science and Law.

On April 10, the 2019 Belt and Road International Logistics Exchange and Cooperation Conference was held in Xi'an.

On April 18, the press conference of the 2nd anniversary on Xi'an Economic Development Functional Zone of Shaanxi Pilot Free Trade Zone, the Belt and Road International Capacity Cooperation and Private Enterprise Development Forum were held.

On April 20, the Belt and Road Shaanxi Xi'an (Samsung) 2019 City Wall International Marathon kicked off.

On April 22, Xi'an City and the Croydon City of the UK signed a letter of intent to develop friendships.

On April 24, Shaanxi Province and North Kazakhstan Oblast signed a letter of intent to develop friendships.

On April 25, the 2019 China-Russia Silk Road Industrial and Technological Innovation Forum was successfully held.

On May 13, Shaanxi's first fifth-freedom rights route "Seoul-Xi'an-Hanoi" successfully made its maiden trip.

On May 20, Silk Road (Xi'an) Qianhai Park project was contracted.

On May 28, the first Xi'an-Minsk cross-border e-commerce export train, Chang'an China-Europe Freight Train, departed.

On June 4, Longi announced that it plans to invest 957 million yuan to build a monocrystalline battery project with an annual output of 1.25GW in Kuching, Sarawak, Malaysia.

On June 11, the China-Brazil Agricultural Biological Resources Research Center was established at Northwest A&F University.

On June 14, President Xi Jinping proposed at the 19th meeting of the Council of Heads of Member States of the Shanghai Cooperation Organization that "China is willing to establish a Shanghai Cooperation Organization Demonstration Base for Agricultural Technology Exchange and Training in Shaanxi to strengthen cooperation with regions and countries in the field of modern agriculture."

On June 18, Xi'an Xianyang International Airport was approved as a designated supervision site for imported meat.

On July 2, FastMaz laid the foundation stone in the China-Belarus Great Stone Industrial Park.

On July 27, the Silk Road Cultural Development Forum was held at Qujiang International Conference and Exhibition Center.

On August 15, the third southern corridor and station apron project of Xi'an Xianyang International Airport was officially opened.

On September 3, Schneider Electric's two global design centers settled in Shaanxi.

On September 29, China's first batch of new supply chain finance model "Central Bank-Chang'an Ticket and Transportation Pass" was officially launched in Xi'an International Trade and Logistics Park.

On October 18, the Shaanxi Capital Market Service Base of Shenzhen Stock Exchange was officially unveiled.

On November 1, Shaanxi opened its first multimodal China-Europe freight train and used unified waybills for the first time to achieve "one order to the end."

On December 9, Shaanxi Province and the Chinese Academy of Sciences signed a strategic cooperation agreement to jointly create the Yulin National Energy Revolution and Innovation Demonstration Zone.

On December 17, Shaanxi's first "National Traditional Chinese Medicine Service Export Base" was approved.

On December 26, Baoji Comprehensive Bonded Zone was officially approval by the State Council.

In 2020

On January 15, the Overseas Scientific and Technological Achievements Transformation Research Institute of Shaanxi Overseas Chinese Federation was unveiled.

On January 22, Shaanxi Xixian Airport Comprehensive Bonded Zone (Phase I) was officially closed for operation.

On March 20, the National Center for Molecular Medicine Translational Science began to construct.

On March 25, the *Development Plan for Xi'an Silk Road Financial Center* and the *Action Plan for Development of Xi'an Silk Road Financial Center*(2020-2022) were released.

On March 27, *Several Measures of Supporting High-quality Development of Chang'an China-Europe Freight Train* was released.

On March 30, Xi'an Xianyang International Airport's first flight carrying epidemic prevention supplies flew to Germany, Europe.

On April 23, General Secretary Xi Jinping pointed out during an inspection in Shaanxi that, "For Shaanxi, insufficient opening up is the biggest shortcoming restricting the development," "Shaanxi must deeply integrate into the overall pattern of the Belt and Road Initiative."

On May 8, the *Strategic Plan for Xi'an International Aviation Hub* jointly issued by the Shaanxi Provincial Government and the Civil Aviation Administration of China was officially released.

On June 9, the Shaanxi Silk Road Archaeological Center was unveiled.

On June 30, the groundbreaking ceremony of Suning Logistics Industrial Park was held in Xi'an International Trade and Logistics Park.

On July 2, the Multilingual Translation Center for International Cooperation in Modern Agriculture was unveiled in Yangling.

On July 6, the Xi'an Assembly Center of China-Europe Railway Express was included in the national demonstration project and received investment from the central budget.

From July 10 to 12, the 2020 Shaanxi International Science and Technology Innovation and Entrepreneurship Expo was held in Xi'an.

On July 22, the third phase of the Xi'an Xianyang International Airport project started construction.

On August 1, STO International Xi'an Port Transshipment Center was unveiled in Airport New City.

On August 8, the Belt and Road Cultural Communication and Economic Development Forum was held in Xi'an.

On August 14, Xi'an Customs issued Shaanxi's first digital "Inspection and Quarantine Certificate for Entry Goods."

On August 27, the online exhibition of Western China International Sourcing Exhibition was held in Xi'an.

On September 14 and 15, the 2020 Global Automotive Logistics Conference was held in Xi'an for the first time.

On September 16, the Shaanxi Provincial Government and China Export & Credit Insurance Corporation signed a strategic cooperation agreement in Xi'an.

On October 10, the Xi'an Branch of the People's Bank of China and the Shaanxi Branch of the State Administration of Foreign Exchange issued the *Opinions on the High-quality Development of Financial Support to the China-European Freight Train (Xi'an) Assembly Center and the Pilot Free Trade Zone of China (Shaanxi)*.

On October 22, the SCO Demonstration Base for Agricultural Technology Exchange and Training was officially unveiled.

On October 23, Shaanxi's first "International Aviation Supplies Supermarket" Xi'an International Aviation Supplies Supply Chain Management Center was unveiled in the Airport New City of Xixian New District.

On November 18, Shaanxi Province's first online verification business of tax filing information for external payments under service trade was launched.

On December 13, the National Artificial Intelligence Vocational

Education Industry-Education Collaborative Innovation Alliance was established in Xi'an.

On December 28, Xi'an Aerospace Base General Airport officially obtained the certificate for operation.

In 2021

On January 27, the Shaanxi Province launched the imported goods port circulation information management platform online.

On January 27, the Belt and Road international intermodal transport smart logistics hub platform - "Inland Port Cloud Wharf" officially entered the trial operation stage.

On February 3 and 4, the 2021 Silk Road Carnival · A Promise of Harmony and Beauty - Silk Road Online Spring Festival Gala links five continents.

On February 18, the world's largest aviation-grade titanium alloy rod production line was opened in Shaanxi.

On March 18, Baoji was selected as a national cross-border e-commerce retail import pilot city.

On March 19, Xi'an Xianyang International Airport won the Healthy Airport Certification from Airports Council International (ACI).

On March 19, Shaanxi Pilot Free Trade Zone Energy Gold Trade Zone Functional Zone and Shaanxi Branch of Bank of China signed the "Free Trade Pilot Zone Financial Collaborative Innovation Cooperation Agreement".

On March 24, Xi'an International Trade and Logistics Park held the launching ceremony of the "China-Europe Talent Train."

On March 30, the Silk Road International Water Technology Innovation Park project laid the foundation stone in Jinghe New Town, Xixian New District.

On April 9, China (Shaanxi) Joint Working Group to Tajikistan was awarded the "International Friendship Contribution Award."

On April 21, Xi'an International Inland Port Investment & Development Group signed a memorandum of understanding on strategic cooperation with the Belgian North Sea Port Group and Oostende-Brugge International Airport respectively.

On April 25, the *Shaanxi Province's Key Work Points for Promoting the Belt and Road Initiative in 2021* was issued.

On May 1, the *Regulations for China (Shaanxi) Pilot Free Trade Zone* officially came into effect.

On May 12, China (Shaanxi)-Korea Economic and Trade Cooperation Fair was held in Xi'an.

On May 13, the 2021 EU-China Economic Cooperation Forum of Yulin City was held in Xi'an.

On May 20, the Yulin international freight train on the New Western Land-Sea Corridor officially opened for operation.

On June 16, the first cross-border commodity display and trading center in Baoji Comprehensive Bonded Zone - Shaanxi Fruit Technology Group Co., Ltd.'s cross-border experience store opened.

On June 18, with the strong support and precise guidance of the State Administration of Foreign Exchange, the cross-border financial blockchain service platform Chang'an China-Europe freight train application scenario was officially launched.

On July 1, the Ministry of Agriculture and Rural Affairs, the Ministry of Foreign Affairs, the Ministry of Science and Technology and the People's Government of Shaanxi Province jointly issued the *Construction Plan for Shanghai Cooperation Organization Demonstration Base for Agricultural Technology Exchange and Training*.

On July 5, the "Qin | Modern Art Exhibition on the Past and Present - Terracotta Warriors and Horses" was officially launched in Nepal.

On July 7, the Malaysian comprehensive phosphorus chemical EPCC project undertaken by SCEGC Installation Group Company Ltd. was put into operation.

On July 15, Airport New City established an overseas talent service window.

On August 20, the "Cloud Recommendation for China-Russia Business Enterprise Resources" was held.

On August 12, the UCLG Local Action Port High-level Youth Dialogue Forum was successfully held at Xi'an Jiaotong University.

On August 22, Northwest University's "China-Central Asia Human and Environmental Belt and Road Joint Laboratory" was approved for establishment by the Ministry of Science and Technology.

On August 23, the "Silk Road E-commerce" Shaanxi cross-border e-commerce RMB settlement service platform was connected to the RMB cross-border payment system.

On September 30, Shaanxi's first fifth-freedom cargo route for the BRI countries was opened.

On October 23, the *14th Five-Year Plan for Shaanxi Province to Deeply Integrate into Belt and Road Cooperation and Develop into a Highland of Opening Up* was issued.

On October 23, the SCO Demonstration Base and Practical Training Base for Agricultural Technology Exchange and Training was unveiled.

On October 28, the 2021 Silk Road International Industry-University-Research and Application Cooperation Conference opened in Xi'an.

On December 29, the Shaanxi Provincial Department of Commerce, Xi'an Customs, the Shaanxi Provincial Tax Service under the State Taxation Administration, and the Xi'an Branch of the People's Bank of China jointly issued the *Action Plan for Comprehensively Aligning with the New Rules of RCEP Economic and Trade and Solidly Promoting High-level Opening Up to the Outside World* to fully align with the new RCEP economic and trade rules, deepening economic and trade cooperation between Shaanxi Province and RCEP member states.

In 2022

On March 31, the 11th APEC Small and Medium Enterprises Technology Conference and Fair was held.

On April 18, the first China-Europe freight train to enjoy the tax refund policy for the land port departed from Xi'an Guojigang Railway Station. Xi'an Port became the first pilot inland port in China enjoying tax refund policy.

On May 18, the People's Government of Shaanxi Province issued the measures for *Promoting the Pilot Project of Cross-border E-commerce Retail and Import of Certain Pharmaceuticals and Medical Devices*.

On June 8, the 12th Meeting of BRICS Ministers of Agriculture and the BRICS Symposium on Rural Development and Poverty Alleviation were held.

On June 21, the Chang'an China-Europe freight train (Haifang-Xi'an-Almaty) departed from Xi'an Guojigang Railway Station. It marks the connectivity of the Chang'an China-Europe freight train and the New Land-Sea Corridor for the first time.

On July 7, the *SCO Agricultural Base Construction Plan* was released.

On August 9, the 2022 Media Cooperation Forum on Belt and Road opened in Xi'an.

On August 14, China (Shaanxi)-Uzbekistan Economic and Trade Cooperation and Cultural Tourism Promotion Conference was held in Xi'an.

On August 15, the Belt and Road Forum on Agricultural Trade and Rural Revitalization was held in Xi'an.

On August 15, the Belt and Road Summit on Intelligent Manufacturing was held in Xi'an.

On August 16, the first Belt and Road Forum for Commercial and Legal Cooperation was held in Xi'an.

On September 7, Shaanxi issued the first certificate of origin for goods exported to RCEP member countries.

On September 15, the 2022 SCO Modern Agriculture Development Roundtable was held in Yangling Demonstration Zone.

On September 27, the 5th China-Central Asia Cooperation Forum was held in Xi'an.

On October 13, the Shaanxi Provincial Administration of Traditional Chinese Medicine and the Shaanxi Provincial Development and Reform Commission issued the *14th Five-Year Plan of Shaanxi Province for the Development of Traditional Chinese Medicine*.

On October 26, the first China-Europe train with complete timetable departed from Xi'an.

On November 29-30, the first Asia-Europe Youth Leaders Exchange Camp and Asia-Europe Youth Green Development Forum was held in Xi'an.

On December 21, the China (Shaanxi) Commodity Exhibition and Trading Center of SCO Agricultural Base was opened.

On December 23, the China-Kazakhstan Center for Traditional Medicine was established in Kazakhstan.

In 2023

On February 21, Shaanxi Province and Syr Darya Oblast of Uzbekistan signed a memorandum of understanding on the development of friendly cooperation relations.

On March 27, the International Cooperation Working Committee of

Shaanxi Provincial Federation of Industry and Commerce was established in Xi'an.

On March 22, the founding meeting of the Shaanxi Provincial Social Organization International Exchange Promotion Association was held in Xi'an.

From April 24 to 26, the Asia Cultural Heritage Protection Alliance Conference was held in Xi'an. This was the first large-scale, high-level international conference held offline since its establishment.

On May 17, while hearing the work report of the Shaanxi Provincial Party Committee and the Provincial Government, General Secretary Xi Jinping emphasized that Shaanxi should open up wider and develop the inland province into a highland for reform and opening up, integrate and serve the new development pattern more proactively, and be more deeply integrated into the overall pattern of jointly building the BRI, so as to strengthen Shaanxi's momentum and vitality in expanding opening up and open a new development landscape.

On May 18-19, the China-Central Asia Summit was held in Xi'an. During the summit, China and the five Central Asian countries reached a series of consensuses on cooperation.

From June 27 to July 1, the Governor of Shaanxi Province Zhao Gang led Shaanxi Provincial delegation to pay a goodwill visit to Turkmenistan to actively implement the important consensus reached by the two heads of state and the results the China-Central Asia Summit related to Shaanxi.

On August 1, Shaanxi held a meeting of Shaanxi Provincial Leading

Group for Promoting the Belt and Road Initiative and the leading group for the China (Shaanxi) Free Trade Pilot Zone.

From September 1 to 8, Zhao Yide, Secretary of the Shaanxi Provincial Party Committee and Director of the Standing Committee of the Provincial People's Congress, led a Shaanxi delegation to pay a goodwill visit to Uzbekistan, Kazakhstan, and Kyrgyzstan to actively implement the important consensus reached by the heads of state and the results of the China-Central Asia Summit related to Shaanxi.

On October 10, the Information Office of the People's Government of Shaanxi Province held a series of press conferences on the 10th anniversary of the joint building of the Belt and Road Initiative (the first one).